Also by Adrian Forsyth

Mammals of the Canadian Wild
A Natural History of Sex

TROPICAL NATURE

*Adrian Forsyth
and Kenneth Miyata*

Illustrations by Sarah Landry

A TOUCHSTONE BOOK
Published by Simon & Schuster
New York   London   Toronto   Sydney   Tokyo   Singapore

TOUCHSTONE
Rockefeller Center
1230 Avenue of the Americas
New York, NY 10020

First Touchstone Edition 1995

Library of Congress Cataloging-in-Publication Data
Forsyth, Adrian.
  Tropical nature.

  Bibliography: p.
  Includes index.
  1. Rain forest ecology—Central America.   2. Rain forest ecology—
South America.   I. Miyata, Kenneth.   II. Title.
QH108.A1F67   1984   574.5′2642′098   82-42640
ISBN 0-684-18710-8

Manufactured in the United States of America

10 9 8 7 6 5

To the memory of Ken Miyata

CONTENTS

ILLUSTRATIONS

FOREWORD

Belém, the Amazon's port city, lies but $3\frac{1}{2}$ hours from Miami, but seems as remote as if the journey were possible only by sail. Even to me as a naturalist, the Amazon seemed remote when, in 1965, it was first suggested that I visit. Only then did I really register that such a city existed, let alone that it dated from 1616 and contained half a million people. I felt embarrassed to be so unaware.

All tropical forests seem touched with this perception of remoteness, even more than the savannahs of Africa with all their great mammals. In large part this is because tropical forests are a world for biological sophisticates, a world the wonders of which only become apparent with considerable patience and background.

I was no exception that June afternoon when I first entered the tropical rain forests on the outskirts of Belém. The first impression was not of tremendous variety as the books of the great naturalist-explorers had taught me to expect. Rather, the mass of vegetation conveyed a sense of green, and of sameness. It was wet and warm but not blistering hot as it was in the sun outside the forest. It was quiet. Little moved except ants.

Superficial as they might seem, these were quite accurate and appropriate perceptions. Ants are a dominant feature of these great forests. The plentiful variety of plant species has been shaped similarly to shed water and discourage epiphytic growth.

Most species of plants and animals are relatively rare and most animals are occupied in *not* attracting attention.

If that is as far as one gets in making the acquaintance of these wonderful forests, the remaining impression is likely to be one of vague unease about unseen tarantulas and snakes coupled with a sense that the forests are probably, after all, unremarkable. The only cure for such inappropriate ennui has been to see the forest in the company of a modern tropical naturalist, or read the works of those of the nineteenth-century naturalists—books always a bit hard to find and, except as reprints, not to be subjected to the rigors of field conditions.

This volume bridges the problem, providing a modern introduction, to those who have cut their naturalists' teeth in the temperate zone, to the tropical forests, most particularly those of the New World. A very comfortable introduction it is, providing the most recent insights in tropical biology, in highly readable form. A journey in itself, it is my hope and that of the authors, one of whom died tragically young, that this will be but bait to lure ardent naturalists to partake directly of the fascination of tropical nature.

Timely it is for people to acquaint themselves with the wonders of tropical biology and the problems of tropical deforestation. Tropical biologists such as the authors and myself can take heart in the plight of tropical forests' appearing on the front page of the *Washington Post* on New Year's day 1984. Yet, are not most people on reading that touched with the same feeling of remoteness that affected me in 1965?

In the meantime tropical deforestation progresses at a terrifying rate, variously estimated, but in the vicinity of fifty acres a minute. In most instances, because of the peculiarities of tropical ecology, the land becomes rapidly degraded and worth little to society. At the same time, the major portion of our stock of biological resources—the half or more of all species of animals and plants of the entire planet that reside in these forests—becomes seriously threatened. Substantial number of species, many never seen by scientists, have probably already disappeared, while enormous numbers (hundreds of thousands of species) are likely to be lost in the next two or three decades. There is no greater environmental problem.

There are many reasons to be concerned. The forests are important for the useful species and ecological processes they harbor and produce. They are important because laying waste to the land helps no person and creates problems that can reach out and affect the most powerful of nations.

But most of all they are special because this is where life on earth reaches its utmost expression, where systems are richest in numbers of species and where biological systems reach their greatest complexity. Here science is likely to find kinds of arrangements of life forms to be found nowhere else. Surely, to the extent that biology, the study of life, is of value to us as living entities ourselves, it makes sense not to erase the evidence from which to build our knowledge?

Further, in these forests lies a virtually limitless supply of excitement, joy, and wonder to be encountered in new illuminations on the constructs and workings of life on earth.

THOMAS E. LOVEJOY
World Wildlife Fund

PREFACE

This book is based on the ideas and experiences of two different people who have done field work both together and apart. We have chosen to write in the first person plural when writing of experiences we shared, and in the first person singular in our accounts of experiences of only one of us. We found this preferable to relegating our thoughts and observations entirely to the blandness of the third person. Readers who wish to know which "I" speaks can bear in mind that narratives from Ecuador are usually by Ken Miyata and those from Costa Rica by Adrian Forsyth.

We have asked friends and colleagues to read chapters of this book, to make sure that we made no egregious misstatements of fact. They didn't always agree with our interpretations, but we are grateful for their helpful comments. We thank Dr. Ernest E. Williams of the Museum of Comparative Zoology, Harvard University, Dr. W. Ronald Heyer of the National Museum of Natural History, Smithsonian Institution, Dr. Roy W. McDiarmid of the United States Fish and Wildlife Laboratories, and Dr. Jerry Coyne of the University of Maryland for their efforts to keep us honest. We are also grateful to Sally Landry, our illustrator, and Michael Pietsch, our editor at Scribners, for their helpful suggestions from a nonbiologist's perspective.

We have made dozens of trips to the New World tropics over the years and we are grateful to all who have helped fund our research. We thank in particular the Center for Field Research and Earthwatch of Belmont, Massachusetts, for their efforts to get us out of the country over the years. The National Science Foundation, the Richmond and Anderson Funds of the Department of Biology at Harvard University, the Barbour Fund of the Museum of Comparative Zoology, Professor E. O. Wilson of Harvard University, and Dr. Paulo Vanzolini of the Museu de Zoologia of the Universidad de São Paulo have all contributed generously to our wanderings in the tropical rain forests of South and Central America. The Friends of the Museum of Comparative Zoology and Hanns Ebensten Travel also indirectly funded some field work by covering travel expenses when we served as naturalist leaders for their tours.

We are grateful to the many people who have accompanied us on our wanderings. Some were biologists, and we learned a great deal from them, particularly things that fell outside our areas of specialization. Others were students and Earthwatch volunteers, whose enthusiasm constantly allowed us to look at the tropical forest from a fresh perspective. Most turned out to be friends and helped make our stays even more enjoyable. Although there isn't space to list them all, we would like to extend special thanks to Joe Brenner, Jerry Coyne, Cal Dodson, Alfredo and Tina Garzon, Paul Greenfield, Bill Haber, Russ Lande, Roy McDiarmid, Fernando Ortiz-Crespo, Gene Schupp, Phil Ward, and Richard Webster.

We are also grateful to the institutions that have provided working space and access to libraries and collections. The Museum of Comparative Zoology at Harvard University was our home for many years, and their superb library was called upon many times for important references. Much of this book was written while one of us was a postdoctoral fellow at the Smithsonian Institution, and we are grateful to those responsible for this program. Gabrielle Dundon of the Friends of the Museum of Comparative Zoology kindly allowed us the use of the computer printer that typed much of the final manuscript.

IN MEMORIAM

The galleys for this book arrived on Ken's desk just after he set out for a trout-fishing trip to Yellowstone. Ken never returned, never saw this book completed. On October 15, 1983, he drowned in a treacherous rapid of the Big Horn River.

"A legend is dead," the newspapers said. They spoke of Ken's expertise in the art and biology of trout fishing. To his many friends the legend went further. He was a brilliant photographer, a superb field biologist with a taste for pure waters and virgin forest. Above all he was a complex person with a penchant for the bizarre and diverse extremes of life. It is no accident that he gravitated to the rich and exotic forests of the Neotropics. He knew they were the ultimate biological experience.

As we wrote this book we both labored under the knowledge that the richness of rain forest would ever exceed our ability to describe it. Words are no more able to celebrate and pay tribute to all the complexity that was Ken. This book can only give mere glimpses of him. Yet in its intent, in the celebration and preservation of rain forest, perhaps there is a monument and memorial worthy of him.

TROPICAL NATURE

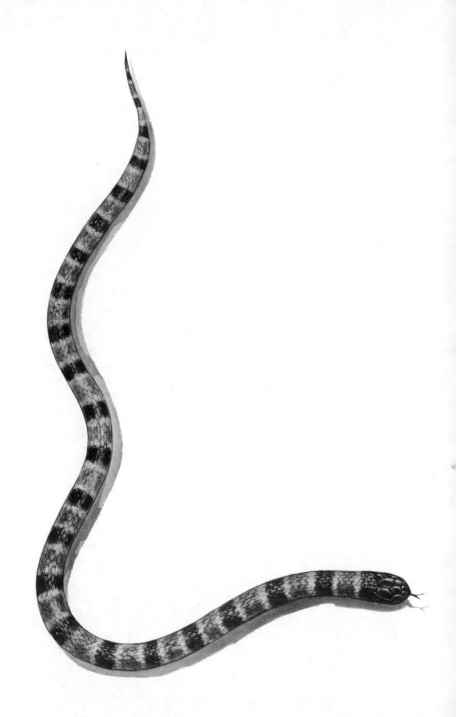

INTRODUCTION:
A TEMPERATE VIEW
OF TROPICAL LIFE

> *Epithet after epithet was found too weak to*
> *convey to those who have not visited the*
> *intertropical regions, the sensation of delight*
> *which the mind experiences. . . . The land is one*
> *great wild, untidy luxuriant hothouse,*
> *made by nature for herself.*
> —CHARLES DARWIN
> Voyage of the Beagle

A naturalist can find complexity in any habitat. Life almost everywhere on our planet involves a complex intermingling of resources and energy by hundreds of different species, and these patterns are not static. They shift and change not only with the vagaries of weather and season but also with evolutionary changes in the organisms themselves. Sometimes the patterns may be evident, but much of what goes on in natural communities defies simple interpretation and provides profound intellectual challenges to anyone with a curious mind.

It is the mix of ecological complexity and pattern that commands the attention of a naturalist; complexity excites the mind and the discovery of pattern rewards it. While there is no shortage of intriguing questions to explore in regions with a temperate climate, the wealth of life in the tropics beckons strongly to anyone with an interest in nature. The great complexity and diversity of life in the humid regions of the tropics offers the most seductive challenges available to any naturalist.

But the tangle of diversity that characterizes life in the humid tropics can perplex and confuse on first exposure. It can be extremely difficult to identify some of the most conspicuous organisms in a tropical rain forest. Ecuador, a country no larger than the state of Colorado, has over 1,300 species of birds, almost twice as many as in all of Canada and the United States. Up to 500 of these species may be found in a small area of forest in the lowlands east of the Andes, and there are no comprehensive field guides of the sort we take for granted to make field identification easy. A naturalist in New England can easily learn all the species of native trees in the region in a single summer, but there are few people who, even after a lifetime of study can confidently identify most of the trees in a patch of tropical American rain forest. Without a flower to examine carefully, even the most expert botanist may be unable to place a tropical plant in its proper family.

The difficulty of identifying common plants and animals underscores the difficulty of detecting patterns amid the exuberance of tropical life. Life in a temperate zone habitat may course through hundreds of coexisting species, while life in a tropical rain forest may involve tens of thousands. The first visit to a tropical rain forest can be a profoundly stimulating experience for any naturalist, but it can also be a drastic shock. An endless stream of information bombards the senses from the richness of tropical nature, yet it arrives as if in a garbled foreign tongue. One is lost without a guide.

This book grew partly out of our own clumsy initial contacts with the lowland rain forests of the New World tropics. When we first visited this realm more than a decade ago, we found little to prepare us for our initial encounter. The books and articles we read seemed polarized between exaggerated, sometimes hysterical popular accounts and dry, specialized academic prose that conveyed little of the excitement of tropical nature. Somewhere in between were the wonderful accounts of travel and natural history written by Henry Bates, Thomas Belt, Richard Spruce, and Alfred Wallace; but these were Victorian works that lacked much of the insight of post-Darwinian biology and addressed a world long past. We felt a need for a book addressing the natural history of tropical rain forests that would be accessible to the legion of naturalists and interested laymen in the temperate zone who might wish to learn something of this remarkable world today.

This book is not meant to be an exhaustive guidebook to tropical nature. We have limited its scope to the lowland rain forests of the New World tropics, though we cannot pretend to cover all aspects of the ecology of that realm. While in certain chapters we give an overview of essential features of the rain forests of the American tropics, most of the time we take close looks at some of the topics we have found most fascinating. We have tried to focus on phenomena that can be observed by anyone on a visit to a tropical American rain forest.

The rain forests of the New World tropics constitute so vast an area that no one can claim to be familiar with all of it. Between us we have made several dozen trips to the American tropics and have spent a total of six or seven years wandering about in various parts, but there is much that we haven't seen. Neither of us has visited the blackwater drainages of the Amazon, the rapidly disappearing forests of southeastern Brazil, or the extremely wet rain forests of the Pacific coast of Colombia. In the past dozen years we have visited rain forests in Brazil, Colombia, Panama, Peru, and the Yucatan; but the bulk of our time has been spent in the forests of Costa Rica and Ecuador. It is from these places that we draw most of our observations.

We have avoided using a textbook or encyclopedic approach in writing about tropical nature for two reasons. First, the ecology of tropical rain forest is still a virtually unexplored academic frontier. Some of the most fundamental biological details of this region are all but unknown. Only a small part of the plant and animal species that live in the rain forests of tropical America have been described and named, and only the tiniest fraction of these have received careful scientific study. Not only do millions of insect species remain unknown to science, but many tropical vertebrate groups also contain a wealth of unknown species. More than a quarter of the almost 700 known species of Ecuadorian reptiles and amphibians have been discovered and named only since 1970, and there are still new species of birds yet to be discovered and described from the forests of South America. Given our profound ignorance of the composition of Neotropical rain forest flora and fauna, any attempt to write generally of processes must involve speculation. Textbooks and popular treatments of science often fail to convey the role of intuition and speculation in the development of a science. Speculation based on fact is the essence of science, particularly in its early stages when all the facts can do is point in interesting directions that warrant further inquiry.

Our second reason for avoiding a straightforward textbook style is more compelling than the infancy of our knowledge of tropical nature. Academically cautious discussions about the ecology of tropical rain forests certainly serve valuable scientific ends, but they are not likely to hold the interest or pique the curiosity of anyone other than a professional biologist. Alexander Skutch, a well-known tropical naturalist, has suggested that naturalists have motives fundamentally different from those of scientists. A scientist whose "triumph is to summarize his observations in a neat graph or mathematical formula," as he points out in *A Naturalist in Costa Rica*, may bear little resemblance to a naturalist, for whom "the concrete significance of living things in their natural setting is at least as precious as any generalization."*

Of course many naturalists are good scientists and many scientists are good naturalists, but we think there is much truth in Skutch's simple dichotomy. In the chapters that follow, we draw upon our own observations and those set down in the scientific literature. We are the first to admit that some of our statements and conclusions rest on evidence no more substantial than a strand of spider silk. But our web of fragile evidence is not without value. Our facts are unimpeachable—plants and animals do the things we say they do, at least in some places and at some times. It is the underlying causes that are poorly understood. Our purpose is not merely to set down a compendium of interesting facts about tropical nature but to provoke curiosity about how such a complex world might function and how it might have evolved. Future research will no doubt alter some of our ecological and evolutionary generalizations and new facts about tropical nature come to light every day. These changes, which are signs of a young, healthy science, would quickly render a definitive book about tropical nature obsolete.

It is not enough to restrict the wonders of tropical nature to

* Bibliographical information about books quoted in the text as well as other works related to tropical nature can be found in Further Reading, page 235.

professional biologists. The rain forests of the American tropics are rapidly disappearing, and without a broad public interest in this vanishing habitat they may be transformed into pastures, hamburgers, and chipboard long before their fundamental composition and natural history have been documented. If this happens, ecological generalizations about life in the tropics, no matter how elegant, will be useless and irrelevant. There has been considerable concern over the rapid rate at which rain forest is disappearing, but this concern has largely been focused on the wealth of plant and animal species that may hold unknown potential benefits for human welfare and are in danger of extinction should we lose the tropical rain forest.

We hope to show you that the diversity of a tropical forest is far more than a list of the plant and animal species that live there. The complex interactions—the food webs, dispersal systems, and mutual interdependencies—that thread through the rain forest are the true essence of tropical nature. The lowland rain forests of the New World tropics are the most complex biological communities that exist; even if a cure for cancer is not to be found in one of the unnamed or unstudied plants of the tropical rain forest, the fact that rain forests are the single greatest reservoir of genetic diversity and the ultimate realization of biological complexity makes them worthy of study, admiration, and preservation.

Chapter 1

IN THE REALM
OF THE TROPICS

*The "tropics" are not a plot of convenient forest
in Costa Rica; they are an enormous realm of
patchiness, and any theoretical thinking based on
presumed general properties is bound to become
an in-group exercise in short-lived futility.*
—PAULO E. VANZOLINI

Tropical America encompasses a great diversity of habitats. In a single day's drive in Ecuador it is possible to pass through Andean páramos (moors at a high elevation), cloud forests, lowland rain forests, marshes, mangrove swamps, and even desert beaches. These habitats are all tropical, yet they have little in common except geographic proximity. It would be difficult to describe them all in a single short book.

The lowland forest—the jungle of common parlance—is the subject of our discussion. But there are many kinds of forest in the tropical lowlands of South and Central America. We will focus in particular on the lowland rain forest.

The greatest expanse of this forest is in the Amazon basin. The Amazon forest is one of the wonders of our planet, and this vast expanse is the largest tract of rain forest in the world. But not all rain forests in tropical America are Amazonian, and although they may look insignificant on the map, the total area of these other rain forests is substantial. The most important of these non-Amazonian rain forests are those along the Caribbean coast of Central America, the northwest coast of South America, and southeastern Brazil.

Tropical rain forests are not accidents of nature, randomly placed on the earth's surface. There is an order to their distribution, and to understand this order we must consider how our planet hurtles through the universe.

The earth rotates about its axis once each day and travels around the sun once each year. This means that every point on the earth's surface receives the same amount of daylight each year, a total of 4,380 hours (give or take a few minutes, which we make up every so often in leap years). Our long summer days are precisely as long as our long winter nights and we finish the year in balance. This is true even in the polar regions, which have constant daylight during the summer and constant darkness during the winter. But the axis of the earth's daily rotation is not perpendicular to its orbit, and this inclination has several implications. It explains the familiar seasons of the temperate zones—during the winter we are tilted away from the sun and during the summer we are tilted toward the sun. It also explains why the seasons are reversed in the southern hemisphere, because when the north is tilted toward the sun, the south is tilted away. What may be less obvious is that only part of the earth's surface ever receives direct overhead sunlight: those places that lie between two lines of latitude, the Tropic of Cancer in the north and the Tropic of Capricorn in the south. Within these borders, daylength remains more or less constant through the year. These are the tropics, or as Darwin was wont to call them, the intertropical regions.

The tropics are characterized by climatic features that residents of the temperate zones find unusual. There is little seasonal change in temperature, the type of seasonality we are accustomed to. Days and nights are about the same length throughout the year. In the tropics you don't have to worry about sending your children off to school on dark winter mornings, but you miss out on lingering, lazy summer evenings.

The intensity of tropical sunlight is difficult to describe, though the reason for its intensity is clear enough. It is related once again to the tilt of the earth. A beam of sunlight striking the earth in the temperate zones always strikes at an angle because the sun is never directly overhead. The radiant energy of this beam of sunlight is therefore spread out. In the tropics, the same beam of sunlight strikes the earth perpendicularly, or at least more directly than in the temperate zones, and the same amount of energy is therefore focused on a correspondingly smaller area. This effect is further intensified by the earth's protective mantle of air. Sunlight hitting the temperate zones at an angle passes through more energy-absorbing atmosphere than it does before striking the tropics. The intensity of tropical sunlight can be awesome. Newcomers must always be wary of its power, particularly if they are sporting pasty winter complexions; a shirt may not offer enough protection from the sun, and we have seen some visitors blister beneath thin coverings.

The intense tropical sunlight warms the air, and tropical latitudes are characterized by warm temperatures. Since daylength is more or less constant through the tropical year, there is relatively little fluctuation in temperatures through the year. Those of us who live in the temperate zones are accustomed to heatwaves during the summer and cold spells during the winter, both of which are consequences of varying daylengths. The long summer days heat the air, and if the air is stagnant, this heat accumulates and can't be lost during the short nights. The perpetual darkness in the Arctic region during the northern winters allows ample opportunity for air to lose its heat, and when this frigid air pushes into our more temperate latitudes it can cause devastating cold spells. But in the tropics the uniformity of daylength means that there are no such opportunities for heat to build up or be lost. Although there may be seasonal fluctuations in temperature, they tend to be minor.

The tropics are not necessarily characterized by high temperatures; if anything, they lack truly hot weather. The hottest place we have visited in tropical America was near Lake Maracaibo in Venezuela. We were searching for a mysterious little lizard, known from a single specimen collected in the early years of the century; but the heat made it difficult for us to work efficiently. The entire basin seemed suspended in still, hot air, and there were times when it seemed thick enough to eat. This was thornscrub rather than forest, and the scanty vegetation seemed to intensify the heat; yet as far as we recall, the temperature never reached 100 degrees Fahrenheit. This heat was exceptional apparently even for the region, and in general we rarely encounter temperatures over 90 degrees in our travels in the American tropics. When we lived in Arizona the summer temperatures were routinely over 100 degrees, occasionally exceeding 115 degrees, and summer heatwaves often bring temperatures over 90 degrees even in New England. So the lowland tropics we know are not extremely hot. But they are very warm, and they may seem even warmer because of the high humidity.

There is an exception to the rule of the warm tropics. As you climb a tropical mountain, the air temperature decreases at a predictable rate: for every 1,000 feet you climb, the temperature drops about 3 degrees Fahrenheit. When air rises it expands. Expanding air does work, and work requires energy. If the energy needed to expand comes from the air itself, heat is lost during the work and the air cools. Anyone who has felt the cold air coming from a deflating inner tube after a hot summertime float trip can attest to the cooling nature of expanding air. This cooling with elevation is typical of any mountainous region, but it seems particularly noticeable in the tropics, perhaps because it can be so unexpected and so refreshing. Whenever we wish respite from the uniform warmth of the tropical lowlands in Ecuador, all we have to do is find our way to Quito, the capital city perched 9,000 feet high in the Andes, where we can enjoy a climate as pleasant and invigorating as early fall in New England.

The difference in the intensity of sunlight on a tilted earth has other effects. It accounts for the major global patterns of air and water circulation, which in turn determine patterns of rainfall. Warm air is less dense than cool air, and when tropical air is warmed by the intense sunlight, it rises. As it rises, cooler air from the temperate latitudes takes its place, and the resulting flow of cool temperate air into the tropics has played a major role in both human and natural history. These steady winds, formed by the warming and rising of tropical air, are the trade winds, and as any sailor knows, trade winds move in predictable directions.

The direction in which they blow is another consequence of the earth's rotation. The surface of the earth moves faster at the equator than in the temperate latitudes. This may not seem right, but it is true. The earth is more or less spherical, and its greatest circumference is at the equator. Since the earth rotates around its axis once a day, a church steeple in Quito actually travels 24,000 miles in an easterly direction every day. In the temperate latitudes, the diameter of the earth is less: at the latitude of Minneapolis, for example, the earth is less than 17,000 miles in diameter, and a church steeple there moves some 300 miles per hour more slowly than its counterpart in Quito. If a mass of air moves from the equator northward, it should veer in an easterly direction because it is moving faster than the surface of the earth in that direction. Likewise, an air mass moving from the north to the equator veers in a westerly direction because it is moving more slowly than the surface of the earth and loses ground in a direction opposite the rotation. If the air moving to the equator should be cool air replacing the warm rising air, the winds that result come from a northeasterly direction. These steady trade winds also push ocean water, and when this water meets land, it must go somewhere. The northeasterly trade winds in the Caribbean push water against the Central and South American coast. As the water deflects northward, it moves in a northeasterly direction and is called the Gulf Stream. This tongue of warm water flows atop the cold temperate Atlantic Ocean.

Winds and ocean currents on a rotating, tilted earth help explain major patterns of rainfall. The trade winds pick up moisture as they flow across the ocean. Warm air can hold more moisture than cool air, and as the northeasterly trades enter the American tropics, they pick up moisture from the sea. As the air warms further, it begins to rise, and rising air loses heat. When the air cools, its capacity for holding moisture drops, and the excess water falls as rain. The abundant rains produced by the cooling of moisture-laden tropical air give birth to the lush forests of tropical America—the piece of tropical nature that we find so fascinating.

Rain forest requires abundant rain, but a large amount of rain is not in itself sufficient to nurture an evergreen rain forest. Tropical climates may show little seasonal variation in temperature, yet they often show marked seasonality in rainfall. It is this seasonality of rainfall that defines the rain forest. If the dry season is long enough and dry enough, trees shed leaves to reduce water

loss. Tropical deciduous forests are sere expanses of brown and
gray during the dry season, the only spots of color the green cactus
trunks growing amid moribund gray trees. Yet come the rains, these
forests quickly leaf out to look as verdant as any rain forest. When
the rains quit for the year, the trees lose their leaves once again;
but before they slip into dormancy, many of them burst into flower.

In some forests it never becomes dry enough for all the trees to
lose all their leaves. Even during the driest months of the year
these forests look green. Here and there may be scattered leafless
trees, but the signs of water shortage are evident elsewhere, though
they may be subtle. Streams are crystal clear, shrunken, and seem
to hold far more fish than they can possibly support. You can
hear dead leaves crackle underfoot when you walk through the
forest. These tropical moist forests are transitions between forests
that have abundant moisture throughout the year and forests that
are parched for part of the year; the plants and animals that live in
them show affinities to both.

The boundaries of true rain forest are difficult to define. Natural
boundaries, unlike political boundaries, are seldom sharply de-
marcated and there may be complex interdigitations of one type
of vegetation into another. Tropical rain forests may shade im-
perceptibly into tropical moist forests, which in turn may shade
gradually into tropical deciduous forests. The forest that lines the
banks of tropical rivers in seasonally dry habitats can more closely
resemble a rain forest hundreds of miles away in both structure
and species composition than it does a patch of deciduous forest
several hundred yards away. There are trees that lose their leaves
even in the wettest rain forest, but they seem to do so in response
to their own cycles rather than to real shortages of moisture. Even
during the driest months rain forest does not want for water. This
doesn't mean that it has to rain heavily every month, but if there
is not much rain there should be little evaporation.

One of the rain forests we are most familiar with gets little rain
during part of the year. During this dry season, however, the
region is almost constantly cloaked in a layer of damp clouds.
The relatively cool, moisture-saturated air ensures that plants lose
little water to the environment, and the forests remain lush and
green throughout the year even though the total annual rainfall
is not that great. In general, lowland rain forests in tropical
America receive at least 100 inches of rainfall annually, and

monthly rainfall rarely drops below 6 inches. This is enough moisture to prevent most trees from losing their leaves, so that the rich lowland rain forests present a uniformly green aspect to the visiting naturalist regardless of when he or she is able to travel.

There are some rain forests that show no real dry seasons. Although rainfall may be cyclic, there are no dry and wet seasons; these places are often said to have wet seasons and flood seasons. The wettest forests in tropical America, and perhaps in the world, are found along the Pacific coast of Colombia. In this area the warm El Niño current lies offshore, while the Andes protect the land from the northeasterly trade winds that might blow the moisture-laden clouds out to sea. Warm, moisture-laden air wafts in from El Niño. When it hits the steep western face of the Andes Mountains and cools, prodigious amounts of rainfall result. The average annual rainfall may exceed 360 inches in some parts of the Colombian Chocó.

The Pacific coast of tropical South America shows clearly the relationship between ocean currents and rainfall. The warm El Niño is a small backcurrent that circulates off tropical America. Water is a marvelous heat trap, and tropical oceans often are warmer than the air over tropical lowlands. If warm, moisture-saturated air crosses cooler land, rain will fall as the air cools. If there are tall mountains, it rains more because the air cools even more as it rises. The major current lapping western South America is the Humboldt Current, a tongue of cold Antarctic water driven by the southeasterly trade winds of the southern hemisphere. Cold air picks us little moisture from a cold ocean, so when these cool breezes drift over warm land, rain doesn't fall. Parts of the Atacama Desert in Chile have never recorded a rainfall, and even Lima, the capital city of Peru, rarely receives rain. The arid coastal deserts of Peru and Chile give way to the lush rain forests of Pacific Colombia suddenly. Where El Niño holds sway, the rains fall and the land is cloaked with lush rain forest. Where the Humboldt dominates, the rain rarely falls and the land may appear barren of life.

There is a zone of transition in western Ecuador very close to the equator, and here El Niño and the Humboldt fight for control each year. The currents shift slightly from season to season, and when El Niño prevails, there is a rainy season that is sufficient to foster the growth of forest. The effects of this warm current are usually felt around Christmas; it is the life-giving nature of the rains that gives the current its name (the Child).

This brief characterization of rain forest in tropical America is necessarily simple. The climate of tropical rain forest is uniformly wet and warm, yet these terms are relative, not absolute. There is a distinction between climate and weather. Within the human time frame the climate of tropical forest is reasonably predictable; but weather can be as capricious and unpredictable in the tropics as it is in the temperate zones.

I was once in southern Peru, along the Rio Tambopata, during a cold spell. This region is reputed to have the richest fauna of any single area in the world; more species of birds and butterflies have been recorded there than anywhere else. Giant otters still swim undisturbed in lagoons they share with black caimans, and jaguar sign is seen regularly. My stay was to be brief, but I hoped to see as much as possible during the short time available. On the first night a strong wind blew in from the south, bringing rain and cool air. It got colder and colder, and by morning I was chilled to the bone beneath my thin sheets. The gray skies and scudding low clouds reminded me of an early spring storm in New England, and I shivered all day in the cold rain and wind. This was not the weather I had expected in a lowland Amazonian forest, but apparently these cold storms are a regular, if unpredictable, element of the region's climate.

Freak storms are not the only vagaries of tropical weather. Wet and dry seasons are predictable only in a general sense. We once wanted to study the burst of frog-breeding activity that occurs when a tropical pond fills. The rainy season in western Ecuador was supposed to begin in January, and we greeted each new heavy rain with anticipation, hoping it would signal the beginning of the deluge, but they were always false alarms. Finally, in the middle of February, we grew tired of the wait and struck off in search of greener pastures, only to return a week later and discover we had missed the big event. The pond, which had been a damp depression the week before, was a full-fledged little lake when we returned and the initial concupiscence of the frogs was spent.

Annual averages concerning climate should also not be taken too seriously. The rain forests in eastern Ecuador receive about 200 inches of rain each year, and rarely does a month pass without at least 8 inches to keep the trees green. The last time I visited this rich forest, a curious brownish pall hung over the horizon as far as I could see. Even though I was born and raised in Los Angeles, the brownish haze seemed excessive. It was the smoke of countless fires, some burning in the rain forest itself, but most burning in the grassy llanos hundreds of miles to the north. The upper Amazon was in the throes of drought, and it was the only time I have ever been there when leaves crackled beneath my feet. Eventually the rains resumed, and the forest probably did not suffer much for the drought; yet the annual rainfall that year was far below normal.

The tropical rain forest may not have a perfectly regular and predictable pattern of weather, but there is no question that weather forecasters in Panama lead a less stressful life than their colleagues in New England. They could probably tape their forecasts twice a year, once during the wet season and once during the dry season, play these back without modification on the nightly news, and be right more often than the most diligent and experienced meteorologist in the eastern United States.

Although lacking the drama of seasonal change that North Americans are accustomed to, the warm, damp, relatively aseasonal climate of the tropical lowlands more than compensates by the wealth of life it supports. This is the climate responsible for nurturing the incredible diversity of life in the Neotropical rain forests.

Chapter 2

FERTILITY

*Quick are the mouths of earth, and quick are the
teeth that feed upon this loveliness.*
—THOMAS WOLFE
Look Homeward, Angel

Many of the Europeans who first prospected the rain forests of
tropical America in search of farmland suffered from a delusion.
They saw visions of fertility, mirages of fecundity, in the towering
forests that covered so much of the land. The lush forests and the
thick tangle of riparian vegetation they encountered as they
traveled the interior were manifestations of what they thought
had to be tremendously productive soil. How else could such an
abundance of life be sustained?

It was a reasonable yet tragic piece of logic. The forests were
immense and rich; they covered vast expanses of the South
American continent; and any given area contained twice the
vegetative mass of an equivalent parcel of European forest. But
when these forests were cut and the slash burned off, a few crop
plantings showed the soil weak and easily exhausted. Where there

once flourished massive trees and a wonderland of lianas and vines, fields of manioc and maize gave only mediocre and ever-decreasing yields. Viewed against the lush backdrop of primeval forest, the crops were thin and pitiful. This was a mystery wrapped in misery. As the soil died and the crops failed, the hungry settlers moved on, slaughtering more forest and destroying pieces of the puzzle as they went.

It is perhaps only with the wisdom of hindsight that we can claim the clues to solving this paradox were obvious. A perceptive naturalist from temperate latitudes will stumble on one such clue immediately: there is a striking difference in the way the tropical forest *feels*. The resilient spring of conifer duff and the deep layers of deciduous leaf litter that characterize forests in the northern temperate zone are absent. The soft bed of loamy soil, fragrant with the rich smell of humus that tired hikers find so comforting, will not be found in the rain forests of the upper Amazon basin.

The rain forest floor has litter, but it is often a thin layer, rarely more than a few centimeters deep. If you brush it aside with your boot, an intricately interwoven mass of white threads will be revealed just under the surface. This pallid, tangled mass consists of the rootlets of forest trees and strands of fungal mycelia. And if you carefully trace the wandering path of a fungal thread from a rotting fruit or a decomposing leaf, you will often find that it leads to the tiny rootlet of a large tree. The root systems of the massive forest giants are bound together with lowly fungi in complex, mutually beneficial relationships. These relationships, known as mycorrhizal associations, seem to operate in much the same manner as do lichens, a familiar temperate zone symbiosis between fungi and photosynthetic algae. Each member of the association special-izes in the production and uptake of different nutrients: the photosynthetic trees provide important sources of energy and the nonphotosynthetic fungi provide certain critical minerals.

The fungi are particularly adept at recycling phosphorus and potassium, minerals that are often in short supply in rain forest yet are critical to tree growth. These minerals are quickly lost from fallen fruits and leaves, and unless recovered rapidly they can be washed away in the heavy rains characteristic of this type of forest. The fungal mycorrhizae can quickly recycle these soluble minerals, and they can return almost twenty times as much phosphorus and potassium to the trees as is lost to the rains. The constant temperature and high humidity of the rain forest floor provides a perfect environment for fungi—one that allows particularly rapid growth. Fungi can invade new sources of fertility far more rapidly than a tree rootlet can, and this rapid capacity for growth and colonization lessens the loss of valuable nutrients from the forest ecosystem. Under the silent, relentless chemical jaws of the fungi, the debris of the forest quickly disappears. The leaves that constitute much of the litter vanish within a few weeks, and even the massive boles of fallen forest trees often erode away within a few years. This digestive process goes on much more rapidly in tropical rain forest than it does in temperate forests.

Tropical rain forests provide few large accumulations of fertility. In temperate zones the first awakening rove beetles each spring find a cornucopia as the stirring landscape reveals the thawing corpses of chickadees and porcupines killed during the winter. But in the tropics you are unlikely ever to stumble across a corpse; such treasure troves of spent life are quickly broken down and returned to the world of the living.

There is a dynamic balance in this rapid turnover of life and death. The tropical lowland rain forest is what some ecologists would call a mature ecosystem; it has reached a steady state in which the products of growth, upon dying, are quickly transmuted and transported back to the world of the living. There is no surplus of nutrients, no bank of minerals to rely on when the system is stressed. In a black prairie chernozem soil or the loam of a temperate forest, humus—the true organic fat of the land—builds up quickly and deepens with each passing year. This does not happen in many tropical forests. Nutrients crucial to plant growth may be leached away quickly and lost, or they may be trapped by the mycorrhizal mat and returned to the living forest. Some studies have shown that as little as one tenth of 1 percent of forest nutrients ever penetrate below the first five centimeters of soil in tropical rain forest. The mycorrhizae are agents of rapid digestion as well as efficient assimilators. This efficiency accounts for the poverty of the soil, while the close association between these fungi and the giant forest trees helps explain how such a thin soil can support such a tremendous mass of life.

Given the intense competition for nutrients that prevails in many, if not most, lowland tropical rain forests, it should be apparent that fertility cannot be maintained by the crude techniques of pioneer agriculture. The slash-and-burn or swidden agriculture employed by some of the Amerindians of the rain forest is certainly crude by modern agricultural criteria, and might not seem all that different from the practice of early European settlers. But Amerindians lived in low densities. Their fields were small and short-lived, so that the area of destruction could be renewed by detrital input from the surrounding forest. When they moved on, the closeness of mature rain forest provided a ready supply of seeds and shoots to recover the abandoned fields.

Animals also contribute to the rapid recycling of nutrients. If you sit quietly, you can sometimes even hear this process. Large long-horned beetle larvae generate an audible crunch as they chew through solid wood and the trundling steps of millipedes are always near. Less obvious but far more significant are the termites, who toil in the dark of night or under the cover of bark or soil. Their large nests, which look like immense boils or galls, are often conspicuous on tree trunks high above the ground; but these visible nests give only a hint of the true abundance of these creatures. Termites appear to devour raw cellulose in its crudest form, and although this food may not be tainted with poisons, it is gastronomically formidable because of its low nutritional quality. Termites can do this only with the aid of protozoan symbionts that dwell in their guts. The protozoans make quick hash of coarse organic debris like wood, rendering it palatable for the hungry termites. With the aid of their gut symbionts, termites are the cattle of the litter zone, shredding the roughage and ultimately producing more fodder for the ever-present fungi.

The waste products of litter animals are rich in nutrients in a form easily used by plants and fungi. But this is not the only way small arthropods contribute to mineral recycling and fungal welfare. In the wet tropics even lowly fungi can become predators on the living—and they needn't wait for death to provide them with fuel. It is not unusual to find a moth or a spider, or perhaps a large ponerine ant, rigidly clutching a plant, with a *Cordiceps* fungus already fruiting wildly from its corpse.

The net result of all this rot is a rapid turnover of the nutrient pool that is the living forest. Yet the rapidity of this process is not well conveyed by staring at a mycorrhizal mat on the forest floor. Despite all of its implications, this static mass conveys no intimation of the rapid pulse of nutrient exchange in tropical rain forest. Fortunately, a far more spectacular embodiment of this rapid turnover is readily available to any naturalist blessed with an open mind and a healthy appetite.

Tropical rain forest is not yet considered a suitable playground for the rich and indolent, and there are few luxury hotels close to lowland rain forest, so most naturalists who visit tropical rain forest must lodge in a modest *pension* or field station, camp in a national park, or stay with one of the local citizens. This inevitably exposes temperate zone naturalists to a diet consisting of some combination of beans, starch, and grease, a cuisine notable for more than its simple and bountiful gastronomic delights; when combined with a cup of strong coffee, it is renowned for generating large, healthy bowel movements. Aside from the biological necessity of this activity, it has great educational attributes when performed in the tropical rain forest.

What happens to dung on the rain forest floor is one of nature's vast spectacles on an intimate scale, competition for a precious resource at its most intense—a battle and scramble full of color and pattern. It is simple to witness. After nature calls, do not beat a hasty, embarrassed retreat but sit quietly nearby. The earliest contestants will arrive soon after you settle down. First are the tiny dung scarab beetles and metallic ottitid flies. The flies quickly set up for mate acquisition, a contest in which males engage in vigorous charging bouts accompanied by wing-flipping. While this is happening, the little dung scarabs go about their simple business: they plunge in and begin feeding. Many of the females are ripe with eggs ready for laying, and they may bury some eggs as they gobble contentedly away.

The later arrivals are larger and behaviorally more complex scarab beetles. They are less adept at homing in on the odor, and unlike the smaller early arrivals who plunge directly in, they often overshoot their target before finally converging on it. Upon landing they embark on a series of maneuvers designed to secure a private cache of food that they will either eat themselves or barter for copulatory rights. Some dung scarabs, such as the various *Canthon* species, slice off balls of dung using specially modified hind limbs, then roll their loot away from the churning battlefield using the same hind limbs. Speed is essential. If the dung ball is contaminated with the eggs of flies or small beetles, it will be useless to *Canthon* because their larvae grow relatively slowly and the dung will be gone before they can develop. Those who dally also risk having their prize usurped by a larger rival unwilling to go through the work of preparing a dung ball.

Female *Canthon* select their mates by the size of their balls. They jump aboard the rolling dung ball, scrambling to stay aloft as they ride away on the spinning nuptial globe. The ardent male pushes his ball and passenger over sticks and other obstacles with unabashed Darwinian zeal. After rolling his treasures several yards, the male stops to excavate a burrow for the ball. Only then will his rider allow him to mount her. The couple may pause for a brief meal, scraping some dung off the ball before it is buried to provide sustenance for the coming brood.

The sequestering of dung is a more cooperative venture for other scarab beetles. In these species, the male drags great loads of dung to a hole that the female busily excavates. He deposits his load at the burrow entrance and the female carries it inside, where she molds it into egg-shaped masses that become provisions for the larvae's pantry. In these species the males often fight furiously over both dung and females, and it is not surprising that many of these combative males sport large, rhinoceros-like horns. Females of the large burrowing species often remain with their brood balls for several months, rotating them from time to time to guard them against attack from fungus and burrowing insects. The males linger only briefly by the burrows; they stay only long enough for sex and a quick meal before departing in search of an encore.

While the scarabs are carting away dung, long, sleek staphylinid beetles arrive on the scene. Agile and voracious, they burrow under the dung mass in search of their prey. They are not after the rich dung; what they are looking for are the small scarab beetles, fly larvae, and insect eggs that abound under the heap after it has sat for a while. Black oval histerid beetles churn through the dung like small bulldozers, devouring insect eggs as they go. Stingless bees carefully gather loads of dung in special pockets on their legs and carry them back to their nests. They disappear into the entrance tubes of their nests after signaling their nest mates where the riches are, but what they do with the dung is not known.

Of all the dung deposited in tropical rain forest, human scat is the most avidly sought and the most quickly removed. More than fifty species of dung scarabs may converge on a pile of our manure before it is gone. For some reason, perhaps our protein-rich diet, our scat is much more attractive than that of other rain forest mammals. Carnivore dung consists mostly of bones, feathers, and hair, and offers few rewards to the diligent beetles. Bird droppings, with their high concentrations of uric acid, are savored only by a few ants and butterflies. These less desirable dungs may remain visible on the forest floor for days as they are slowly broken down and utilized. But since dung beetles are so enamored of the human product, it often takes only a few hours before all evidence of the intense struggle has been buried and dispersed.

We have spent many hours studying this struggle and pondering its lessons. It is a revelation to see this despised substance sought so eagerly by so many beautiful creatures, but our attempts to interest friends and students in such events have not been completely successful. Raw fertility is not pretty, and Western man's loathing of excreta, recent though it may be, seems deeply ingrained. Unless we are gardeners or farmers, we become divorced from the fertile byproducts of ourselves and our fellow creatures. Some may argue that this revulsion is an adaptive avoidance of a source of pathogenic organisms, and there is certainly no doubt that human dung plays a major role in disease transmission in many parts of the world. But we wonder whether a Chinese farmer exclaims "Shit!" when something distasteful happens?

Perspiration is another case in point. Although sweating is beneficial to one's health, large amounts of the resources of American society seem to be directed at eradicating or hiding it. The rain forest affords us a more enlightened appreciation of our own exuviae. In an environment where there is a great demand for nutrients like potassium, our perspiration is not merely the foul precursor of a socially aggressive pheromonal musk. To the clear-winged ithomiid butterflies—diaphanous pale creatures winged with translucent membranes and delicately etched veins— the value of our sweat is clear. They sit eagerly on our shirts probing for its salty treasures when we pause to rest in the forest. To these elegant little creatures, we are oozing not a malodorous substance but a prized resource no different from the sweet nectar of a tropical blossom. In the tropical rain forest the intense demand for nutrients can imbue our cast-off byproducts with a biological significance that far outweighs our cultural taboos.

If the prospect of dung-gazing fails to strike your fancy, you may find some consolation in the fact that a rotting pile of fruit will present a similar, although less intense, set of events. Indeed, any concentration of fertility will be the object of great interest in most lowland tropical rain forests. And although such pockets may be rare, they do exist.

Another example of the intensity of competition for nutrients in tropical rain forest was brought to our attention by Daniel Janzen, a tropical ecologist at the University of Pennsylvania. He suggested that rain forest trees have evolved a tendency to develop rot in their cores, since the rotted cores become hollows that often harbor animals and their nutrient-rich excreta. These trees, Janzen argues, may be trading off some structural stability for an increased access to fertility.

We balked at this proposal when first we heard it. It seems far more likely that a tree with a rotten, hollowed-out core is simply a loser in the battle with saprophytic fungi, termites, and wood-boring beetles. But after considering the idea for several years we find it less and less far-fetched, if yet unproven. Hollow tropical trees are in great demand for use as roosts and nest sites by many animals, ranging from bees and wasps to bats and opossums. When such a tree is occupied by an owl, a nutrient bonanza is evident because owls typically deposit pellets and defecate where they roost. There may be quarts of rodent bones and guano heaped within the hollow core of a living tree, and these are substances fertile enough to inspire lust in the souls of even the mildest of gardeners.

It was after seeing one of these hollow tree middens that we first began to warm to Janzen's notion. This particular deposit was the work of a single bat, a solitary individual of *Vampyrum spectrum*, largest of the New World bats. This uncommon creature has a wing span of almost a yard, and its massive jaws give it a frightening aspect in keeping with its predatory habits. *Vampyrum* is not like the giant fruit-eating bats of the Old World tropics; it sweeps the Neotropical night searching sonically for birds and lizards sleeping amid the foliage. It brings its victims home to a hollow tree core to meet their fate, and there it shows a casual disregard for the trifles of etiquette and hygiene as it dines sloppily away.

While working in Costa Rica I heard of a *Vampyrum* roost within my study area. I was concerned primarily with six-legged creatures at the time and felt no particular urge to locate the roost. My nonchalance continued until a brief but intense encounter with this magnificent predatory bat.

I was sitting by the edge of the forest one still evening when a startling rush of air and a terrific flurry of beating wings shattered my reverie. Alarmed by the suddenness of the sound, I turned to confront its source. But there was only a massive black shadow weaving its way into the fading light at great speed and with the peculiar cadences of bat flight.

Entranced by this fleeting glimpse of the great predatory phantom, I returned to the area in daylight and searched for the roost, aided by the directions of a friend familiar with its haunts. When I found it, I was surprised that I hadn't noticed it before. The roost tree was surrounded by a profusion of feathers, the sometimes bright and sometimes dull remains of anis, parrots, and a host of other birds. I peered inside the hollow core of the tree, and although I couldn't see its sleeping resident, the floor of the hollow bespoke its presence. The bottom of the roost hole was several inches deep with the remains of its victims. It seemed to be a living carpet of bones, dried blood, and bat guano, the surface seething with the energetic feeding of insect larvae and adult beetles. This lodestone of fertility could be an enormously valuable resource to a nutrient-starved tree. Such a wealth of nutrients would seem to be worth the loss of structural stability that a hollow core dictates, and Janzen's hypothesis took on new significance.

Although concentrations of nutrients occur in the rain forest, most of the fertility of tropical nature is tied up in the trees themselves. When the forest is cut and the trees left in ashes, the soil is exposed. As the sun beats down unrelentingly on this fragile substance, its temperature increases and it begins to dry out. The process accelerates the loss of organic material and kills off the mycorrhizal mat. The loss of tree ashes to erosion is not easily rectified, and the input of new nutrients through rainfall is an exceedingly slow business. Hundreds of years may be required to replace some of the important nutrients. Moreover, many tropical soils lack weatherable minerals like silicates, which are needed to build new soils. Tropical soils are often lateritic; they are poor soils, stained red with iron compounds that quickly lose their fertility and react with the sun and rain to bake as hard as pavement. Once these fragile soils are exposed, they die, and forest returns slowly if ever.

It is in the trees that the nutrient wealth of the rain forest resides. In the dimly lit understory of virgin rain forest few herbs or grasses can exist. The limited productivity of the forest understory has had an uplifting effect on the native inhabitants. There are few large understory grazers in closed-canopy forest anywhere, and the Neotropical rain forest is no exception to this rule. Understory herbivores like peccaries and tapirs are less common than their temperate zone counterparts, a fact that led many European settlers to regard the rain forest as a gastronomic desert.

The scarcity of earthbound red meat also had an impact on the human residents of the rain forest. Some anthropologists believe that competition for mammalian protein is one of the primary forces driving intertribal warfare. When a Mundurucu tribesman returns home from a raid carrying the head of a neighboring villager, he is given the title "Mother of the Peccary." The Yanomoma chant "I am a meat-hungry buzzard" prior to setting out on a homicidal raid.

Although some anthropologists dispute this interpretation, the fact remains that most rain forest browsers and foliage eaters spend their time foraging in the upper levels of the forest canopy, where they attempt to exploit the limited supply of available greenery. Although the lush visual aspect of rain forest belies this limited supply, these forests actually have a low percentage of green growth compared with even Arctic tundra or boreal forest. This is because most of the nutrients in rain forest trees are tied up in the heartwood, and much of what is not is unpalatable (see Chapter 8).

The ultimate expression of the skyward concentration of nutrients available to foliage feeders is found in the sloth. Although sloths are edentates, cousins to the toothless armadillos and anteaters, they have well-developed crushing teeth and a digestive tract that resembles that of a grazing ruminant. It is difficult to imagine a creature more fitted for arboreal life than the sloth. Many of their attributes are well known: the long claws and limbs, the slow, deliberate movements, and the tireless ability to hang upside down from a limb contribute not only to their ability to live in trees but also to the strong associations implied by their name (in many Latin American countries they are called *perezosos*, or lazies). These beasts are camouflaged by their greenish tint, an unusual color for a mammal (mammals more usually tend toward browns and grays); in fact, the color is due to algae that grow in the fur rather than to a green pigment, further testament both to their arboreality and sluggish demeanor.

There is one aspect of sloth biology that seems curiously out of line with these adaptations to arboreal grazing. And, in keeping with the scatological tone of this chapter, this curiosity has to do with the defecatory habits of the sloth.

Sloths defecate small, hard pellets, usually only once a week or so. This makes sense for an arboreal creature because it conserves water, which may not be easy to come by high in the canopy of even the wettest rain forest. But they do not defecate the easy way, which is to say from on high. Instead, they laboriously and deliberately descend from their lofty trees, poke a hole in the ground with their stubby tails, and carefully bury their feces near the base of the tree. This is curious indeed. The sloth expends a great deal of time and energy coming down from its home on high merely to dispose of some waste material. In the treetops it is virtually immune from predation, whereas on the ground it can be eaten by a variety of large carnivores. Howler mankeys, who inhabit the same forests and eat many of the same foods as do the sloths, defecate freely from the treetops and are extremely reluctant to venture onto the forest floor for any reason, even though their great agility and the many watchful eyes of their social groups help protect them from predation. Is there any reason why a sloth, who lacks both agility and social groups, would risk coming down in order to neatly dispose of its dung?

Perhaps the sloth is acting as a recycling gardener, by feeding its tree crops with its own "wastes." This notion may seem absurd at first, but is it any stranger than a rabbit consuming its own feces to conserve Vitamin B?

Consider the sloth of the sloth. Sloths move slowly, to say the least, and their laziness extends to their physiology as much as to their behavior. Their basal metabolism is about half that of most mammals of similar size, which means that they require relatively little energy to maintain themselves. This low basal metabolism is related in turn to their low body temperature, which they do not regulate as closely as most other mammals. Sloths also have small home ranges. Over a period of several months an individual may feed on only fifteen to forty neighboring trees. More significantly, sloths have modal trees—trees in which they spend a disproportionate amount of time. These modal trees may lose almost 10 percent of their total annual production to the resident sloth. If this sounds insignificant, think of it in terms of losing ten to twenty pounds of your body weight. In some cases, modal trees may be used by more than one sloth, and these trees can lose a fifth of their total annual production to their guests. Since about half of the nutrients cropped by a sloth can be returned to the tree via the sloth's feces, their careful deposition of this valuable resource might serve them well in the long run. The modal trees do not lose as much as they might otherwise and sloth feces decompose slowly, providing a long-term nutrient source.

You might wonder how much difference it can make to deposit these pellets at the base of a tree compared to scattering them from high above the ground. No data exist, but it is easy to visualize a cascade of pellets dropping from 100 feet or more being deflected and caught by bromeliads, vines, and branches during the descent. Were they to become scattered on the forest floor, which would surely happen if they were dropped from the canopy, the benefits of fertility would be spread to many plants and not just to the modal tree. Because howler monkeys range so widely through the forest and lack modal trees, there is no need for them to exhibit defecatory behavior like that of the sloth.

This scenario may be pure wishful thinking on our part; there may be a more parsimonious explanation for the hygienic ways of the sloth. But we like to believe that in the arduous, dangerous descent of the sloth there is a metaphor, a message urging humans to show a similar regard for conserving the fertility of the tropical rain forest.

Chapter 3

CANYONS OF LIGHT

> *Tropical vegetation has a fatal tendency*
> *to produce rhetorical exuberance*
> *in those who describe it.*
> PAUL RICHARDS
> The Tropical Rainforest

Richards' admonition was already an old complaint when he voiced it in 1952. Over a century ago, the great Victorian naturalist Alfred Russel Wallace warned his readers that "the luxuriance and beauty of Tropical Nature is a well-worn theme, and there is little new to say about it." Nevertheless, the difficulty of describing tropical rain forest continues to spawn hackneyed descriptions and clichés. The most common of these clichés seems to be to describe the forest as "cathedral-like"; although he probably would not have approved of its use, Wallace may have been responsible for creating this image. It was he who described the large buttressed trees as Gothic-like structures. Marston Bates, in his bestselling *The Forest and the Sea*, greatly elaborated on this metaphor, and the device has since been popularized to a cliché.

In any case, the metaphor is not munificent enough. Cathedrals may be solemn and beautiful places, but they are far simpler than any rain forest. The forms and functions of buttresses in Gothic churches are well understood, while the forms and possible functions of the buttresses of rain forest trees are poorly known. These rain forest buttresses are still the subject of scientific argument many years after Wallace drew attention to them.

Buttresses take on numerous shapes in the tropical rain forest, but they are typical of many of the larger trees. The trunks of these tall rain forest trees are often straight columns extending unbroken by branches until they reach the canopy. But beginning about twenty feet or so from the ground, they extend thin, widely spread buttresses into the ground. A line connecting these narrow buttresses might have a circumference of fifty feet, even though the trunk of the tree just above the buttresses might be only five or six feet in diameter.

The buttresses' most obvious function is mechanical stabilization: they help anchor the tree in the wet and shallow soils typical of many rain forests. But alternative explanations have also been advanced, including contentions that the buttresses assist in water conduction, increase the surface area for oxygen exchange, collect litter nutrients, and inhibit upward-climbing lianas. All of these ideas may have some validity, but anyone who has attempted to uproot a large tree stump with lateral root projections will probably agree that the stability argument seems most likely. Its detractors often question whether stability is an issue for large rain forest trees. These large trees are closed in by dense forest, and the tightly packed canopies they form buffer them from the ravages of wind. Besides, regions of tropical rain forest in most of South America are never visited by hurricanes, so wind is probably not much of a factor. However, this is theory based on casual observations, and it seems weak to us.

It is misleading to assume that wind is a minor factor in influencing the growth patterns of forest trees. We tend to make assumptions about tropical winds from a narrow perspective. Naturalists in the tropical rain forest generally stay near the ground, a part of the forest that is extremely well buffered from winds. The calm of the forest interior often belies the breezes that rustle through the canopy 100 feet above. Even in the strongest winds the forest floor remains calm, and often the only indications we have of the winds that accompany rain storms are the sounds of falling fruits and branches. Trees also live much longer than most human observers. If a region goes ten or twenty years between strong winds, we are likely to dismiss such occasional events as unimportant. But for a tree that may live two hundred years, strong storms at ten-, twenty-, or even fifty-year intervals are significant events.

The rain forest of the Madre de Dios in southern Peru may have the richest animal life of any region on earth. I expected to see magnificent tall forest with an uncluttered dark understory, the type of virgin rain forest I had seen elsewhere in tropical America. But the forest along the Rio Tambopata was low and scrubby, and looked to me more like second-growth forest than primeval rain forest. When I walked through it, the understory was dense enough to force me to stay on the trails. I was disappointed in its aspect and wondered why it looked so scruffy.

The answer came quickly. During the night a howling wind rose up from the south. The plains of Patagonia were gripped in the midst of winter and the wind that reached us was bitter cold for the tropical lowlands. The temperature the next day never rose above 60 degrees Fahrenheit, and the wind snapped off trees and branches throughout the forest. This wind, which lasted almost two days without respite, gave me a new appreciation for the significance of "abnormal" weather in the tropics. Along the Rio Tambopata the only tall trees were nestled in narrow ravines or protected from the south by hills. The strong winds did not come often to the area, but they seemed to have left their imprint on the shape and appearance of the forest.

Even though strong winds may not be typical of the lowland tropics, tree falls are common in rain forest. If wind is not the culprit, perhaps the asymmetry of tree crowns and the stresses wrought by clinging vines and epiphytes account for the high rate of tree falls. Whatever the causes, trees in tropical rain forest fall at a surprisingly steep rate, continually opening up new areas for succession. The result is a forest mosaic of mature canopy-level trees, understory shrubs, and seedlings, mixed with intermediate-sized trees growing toward the canopy. Monstrous trees are mingled with trees of smaller sizes, and the forest has a far more heterogeneous appearance than most people are led to believe. First-time vistors to the tropics bring simple preconceptions. They have read that the trees in the rain forest are arranged in several distinct layers, but they fail to appreciate the dynamic nature of these layers. Few things are obvious in tropical rain forest, and although distinct canopy layers may exist in some forests we have always found it difficult to recognize them even when they are pointed out to us.

Gary Hartshorn, a leading Neotropical forester, measured tree-fall rates in several Neotropical forests and found them to be so high that their turnover time (the time required for a forest to replace itself) is on the order of 80 to 135 years. This means that tropical rain forest may be considerably more dynamic than temperate forests. It also suggests a method by which the hundreds of tree species of a tropical forest coexist. Studies of competition among animal species usually find that they divide resources in a manner that allows each species to exist on a unique subset of the resource spectrum. It is relatively easy to imagine that a few dozen tree species in a temperate forest might apportion soil types, moisture, pH, light, and exposure to permit mutual coexistence. But dividing the same basic resources among the 400 or more tree species of a tropical rain forest seems nearly impossible.

When a tree falls, cleaving its way through the forest canopy, it opens a canyon of light and an avenue of change into the understory gloom. Light is energy, and energy brings change. The new patch of sunlight immediately stimulates great changes in the life of the forest floor. There is often a chaotic proliferation of weedy shrubs and tangled vines. But in the aggregate disorder of shrubs and vines that crowd a forest tree fall, ecologists are beginning to discern the patterns of change that the tree's fatal plunge sets into motion.

Tree-fall gaps are important and complicated resources in the tropical forest. Many trees are entirely dependent on these gaps to become established and to reach maturity—Hartschorn found that 75 percent of the trees in a Costa Rican rain forest depended on them. The gaps vary greatly in size, and the resulting differences in sunlight penetration produce microclimatic differences. Some trees are large-gap specialists, meaning that they require the intense light and high temperatures of large holes in the canopy for germination and growth. Their seedlings cannot tolerate shade. These large-gap specialists can use this intense sunlight far more efficiently than understory species. The plants of the forest understory are not accustomed to so much light and have become adapted to utilize efficiently the small quantities that are their normal lot. When more light is available, they are unable to take advantage of it with a growth spurt. Large-gap colonists typically grow rapidly and quickly spread their broad leaves into an umbrella-like crown that catches the maximum amount of sun. These specialists seem to require a gap of 1,000 square yards or more in order to be competitive with more shade-tolerant saplings. Gaps of this size are relatively rare and locating them presents problems in dispersal.

Most gap colonists have bird- or bat-dispersed seeds. Those species that specialize in large gaps are often prolific producers of fruits packed with many tiny seeds, and they usually bear fruit through much of the season. This shotgun reproductive strategy enhances the likelihood of having a seed present when a large gap in the canopy appears. Early arrival is critical because large gaps quickly sprout a matted tangle of light-thirsty vines and weedy ferns that may chemically inhibit the germination of late-arriving seeds. Many successful colonists in these large gaps are pioneers that reproduce early and soon succumb to competition; but others delay reproduction and continue growing until they become large canopy-layer trees.

Species specialized to grow in small light gaps can usually germinate in the shade beneath the dense canopy, although they require an opening in order to grow to reproductive size. Small gaps in the canopy are, of course, far more common than large ones, and many rain forest trees are adapted to grow under these conditions. These species generally have larger seeds that are dispersed less widely than the large-gap specialists' since their targets are closer and more abundant. The larger seeds facilitate rapid development of large root systems, which in turn result in larger seedlings. The store of carbohydrate reserves in the large seeds enables seedlings to wait for a gap to appear. These small-gap species do poorly in large gaps because they cannot keep pace with the rapid growth of the large-gap specialists.

There is no sharp division between large- and small-gap specialists. Many rain forest plants, notably the understory herbs and shrubs, germinate and grow to maturity in the absence of any gap at all. Gaps of all sizes exist, ranging from almost nothing to entire mountainsides opened by landslides, and the optimum gap size varies for each species. Gaps represent a heterogeneous resource for the plants of the rain forest, a resource that is clearly finely divided. Specialization mitigates competition among species to some extent, but there is also an element of randomness in the system. In the tropical rain forest, with its hundreds of tree species and hundreds of dispersal agents, virtually every gap will be contested by a unique combination of species. It is unlikely that a fallen tree will be replaced by a member of the same species, and it is even more unlikely that we will ever be able to give reliable probability estimates for the various replacement species.

Students of forest turnover in the temperate zones can make probabilistic estimates of what tree species are likely to replace a fallen beech or maple, and they can even predict the composition of the forest canopy in a mature forest. Henry Horn of Princeton University developed probability matrices for the New Jersey forest he studied, but he had to take into consideration only eleven tree species. The difficulties of measuring replacement probabilities for a forest with 200 or 300 tree species are immense. This complexity underscores the difficulties that a rain forest tree attempting to colonize a tree-fall gap must face: it must contend with hundreds of uniquely adapted competitors. Since tree-fall rates and gap sizes vary according to soil type, moisture, slope, and elevation—all of which may change within the dispersal range of a single tree—it is extremely difficult to predict the success of any given species of tree.

The process is further complicated because some of the contestant species have generation times of over two centuries. On this time scale a tree species that is gradually evolving the ability to drive a competitor to extinction may confront a climatic shift or a rare but profound environmental disturbance, such as an earthquake, flood, drought, fire, or volcanism, that will alter the conditions of the competitive contest. With this perturbation and the patchy, random occurrence of tree falls, it must be difficult for tropical forest ever to reach a predictable state of equilibrium. The concept of a climax community, which asserts that the relative abundances of different tree species can be predicted, may work well in the relatively simple forests of higher latitudes; it seems more appropriate to view virgin tropical rain forest as a patchy, constantly changing mosaic generated in large part by unpredictable tree falls.

Tree falls are of great consequence not only to the plants of the forest but also to the animals. A freshly fallen canopy giant is one of the most exciting places in the rain forest. A naturalist with an aversion to heights can glimpse the orchids and insect nests that are normally beyond sight or reach. The canopy contains many unique species, and were it not for tree falls our knowledge of these would be even more limited than it presently is. Even though scientists have now begun to ascend the living canopy of tropical rain forest with ropes and jumars, little is known of the plants and animals that dwell there. These adventurous observers are still confined to single trees, and it may be exceedingly difficult to collect and identify many of the creatures they observe. Fresh-fallen trees remain valuable resources for biologists intent on documenting and studying the diversity of tropical rain forests, and it sometimes seems as though each new fall offers surprises.

The flurry of activity that follows the descent of a large tree is often inspiring, particularly to entomologists. The freshly exposed sap wood of a new-fallen tree attracts noisy syrphid flies and many showy beetles. Long-horned harlequin beetles (*Acrocinus longimanus*) several inches long, striped with geometric patterns of yellow and orange; golden buprestid wood-boring beetles; and large black weevils all alight to sip the oozing sap and to lay their eggs in the massive pasture of wood. Parasitoid wasps interested in the immature stages of the flies and beetles patrol the log, and clouds of fruit flies begin congregating around the fermenting sap. If the gap is large and sunny, vines and shrubs quickly spring into flower. Passion vine flowers lure in butterflies seeking nectar and birds and bats seeking fruit. Morning glories lure bees, while *Aphelandra*, *Heliconia*, and other tubular-flowered plants attract hummingbirds, which vigorously defend each flowering patch.

Many of these pioneer plants grow, fruit, and flower through much of the year, so lighted areas of the forest—riverbanks, islands, river bends, and landslides—where pioneer plants thrive are attractive to many animals. Monkeys and other animals migrate into these super-gaps when the pickings in the rest of the forest are at a seasonal ebb. The premium placed on growth by the pioneer plants allows them to spend little on chemical defenses. Herbivores ranging from insects to sloths avail themselves of these islands of palatable foliage. Some birds are apparently specialized to feed in light gaps, which they may flock to in response to high insect densities. These high insect densities, in combination with sunlight, seem also to draw many lizards into tree falls and other gaps. The hot sun and the abundant supply of lizards may also draw in snakes. It is unproven lore among tropical naturalists that tree falls are the best areas in which to stumble across formidable rain forest serpents such as the terciopelo or fer-de-lance (*Bothrops atrox*).

The animals associated with light gaps must live in tune with the constant jumbling caused by unpredictable tree falls opening up new opportunities, and they may face shifting competitive success as the gaps fill in with greenery. The murky competitive interactions in the rain forest may never settle into a stable, predictable state where interspecific competition eliminates some species. It may be that the richness and diversity of the tropical rain forest is due not to age and predictability but to the constant change and disturbance engendered by falling trees.

Chapter **4**

HANGERS-ON

*At Tauau I first realised my idea of a primeval
forest. There were enormous trees, crowned with
magnificent foliage, decked with fantastic
parasites, and hung over with lianas, which
varied in thickness from slender threads to huge
python-like masses, were now round, now
flattened, and now twisted
with the regularity of a cable.*
—RICHARD SPRUCE
Notes of a Botanist on the Amazon and Andes

It is the epiphytes that tell you you're in a rain forest. Those
ferns, mosses, orchids, bromeliads, cacti, and even trees that live
suspended on other plants are largely responsible for the impression of luxuriance a tropical rain forest gives. The epiphytic life-
style reaches its zenith in the warm lowland rain forests and the
cool cloud forests of the tropics, where sometimes it seems as
though every bit of plant surface is a substrate for other plants.

The epiphytic habit is not unique to tropical forests. There
are epiphytes in temperate forests, but temperate epiphytes belong
to primitive plant groups such as algae, lichens, fungi, and mosses.
Only they can endure the freezing and desiccation that are the
bane of arboreal life in the temperate zones. These stresses are
greatly reduced in the wet and uniformly warm tropics, and whole
families of higher plants and thousands of species have taken up

the epiphytic way of life. Epiphytes account for much of the diversity of plant species in the wet forests of tropical America.

It is hard for a resident of a temperate zone to understand why an elevated life-style is so desirable for plants in tropical rain forest. Treetops don't seem an especially hospitable place, and nutrients must surely be in short supply if there is no contact with the earth. Living on a tree in a tropical rain forest in fact has one great advantage: it allows small plants to partake of strong tropical sunlight. The floor of mature rain forest is cloaked in gloom, and many plants find it difficult to thrive on such a meager diet of light. And there are other advantages to high-rise life. Potential for seed dispersal by the wind is increased. The dense mat of vegetation effectively cuts off any breezes inside the forest, but the canopy level of mature rain forest catches any breath of air, so plants in the canopy can take advantage of these air currents to scatter their seeds widely. Plants that live in the canopy also may have increased access to flying pollinators. The bats and birds that best serve these ends tend to avoid understory navigation.

Life on high is not without its stresses, though. Chief among these is lack of water. It is no accident that epiphytes reach their fullest development in the wettest forests, and it is no coincidence that cacti are common epiphytes in lowland rain forests. Treetop habitats in the tropical rain forest are really not too different from many arid habitats in terms of the availability of water: the humidity is relatively low, the temperatures are relatively high, and breezes add further to evaporative water loss. The high rate of photosynthetic metabolism that epiphytes have chosen to seek in the canopy is thus both a blessing and a curse, because the increased evaporation that inevitably accompanies the increased metabolism can severely strain an epiphyte. Although canopy trees are subject to the same conditions, they do not suffer from water stress so much because they maintain a connection with the ground, which absorbs and holds water until it is needed by the plants. As soon as a plant's roots become divorced from the ground, there is a serious reduction in water availability.

Epiphytes have struck on several ways of reducing their water loss. Orchids, which are primarily epiphytic in the New World tropics, often cope with desiccation by developing bulbous stems in which they store water. Epiphytic orchids tend to have thicker leaves than their soil-dwelling relatives, as well as a different system of carbon dioxide absorption. Plants need carbon dioxide in order to produce carbohydrates during photosynthesis. The carbon dioxide is normally absorbed and used during the day, most plants absorbing it through tiny pores on their leaves called stomata. However, these opened stomata can be a major source of water loss, particularly if the humidity is low and the temperature high. Epiphytic orchids combat such water loss by keeping their stomata closed during the day. They open them at night, when humidity is higher, temperatures are lower, and evaporative water loss is at its minimum. The carbon dioxide gathered at night is stored as malic acid and used in photosynthesis the next day through a process known as Crassulacean acid metabolism.

Similar nocturnal absorption systems have evolved independently in several epiphytic plant groups as well as in some desert-dwelling plants. This type of metabolism may have advantages other than reducing evaporative loss. Trees, like most living things, excrete carbon dioxide as a byproduct of their respiratory metabolism. In the rain forest canopy, many plants may vie for excreted carbon dioxide during the day. Respiration occurs at night as well as during the day, but most plants cannot use carbon dioxide without the sun. Perhaps the epiphytic orchids that have Crassulacean acid metabolism may be able to obtain respiratory carbon dioxide from the other canopy plants more easily in the absence of competition from trees.

Other epiphytes reduce stomatal water loss with humidity-sensitive hairs that surround each pore. When the air is dry, they fold over the openings and retard evaporation, and when the humidity is high, they stand erect and open the pores for free exchange of gases. Epiphytes can further reduce water loss through their exposed roots by surrounding them with a layer of dead cells. These absorb water and expand in a spongelike manner when it is wet, then contract to form a dense protective sheath when it is dry.

Although epiphytes have devised means of conserving water and alleviating water stress, many of them still suffer from a continual feast-and-famine cycle of water availability. In order to even out moisture availability in the same way that soil does, some epiphytes have turned into water-storage tanks. Tank bromeliads have evolved into a clumplike shape, with long, troughlike leaves that funnel toward a central stem. Where these long leaves converge, their bases merge to form a watertight tank. Some bromeliad tanks may store as much as two gallons of water.

Tank bromeliads gain not only by storing water but also by compensating for another drawback that comes with life without soil—low nutrient availability. Epiphytes often face severe mineral shortages. The rain may bring small amounts of nitrogen and other nutrients, but this is not enough to meet the needs of most plants. The rest of the plant's mineral needs must be scavenged. If an epiphyte can germinate in the crotch of a tree that collects debris, its mineral needs can be met from the decaying litter; such sites are therefore in great demand. The tree itself may send aerial adventitious roots out from its bark to mine these lodes of nutrient matter. Some epiphytes, particularly ferns, orchids, *Anthurium*, and some bromeliads, have evolved basket-like shapes that are efficient at catching falling litter.

Tank bromeliads do this tactic one better. They may not be particularly efficient at trapping falling litter, but the pools of water they hold are attractive aquatic environments that lure a variety of animals. The microorganisms feast on debris and in turn become food for a series of insects like mosquito larvae. Many rain forest mosquitoes breed exclusively in tank plants, tree holes, or other plant-held bodies of water. There are also large predatory mosquito and midge larvae that devour their filter-feeding relatives. Voracious damselfly nymphs lurk in the bromeliad tanks and impale anything that moves. The tanks are home, too, to frog tadpoles and salamanders that presumably feed on everything else in the system.

It might seem that the presence of all these animals, most of which leave the tank when they are grown, would constitute a net nutrient drain from the bromeliad. However, the role that their immature stages play in increasing the efficiency of digesting the litter that ultimately feeds the bromeliads may compensate for the loss of adult biomass. The waste products of the microorganisms and animals that inhabit the bromeliad tanks are excreted as water-soluble products, which are easily and efficiently absorbed by the bromeliad. Without the digestive powers of its tenants, the litter that accumulates in the tank bromeliad would be less accessible to the plant.

Tank bromeliads show an interesting convergence with insectivorous plants, even though carnivorous plants typically remain rooted in the soil. Carnivorous plants tend to grow in nitrogen-poor soils, such as those found in acidic bogs. Plants like *Sarracenia, Heliamphora, Darlingtonia,* and *Nepenthes* have modified their leaves into water-holding tubes that trap insects. Some of these plants digest their prey with enzymes, but some also contain living insects, principally fly larvae, that may serve their hosts by making nutrients more readily available. The remarkable similarity between the aquatic systems of tank bromeliads and certain carnivorous plants suggests that it is not the absence of soil so much as the absence of nitrogen that has driven the evolution of bromeliad tanks. It is strange that some tank bromeliads have not taken the step of becoming actively carnivorous. Very little is known about the natural history of these treetop plants, and we would not be surprised if insectivorous bromeliads were discovered in the rain forests of tropical America.

Some epiphytes, including bromeliads and orchids, have become reliant on ants. They offer the ants hollow tubers or other structures for nest sites, and in turn they apparently receive nutrients from the garbage and excreta of the ant colony. If the ants are aggressive, the epiphytes may also derive some protection from herbivores. The majority of epiphytes, however, can apparently eke out a living from dust, litter, rainwater, and even from slowly dissolving tree bark, without the assistance of other creatures. Even so, epiphytes seem especially luxuriant on trees where bats and birds congregate to roost or feed, and this may be due to the rain of nutrient-rich dung these visitors supply.

Nutrient scavenging by epiphytes could be a significant detriment to the host tree. Rainwater may be sucked clean of most of its nutrients by the time it filters through the canopy and hits the tree's roots. Some bromeliads seem to inhibit the growth of their hosts by this type of piracy, and epiphytes can adversely affect their hosts in other ways. The sheer weight of thousands of water-soaked epiphytes must cause the tree to invest more in support than it would otherwise do, diverting resources to structural reinforcement that might otherwise go to reproduction. The thick layers of lichens, algae, and mosses that wrap around tree limbs, and the bunches of ferns and other plants, may also reduce light penetration to other parts of the tree.

Many first-time visitors to the tropics assume that the plants clinging to trees are parasitic. This is a false impression. In fact, most epiphytes use their host plants only as platforms, and do not rob them of nutrients. Tropical mistletoes are true parasites, since they send their roots directly into the host's circulatory system. Some epiphytic orchids may have the same effect, since the mycorrhizal fungi associated with their roots invade the host tree and sometimes digest the cellulose and lignin that the tree uses for structural support. Some of these orchids have reduced root and leaf systems, further implicating them as possible parasites. But most epiphytes are not aggressively parasitic on their host.

Rain forest trees have adopted certain morphological features that appear to be designed to discourage epiphytes. Many have smooth barks that shed water rapidly, and these trees have fewer epiphytes than spongy, rough-barked trees in the same area. Epiphytes often grow on other epiphytes—ferns upon mosses, orchids upon ferns, bromeliads upon lichens. Trees must prevent the initial colonization by algae and lichens because even a thin layer of lichens will facilitate the germination of some orchids and perhaps other epiphytic plants. Virtually all epiphytes have tiny dustlike seeds. These seeds are easily dispersed by breezes wafting through the canopy, but they do not carry a large store of nutrients. Once they land, they may require a layer of organic matter to get started. A tree whose bark and leaves are free of lichens and algae that might serve as a substrate is less likely to become the host of a seedling epiphyte.

It may be the threat of epiphyte loads that has driven rain forest trees to assume similar leaf shapes. A temperate forest containing oak, maple, beech, ash, hickory, and conifers is characterized by a tremendous variety of leaf forms. But the majority of rain forest trees have similar leaves, with a smooth oval silhouette terminating in a drawn-out drip tip. The function of drip tips on leaves is still disputed, but they appear to facilitate the rapid shedding of rainwater. This may help to prevent algae and lichens from getting an initial hold on leaves; nevertheless, you will often find rain forest leaves encrusted with miniature epiphyte gardens.

In addition to smooth bark and drip tips that shed water rapidly, some rain forest trees have evolved flaky skins. Tropical trees such as *Terminalia* and *Bursera* periodically slough off great sheets of smooth trunk bark, a behavior that will dislodge any epiphytes that may have managed to gain a footing. Those trees that retain their bark may impregnate it with chemicals that inhibit seed germination or the growth of algae and lichens.

There is another group of plants whose growth habits and lifestyle prove far more troublesome to a rain forest tree than the free-loading epiphytes. Vines reach a peak in diversity and abundance in the lowland tropical rain forest; 90 percent of the world's vine species are tropical. Like epiphytes, vines are most abundant where humidity is highest. The great size and vigor of these vines lends a magical "Jack and the Beanstalk" quality to the tropical forest. A visitor from the temperate zones is invariably entranced by the massive lianas, as thick as a human thigh, that sprawl across the forest floor and then snake their way skyward. They weave upward in great tangles with other vines or soar straight up until they vanish into the backlit canopy.

Epiphytes tend to rely on far-flung seed broadcasting, followed by tenacious occupancy, to inhabit the brighter strata of the forest, while most trees rise slowly into the canopy. Vines employ a different strategy to reach the same goal. They enjoy the benefits of contact with the soil, just like most trees, but they can grow rapidly into the canopy because they don't have to make a heavy investment in structural tissues. The trees serve as trellises for the lianas, while the vines are tedious parasites to the trees. The vines compete for the same light, nutrients, and moisture that the tree needs; they can further damage the tree by their sheer weight.

Vines pursue the light and the trees that will take them there with sophisticated vigor. Tom Ray, of the University of Delaware, has worked out some of the details of how seedling vines seek out the trees on which they will climb into the canopy. A vine must reach high into the forest canopy, where it can sprawl across the treetops, in order to enjoy the photosynthetic rewards of its flexible lifestyle. To reach the canopy, it must first find a tree. Young vines cannot grow toward light like most plants, because if they did so they would be left lying on the ground in a limp heap in a short-lived sun patch. Ray discovered that one vine, *Monstera gigantea,* found its tree by a peculiar behavior he called skototropism, or growth toward darkness. It is not merely a simple avoidance of light but an active interest in dark places. The darkest places on the floor of a tropical rain forest are the bases of the largest trees, and *Monstera* pursues the dark shadow of these trees. Once it has found such a tree, its behavior shifts and it then begins a light-guided passage upward.

The upward passage is no easy climb. The vine must choose a large tree or it will become stranded in the comparative gloom below the sun-drenched canopy. But climbing a large tree is difficult. Many tropical vines have evolved another approach. Rather than climbing into the canopy, these vines have evolved into scramblers, seeking out openings in the forest canopy and growing rapidly and luxuriantly until the forest once again closes in overhead. Members of the cucumber, passion flower, and morning glory families excel in such light-gap situations. These scrambling vines ramble over other small plants, using tendrils and hooks, weaving a self-trellising system that blankets the lower reaches of a light gap. This approach never requires a long upward reach into the canopy, but the scrambling habits confine the plants to the relatively rare open areas within the forest or along river-banks. As the light gaps fill in, the vines die out. Scrambling vines depend on rapid growth and maturity, and they sacrifice longevity and great size.

The woody lianas that can eventually become huge, long-lived perennials up to 3,000 feet long have a different approach to life. These species usually climb by a combination of twining around the trunks and using tendrils or hooks. The larger the tree, the more difficult this becomes. Charles Darwin, who wrote a book on the climbing habits of plants, demonstrated that twining limits vines to climbing trunks whose diameter is less than the arc of the free-climbing leader shoot of the vine. Since the leading tip of the vine is unsupported, it is difficult for a vine directly to tackle any tree much more than six inches in diameter. Some lianas, such as the strangler figs, circumvent this limitation by starting life in the canopy and then lowering their twining aerial roots toward the ground; but this strategy is dependent on finding a deposit of humus for germination in the treetops. Other vines may use tendrils to climb straight up a trunk.

Tendrils encircle any small projections that they meet along the way. When a tendril bumps into something, the friction triggers hormonal changes on the stimulated side of the tendril, which cause it to bend and eventually spiral around and around. Other tendrils become modified into little wedges that enter cracks in the tree trunk and then swell, giving the vine purchase for its next step. Some vines have evolved hooks or cuplike suction discs that cling to smooth surfaces. However, these devices are not capable of supporting great weight, and plants that do not wrap themselves around the trunk cannot become extremely large.

Small vines may content themselves with using sun patches below the upper canopy. By being smaller and less ambitious, they can occupy the sides of large trees and harvest the light patches that the upper canopy misses. Climbers, such as *Monstera*, which inhabit this zone often show a remarkable polymorphism in leaf shape that reflects their opportunistic use of changes in light density. Where the light is dim, *Monstera* grows small, rounded leaves two or three inches long, which it plasters securely against the tree trunk. These continue straight up the trunk in a tight herringbone formation until the plant encounters direct sunlight. The leaves then change where light is abundant, becoming gigantic structures up to six feet long, with their margins deeply cut by indentations. They no longer remain plastered against the tree trunk, and the stems now project the leaves upward and outward in umbrella-like fashion to capture the sun more efficiently.

Canopy lianas also regulate the placement of their foliage. Vines growing in the shaded forest interior need leaves; but once they reach the canopy, the leaves that lie in the shaded understory are dropped, leaving only bare woody ropes stretching between the ground and treetops. When some vines germinate in direct sunlight, they immediately assume a shrublike or treelike form, becoming vines only when they are shaded over. Other vines proceed to change into a tree when they reach the top of the forest, perhaps eventually emerging above the host and smothering it. These crown-forming lianas ultimately consolidate their ropy stems into a self-supporting trunk and become a tree. So, while certain Neotropical trees use vine tactics to take their place in the canopy, most vines retain their ropy identity. Not only can they gather abundant sunlight by sprawling in a thin layer through the canopy, but there is less danger of falls. A fallen tree is a dead tree; if a vine should fall along with its host tree, it still may be able to regain its place in the canopy.

For a tree's well-being, canopy lianas are disastrous. Once a single liana has established a line from the forest floor to the canopy, it becomes a convenient route for others to climb because of its small diameter. The lianas are free to sprawl almost at will over the trees in the canopy, starving them for light. Canopy lianas often twine through several trees, linking the fates of these trees to each other; if one should fall, the lianas may pull down others. Francis Putz, a botanist who has studied lianas in Panama, has suggested that it may be advantageous for trees to sway out of phase from their neighbors because this would tend to snap vine connections. Swaying out of phase is best accomplished by evolv-

ing different architectures, which in turn result in different flexi-
bilities. The need for out-of-phase swaying might thus promote an
increase in the diversity of rain forest trees. Swaying is an obvious
threat to lianas. Once they have become established in the canopy,
the biggest danger to their supple life-style may be a kink in the
long-drawn-out sap transport system that links roots and leaves.
Many lianas protect themselves from kinks by coiling, twisting,
and bending. These springlike, braided curves, which are responsible for common names like "monkey-ladder," flex and bend
as the trees sway.

There is an alternative to swaying. If swaying fails to shed its
hangers-on, a tree can prune itself, sending a liana tumbling down
into obscurity at little cost to itself by dropping branches and
entangled leaves, particularly if these branches and leaves are
shaded. Palm trees are shedders of the highest order. By periodically sending out new fronds and dropping old fronds, palms rid
themselves of, or at least stay abreast of, both epiphytes and vines.
Tree ferns, with their palmlike form and similar habit of dropping
lower fronds, thrive in the epiphyte- and vine-rich cloud forests,
presumably because they remain relatively free of unwanted guests.

Canopy trees with large woody limbs may be doomed once a
liana gains a footing in their crown. Yet, although lianas may spell
the beginning of the end for these trees, they have already lived
long lives. From an evolutionary perspective they have been successful—they have found their way into the canopy, where they
could mature and pass on their genes. Lianas merely accelerate
their eventual demise, perhaps clearing the way for another bout
of competition that will end in another successful canopy tree. A
full and successful life is not available to the young trees that face
scrambling vines in light gaps. These youngsters must rely on
rapid growth, swaying, and bark-shedding to outdistance the green
blanket of twining vines so that they can find their way into the
canopy.

The epiphytes may convey the luxuriant diversity of rain forest,
but it is the vines and lianas that best convey the tropical quality
of a rain forest. The rain forests of the foggy temperate coasts are
heavily laden with mossy epiphytes but the trees are free of vines.
Vines such as wild grape, *Smilax* brambles, bittersweet, and
Virginia creepers penetrate well into Canada, but only as sprawlers
in open habitats. Temperate zone vines are weedy species, absent

from tall forests even though the rough bark of many temperate trees offers abundant holdfasts. Tropical warmth and moisture may be more critical to the success of vines than they are to the epiphytes. The flexibility and capacity for lateral movement through the forest that the vine life-style requires is bought at the cost of a high surface-to-volume ratio. This means that the chances of desiccation and frost damage are inherently high for vines, particularly if they are exposed to the increased sun and air movement 100 feet above the forest floor. Vines also have water-transport problems. Conducting water through hundreds of feet of thin tubing presents serious engineering problems. If evaporation from the leaves is high, the resultant suction may snap or collapse the vine's transport tubing. Thus, high humidity makes life easier for long thin plants by reducing evaporation.

The association of vines and vascular epiphytes with warmth and humidity suggests one of the fundamental causes of the rain forest's tremendous diversity. Life on our planet is based on liquid water and protein-catalyzed chemical reactions. In the humid lowland tropics, temperatures never fall to the point where the abundant water freezes and solidifies, and they rarely rise to the point where proteins coagulate and denaturize. Whenever it gets colder and drier, even in the tropics, vines and epiphytes tend to decrease in abundance, and diversity declines in general.

Many hypotheses have been put forward to explain global patterns of species diversity and the particularly rich flora and fauna of the Neotropical rain forest, invoking arguments concerning predation, time, productivity, and other involved biological factors. These factors are no doubt valid, but perhaps the most important is that suggested by the vines and epiphytes. Life is difficult for vines and epiphytes in most of the world, where physical constraints limit their success. In the humidity and mild warmth of the lowland tropical rain forest, there is a lack of such environmental constraints. This allows a physiological freedom that tolerates the widest range of biological responses to the ever-pressing demands of competition and predation.

Chapter 5

MATAPALO

*He not only grew to a giant stature, but insisted
on wrestling with every stranger that happened
to pass through his Libyan domain. He was
always invincible in these encounters because his
strength waxed with each successive contact
with his mother Earth.*
—WILLIAM MORTON WHEELER
Essays on Philosophical Biology

Scattered across the lowlands of Costa Rica and Panama are a
number of villages called Matapalo. The name means "tree-killer,"
but these villages were not named after some legendary Bunyan-
esque character. Nor were they named after a local hero, perhaps
the first settler who cleared the forest where the towns now stand.
The tree-killer so celebrated is not a person at all, but a tree.
Matapalo is a local name for the strangler fig, one of the most
characteristic trees of the Neotropical forest. There are many
species of such murderous trees, most of which are members of the
subgenus *Urostigma* of the genus *Ficus*, close relatives of some of
the ornamental species that grace Manhattan apartments.

There is a certain injustice and irony in the name matapalo. The
stranglers kill trees, but they are often the only trees left after a
forest is cleared. Their lumber is of poor quality, good for little

save firewood, and their expansive, umbrella-like crowns provide abundant shade after the forest has been cleared. There is little profit in felling them and their shade provides a welcome respite from the tropical sun. Thus throughout the lowlands of the New World tropics the distinctive forms of these killer trees grace pastures and clearings, the sole remnants of butchered forests. But matapalos are never lone killers. Whether they live isolated in a cleared field or in a pristine rain forest, these trees are islands of life and the foci of existence for many creatures.

The broad canopy of a mature matapalo acts as a magnet for many birds and mammals. They come for the figs. Probably all of the 900 or so species of *Ficus* have palatable fruits; matapalos are no exception. Although the half-dozen wild species of *Ficus* we have eaten have been gastronomically inferior to the commercially grown *Ficus carica*, they have all had a sweet and substantial pulp. Some tropical bats thrive on a diet composed almost entirely of wild figs, which suggests that they are quite nutritious. Tropical frugivores relish figs because they are available, in various stages of ripeness, throughout the year. A list of the mammals known to feed on figs in the New World tropics would include dozens of species, and experienced tropical birders are well aware of the attractive forces a fruiting fig tree exerts on the avifauna.

If a matapalo happens to be laden with fruit, the arrival of vertebrate frugivores can be an entertaining spectacle. Nothing rivals the sight and sounds of raucous green *Amazona* parrots and magnificent long-tailed macaws feeding noisily on a fruiting fig, and to many people this vision captures the essence of the tropics. A wealth of smaller birds, most of them brightly colored, are also drawn to these fruiting trees. Troops of hungry monkeys pass by on their daily rounds, leaping from branch to branch as they greedily devour the figs. The larger birds that frequent figgeries are less than refined in their dining habits, and their abandon, combined with the cavorting of monkeys in the crown, knocks considerable quantities of ripe figs to the ground. This attracts a host of less acrobatic fruit-loving beasts, such as peccaries, who shuffle and sniff their way to the figs through the litter. The rain of fruit also lures timid pacas and agoutis, large ungulate-like rodents who gather the fruits watchfully, ever mindful of lurking predators.

Despite appearances, the matapalo does not suffer from this

prandial orgy. Only a few insects, birds, and rodents are meticulous enough to crack and eat the countless small seeds buried in the pulpy flesh of the fig. Indeed, the matapalo gains from the feast it hosts. The luscious, pulpy fruits and tiny, abundant seeds are important, and perhaps essential, characteristics of the matapalo life-style.

When a troop of spider monkeys or a flock of parrots departs a fruiting matapalo with a full stomach or crop, they will soon begin defecating thousands of its seeds throughout the forest. Few other trees spread their seeds as widely as a fig. Moreover, the birds, bats, and monkeys that carry their seeds tend to deposit them into the upper strata of the forest, which is where the strangler begins life. The matapalo seed is adapted for germination far above the ground. Its coat is viscous and sticky, an adaptation shared by the parasitic mistletoes (Loranthacae), who face a similar task of arboreal germination. (Interestingly enough, mistletoes are also called matapalos in some places.) But unlike mistletoes, which germinate quickly and immediately send roots into the vascular system of the host, the strangler fig seed waits.

The matapalo does not tap the nutrients of its host directly. The seed coat of the matapalo must be eroded away by bacterial action, and this adaptation increases its chance of germinating in a place blessed with organic matter. Usually this will be the crotch of a tree that has collected a pile of decaying algae, lichens, and epiphytes, layered into a nutrient-rich pile of compost far above the ground. It is in this organic matter that the fig starts life. The matapalo is not forced to germinate on a living tree as are many parasitic plants, however; when Stephens rediscovered the Mayan ruins on the Yucatan and at Tikal he found matapalos growing thickly over stelae and temples, as well as on trees.

In order to conquer its host, the matapalo must establish a connection with the ground. It begins by sending out one, or perhaps several, aerial roots that drop unhesitatingly downward. If these vinelike roots find another lode of nutrients on the way, they pause long enough to send out rootlets and tap more fuel before continuing to the ground. When they reach the ground they dig in, developing a typical underground network of roots and fungal mycelia. The surge of nutrients carried by this long, thin conduit allows the seedling to grow skyward in earnest. Its leaves are hungry for light, tracking the moving sun just like a sunflower head. Its stomata—those specialized pores through which gas exchange takes place—are recessed below the surface of the leaf, an adaptation that reduces water loss in the growing plant and allows it to bask in the intense tropical sun.

The matapalo has a competitive edge over other forest trees because it starts life in the upper reaches of the forest canopy where the light is bright and it doesn't have to invest in a massive trunk to get there. The matapalo rapidly overshadows its host with its sun-thirsty leaves, and it continues dropping aerial roots as it grows. When these descending roots encounter each other, they graft together, eventually enveloping the trunk of the host tree in a tight sheath. The pressure exerted by this growing, consolidating mass of aerial roots reduces the host tree's ability to transport nutrients to and from its own crown. As the roots of the matapalo meld together to form a trunk, and the canopy reaches ever skyward, the host tree slowly dies. Finally its carcass rots and the matapalo stands as a tree in its own right. The cavity left by the host slowly fills with the expanding, anastomosing trunks and aerial roots of the matapalo. Although it may seem a slow and cruel way to kill, the matapalo is merely speeding up a process begun long before by fungi and beetles. The host trees are often mature trees, ones that have lived long and already flowered and fruited many times.

Mature matapalos may become the largest trees in the forest, and many people find it difficult to believe that these magnificent giants had to kill to get to where they are. But clues to the past are easily seen in the complex and convoluted character of the tree's trunk. Unlike the regular, neatly buttressed trunks of other forest trees, the matapalo's trunk is full of holes and cracks, twists and turns. These are the legacy of the anastomosed aerial roots; almost every strangler, no matter how large it becomes, shows these scars. Their nooks and crannies are the universe to many living creatures.

Just as almost every stone in a temperate-zone meadow becomes the prized solar-heated incubator of an ant colony, or almost every groove in the path of a freshwater rivulet sports the sieving net of a hydropsychid caddis larva, so does almost every dry, protected cavity in tropical rain forest play host to living creatures. Spinoza's claim that nature abhors a vacuum is embodied in life's ceaseless demand for space. It is this demand that accounts for the wealth of life on the trunk of a matapalo, whose niches are almost always occupied. Some ecologists argue that there is no such thing as an empty niche, but when they say this they are speaking in the jargon of their science. In this mysterious dialect, a niche is an "N-dimensional hypervolume" whose form is defined by every factor of importance to an organism. The ecologist's niche therefore depends on an organism to define it. But the denizens of a matapalo trunk are less interested in filling metaphysical niches than they are in occupying the nooks and crannies implied in the traditional meaning of the word.

Each niche on the trunk of a matapalo, be it high or low, narrow or wide, large or small, tends to be occupied by a different sort of creature. This suggests that a resource as hard to visualize as emptiness has considerable value even in a world as full and varied as the tropical forest. Actually, it is not so much the space as the security of the walls defining the cavity that is the valuable resource. These walls provide the protection from predators that is so valuable to its residents. Most of the occupants in the niches of a matapalo search elsewhere for food; and many of them, particularly the smaller forms, earn their livings by roaming over the wide and topographically varied barkscape of the matapalo trunk. These small creatures make matapalo-watching an entertaining pastime for those of us who are ecologically inclined. We could probe the niches with flashlights, optical fibers, or sticks in order to see who hides out where. But it is far more rewarding simply to find a comfortable seat and let the inhabitants of the matapalo reveal themselves according to their own natural schedules.

As the first flecks of sunlight mottle the gray bark of the matapalo at dawn, geckos materialize on the surface of the trunk. Geckos, like most lizards, lead simple lives. Feeding and fornicating are their main concerns, and they pursue these unabashedly in the presence of a discreet observer. These little geckos of the matapalo belong to the genus *Gonatodes*. Unlike many of their gekkonid relations, they are active during the day. The male geckos begin the day languidly, but as their metabolism heats up with the sun they become increasingly ardent and pugnacious. Their heads, dull and rust-colored when they awaken, blossom into an intense orange that contrasts sharply with their deep blue-black bodies. Bobbing their heads and flicking their white-tipped tails, they constantly vie for territory on the trunk surface. Their flamboyant color and behavior no doubt advertises their fitness to the coy and cryptically colored females; at the same time it makes the males glaringly obvious to predators.

This bind, wherein increased sexual desirability is countered by increased vulnerability to predators, is not unusual. Another group of lizards that shares the matapalo trunk with geckos exhibits it in a different way. Male *Anolis* lizards defend their territories on the matapalo and court females with displays involving a colorful patch of extensible skin on the throat. These flaps, known as dewlaps, are often brightly colored and stand out like little flags when they are erected during a display. Such splotches of color, bobbing and flashing passionately in the forest shade, must serve as beacons for predators in much the same way that the loud groaning call of the male bullfrog attracts hungry snapping turtles. Many birds regard geckos and anoles as prime grist for their gizzards. Were it not for the haven that a tight crevice offers when a kiskadee swoops into view, one might imagine that evolution would have colored the male lizards a little less gloriously.

Geckos and anoles are not restricted to matapalo trunks in the tropical forest, but the topographically complex nature of these trunks often allows high concentrations of individuals there. On large matapalos, several adult males of both kinds of lizards can set up territories where they exclude other adult males of the same species. The holders of the prime pieces of real estate will have access to a number of females, who are generally tolerant of the presence of others. Indeed, females who inhabit a given territory may deposit their eggs at a central depot, most often a protected little crevice with a thin layer of decayed plant material.

When a predator looms suddenly on the scene, geckos and anoles cannot duck into just any crevice in their territories on the matapalo trunk. Many of these niches are already occupied by creatures loath to admit anything foreign. Lizard-sized crevices are often used by *Polistes* paper wasps as nest sites. These wasps are large and pugnacious, their picturesque local names, such as *picadura* (hard-stinger) and *ojo de agua* (crying eye) reflecting their formidable nature.

The entrances to *Polistes* colonies are often rimmed with a contingent of workers, who spend the day pecking at ants that venture too near and fanning the nest with their wingbeats for ventilation. Other cavities may be lined with yellowish wasps about half the size of *Polistes*. These *Stelopolybia* wasps are much more formidable than the larger *Polistes* because they typically live in colonies numbering thousands of individuals. Once a colony this size gains control over a cavity, the only creatures capable of evicting them are army ants. Wasps that build their nests outside such a tree cavity, however, are far from immune from destruction despite their formidable stings. They can become the target of hit-and-run artists like monkeys and birds, who are often willing to rip into the exposed brood combs at the cost of a few stings. Life in a tree cavity prevents such rude and destructive intrusions, although it may set limits on how large the colony can grow.

Some of the social insects that commonly nest in matapalo are less hampered by restricted growing space. Wasps who dwell in cavities can be evicted by the tree itself, squeezed out by an ever-growing fig intent on consolidating its many twisted branches into a solid main trunk. Some social insects can get around this. The stingless bees (Meliponinae) control their own destiny when this happens by gnawing away at the wood that encompasses their nests. This is not quite so arduous a task as it might at first seem. Meliponines do not usually construct their nests in the superficial surface cavities of the growing matapalo, choosing instead to begin their colonies deep in the softer central core of the growing strangler. Here there is often a large hollow, an empty reminder of the dead or dying host tree after its carcass has been gnawed away by fungi carried off by wood-boring beetles. Once the bees settle in a cavity, they continue expanding their colony deep inside the living matapalo by removing the soft inner tissues. These colonies can grow to immense bushel basket sizes, and if the colonies can replace their queens they might persist for as long as the matapalo lives.

Such established colonies are often linked to the outside world only by a narrow tube through the tough growing fiber of the matapalo trunk. These narrow, tubelike entrances are defended by workers armed with mandibles that exude a caustic gummy secretion, and the tiny entrances can be defended even against the scourge of the army ants. Indeed, the colony might seem to be impregnable; but nothing in the tropical forest is without an effective predator. The stingless bees' worst enemies are other stingless bees.

One genus of meliponines (*Leistrimella*) has evolved an effective robber strategy. Rather than garnering its nutrients directly from pollens, resins, and nectar, *Leistrimella* steals them from the nests of other meliponines, in much the same way as the temperate parasitic bumblebees (*Psythyrus*). Compared to other meliponines, *Leistrimella* are armored more heavily and have fewer hairs. They are also much more robust, and these characteristics suit them better for grappling and fighting at the nest than for foraging among the blossoms. But *Leistrimella* depends on more than simple brute force when it raids a meliponine nest: it employs a sophisticated chemical screen to batter down the impregnable gates. Social insects rely heavily on chemical channels of communication, and odor rules their daily life.

When *Leistrimella* begin a raid, they release large amounts of citral—a compound that jams and disorients the sensory system of the defenders. The resident bees buzz around in confusion and the *Leistrimella* breach the entrance. Bees of both kinds hover around the entrance in a melee, and corpses accumulate at the base of the tree, to be carted off by foraging ants. The sweet, lemony aroma of citral can be smelled as the carnage goes on. Eventually the robbers depart, taking with them loads of hard-won pollen and honey, and the tattered remnants of the nest can be rebuilt by the survivors. *Leistrimella* act almost like beekeepers, using citral as their smoke and leaving behind a colony that can be raided again in the future.

If a bee or wasp colony succumbs, its nest is soon colonized, often within minutes, by ants interested in its provisions and larvae. There are seminomadic ants—species of *Monacis, Solenopsis,* and *Paratrechina*—that occupy the abandoned nests of bees, wasps, and termites, moving from one shelter to another. There are also ants living in the matapalos that carve their own nests out within the rotting host tree. The carpenter ants (*Camponotus*) that are the bane of many a wooden house in North America are here, too. *Azteca* ants build carton nests in crevices or high on the limbs of the matapalo. These ubiquitous pismires patrol the matapalo, ceaselessly prospecting for caterpillars descending groundward to pupate or for seed bugs crawling upward in search of fig seeds.

They seem less ruled by daily cycles than the other tenants of the matapalo complex, but they show some preference for the dark hours when ant-eating lizards have lidded their eyes and crept away for the night.

The coming of night is a time of awakening on the matapalo. The protective cloak of dusk, heralded by swelling choruses of crickets and frogs, releases a new set of shapes onto the tree's surface. Ominous creatures, black as the night and looking like flattened hybrids between a crab and a spider, ease noiselessly from their narrow crevices. These are amblypygids, or whip scorpions, the nocturnal masters of the matapalo trunk. Amblypygids hunt in a two-dimensional world, roaming the broad expanses of the matapalo trunk. Three sets of long, thin legs jut sideways from their oval body, which is roughly the size of a wolf spider's but without its coarse hairiness. The legs of the amblypygid are lined with sensitive hairs that detect surface vibration and the micro-eddies of air created by passing insects. When a roach ventures close, the amblypygid lunges forward to seize it with a pair of fearsome pedipalpi—armlike mouthparts with a jagged, pointed, basket-like structure at the end. These appendages fold inward, dragging the hapless roach into the hunter's maw. The business of hunting is also facilitated by a set of legs, those closest to the head, which have evolved into long-drawn-out appendages some three to six inches in length. These look and function like long antennae, and like conventional insect antennae they are coated with mechanical and chemical receptors capable of distinguishing friend from foe at a single tap. The antenniform legs of the amblypygid are also used for courtship. Males can be seen tapping and stroking females with these wispy wands with a distinctive rhythm. The females may respond in kind, or they may perhaps menacingly brandish a pedipalp in the air.

Scorpions also lurk at the crevices, awaiting roaches and crickets. Orb-weavers begin the nightly weaving of their elaborate webs between the main trunk buttresses and the banyan-like roots that descend further out from the larger limbs. Bats roosting in the deep upper recesses of the trunk crawl to the edges of their lairs and push off into the darkness. And the meandering creatures of the forest floor ebb up onto the surface of the matapalo. Land snails leave behind slick mucus trails that glimmer silver in a headlamp, millipedes wander about as though hoping a soft mushroom would sprout in front of them, and centipedes that seem like many-legged weasels move constantly on the hunt.

The form of the matapalo may proclaim its murderous past, but even the most moralistic and anthropomorphist naturalists should not condemn it; rather, they should admire it, if only for the richness of other forms that it houses. Although its life history is more blatantly aggressive than that of other trees, its end result is no different from the effect any competitor has on another. The tendency for life to saturate available resources makes almost every living thing a killer of sorts. When we look at the sad manifestations of our own Malthusian predicament, many of us decry competition and aggression, seeking refuge in ideas like "natural harmony" or Hinduism's *ahisma*, the doctrine of harmlessness to all living beings. But this is wishful fantasy. There is a more tangible sense of hopefulness in seeing the matapalos of the world and marveling at the manifold ways in which the living take life from death.

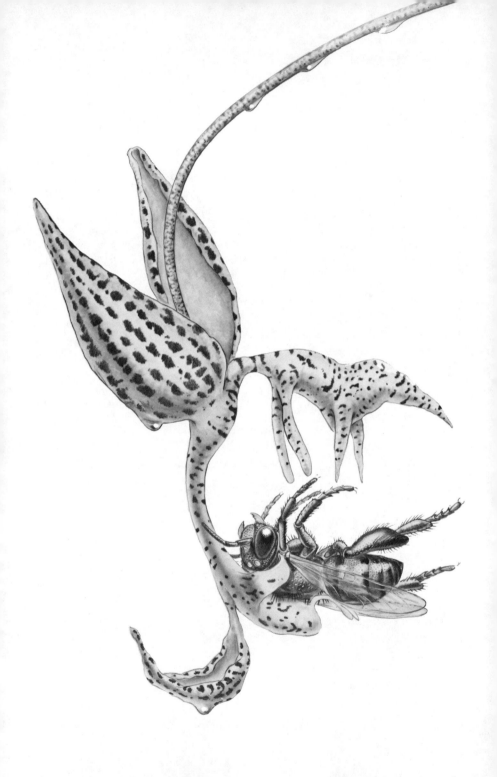

Chapter 6

LISTEN TO THE FLOWERS

"We can talk," said the Tiger-lily, *"when there's anybody worth talking to."*
—LEWIS CARROLL
Through the Looking-Glass

Courtship is a major problem for stay-at-home types like plants. If you are firmly rooted to one spot you can't wander about in search of a mate, and without alternative means of scattering your genes, you sacrifice many of the evolutionary virtues of sex. Organisms that lack mobility often end up sharing most of their genes with themselves or with close relatives. Yet inbreeding erodes the chief virtue of sex, which is the production of genetic diversity. To overcome the sexual handicap of their sedentary life-styles, stationary organisms such as plants and barnacles often use the winds and waters to carry their genes to mates in distant places. But these aids are not universally available. Clouds of drifting birch pollen in the spring are largely a temperate phenomenon.

If you suffer from hay fever, you will quickly notice the lack of windborne pollen in the tropical rain forest, despite the luxuriance of the vegetation and the wealth of flowers. We even know people who have moved to the tropics primarily to escape the curse of their allergies. The dearth of windborne pollen is not due to any lack of wind; plants in the canopy level of the forest are certainly exposed to the wind. Some even employ it to disperse their seeds, but very few entrust their pollen to the breezes. Tropical plants avoid wind pollination because this scattershot method of gene dispersal is effective only if there are lots of targets nearby. And in the tropical rain forest, common species are rare and rare species are common, as Wallace in his *Tropical Nature* was among the first to note:

> If the traveller notices a particular species and wishes to find more like it, he may often turn his eyes in vain in every direction. Trees of varied forms, dimensions and colours are all around him, but he rarely sees any of them repeated. Time after time he goes to a tree which looks like the one he seeks, but a closer examination shows it to be distinct. He may at length, perhaps, meet with a second specimen a half a mile off, or he may fail altogether, till on another occasion he stumbles on one by accident.

A plant looking for receptive targets for its pollen in the tropical rain forest faces the same problems Wallace did. Since there will probably be few individuals of the same species nearby, a plant casting its genetic fate to the wind faces a high risk of losing its investment.

Even a common plant faces selective pressures to conserve or better use its pollen. Pollen is costly to produce, packed as it is with nitrogen-rich proteins, fats, nucleic acids, and vitamins. Some evidence suggests that a higher proportion of Neotropical rain forest plants are dioecious—that is, have separate male and female plants—than in temperate habitats. Mating is more difficult for dioecious plants because they cannot pollinate themselves or another individual of the same sex. Although this problem is shared with dioecious temperate zone plants, the rarefied plant communities of the tropical rain forest render it a particularly tricky one.

Flowers that attract and manipulate animal pollinators are plants' solutions to the problem of aiming their genetic material.

Animals, particularly those that fly, can move easily from flower to flower, and if the plant can attach its pollen to such a mobile creature, then the pollen may be transported to another flowering plant of the same species. Plants accordingly have evolved flowers to entice and attract mobile animals, and they have further evolved mechanisms that induce the animals to visit other plants of the same species. Flowers can offer rewards of nectar, pollen, fragrances, and oils to attract and manipulate a wide variety of animals, or they can dispense with rewards and depend on deceit and trickery to exploit the mobility of their animal pollinators. Whatever method is evolved, tropical rain forest plants depend heavily on animals to act as sexual intermediaries, carrying pollen between widely scattered individual plants in the complex fabric of the forest.

Tropical plants are pollinated by a wide variety of animals. Naturalists from North America and Europe, of course, are familiar with insect pollinators like bees, which play an important pollination role in many temperate zone habitats. But temperate zone naturalists are not as familiar with some of the animals that play an important role in the pollination of tropical plants. Hummingbirds, for example, with their strong flight and their thirst for nectar, are important pollinators of tropical plants. They are found only in the New World, but there is only one species in most of eastern North America. Ecuador has well over a hundred species of these birds, and it is not unusual to find ten or more species in a lowland rain forest anywhere in tropical America. Bats are also significant pollinators in the tropics, and there are even a few small rodents that pollinate some Neotropical plants. But the majority of pollinators in the tropics, just as in the temperate zones, are insects—in varieties that would amaze any temperate zone naturalist. Animal pollinators, insects and otherwise, offer plants the power of long-distance selective gene dispersal necessary in an environment where individual plants may be spread sparsely.

Plants must deal with two sets of problems when they set out to exploit an animal. They must entice the animal to visit the flower and pick up the pollen, and they must make sure that the animal visits another plant of the same species after it leaves. These problems are relatively simple to deal with in temperate zone habitats, where plants of the same species may bloom synchronously in high densities. Insects will naturally flit from plant to plant as they sip nectar, and the pollen will follow.

The richness of the tropical rain forest flora and the relative rarity of most species of plants does not allow such a casual approach to pollination. A tropical forest plant can't afford to depend on random insect movements alone. There are too many other plants, many of which might be in bloom at the same time, and the nearest individual of the same species may be far off through the trees and vines. If the nearest suitable mate is a mile or two away in densely vegetated forest, the plant must somehow convince its pollinator to ignore flowers of other species and search for another individual of the same species. The combined problems of attracting and directing pollinators have resulted in a co-evolutionary process in which plants become specialized to attract certain pollinators and pollinators become specialized to be attracted by certain plants.

Plants can attract pollinators by offering a substantial nutritional reward. If a plant offers such a reward, it should evolve a way of proffering it selectively to specific types of animals. This cuts its losses to inefficient pollinators and flower robbers while increasing the likelihood of the visitor moving on to sample the rewards of other conspecific individuals rather than members of another species. Once a plant has settled on a certain type of animal for pollination, it can fine-tune its morphology and ecology to match those of its pollinator. This proces results in flowers evolving suites of characteristics that make their nectar available only to specific types of animals. The form, color, and behavior of flowers that depend on the same types of pollinators show many parallels even when the plants are derived from independent evolutionary lines. Flowers are pleasing puzzles for naturalists to contemplate. Detailed observations and careful study are needed in order to determine which animals pollinate a specific plant, but an observant naturalist can infer a great deal about the type of animals that probably pollinate a plant by simply looking at and smelling a flower.

If you wander through the tropical rain forest, you will come across a wide variety of insect-pollinated flowers. Blossoms pollinated by butterflies are often red or orange; they are typically platform-shaped, with a mild odor and recessed nectaries, and are particularly common in tree-fall areas. These floral characteristics match the biology of butterflies, which are among the few insects able to see well on the red end of the spectrum and who need the warmth of the sun and a flat perch from which to drink the mild nectar that maintains their life-style. But not all tropical rain forest flowers are colorful and fragrant, and many of them would be sorely out of place in a flower shop. You will find rank-smelling aroids whose flower spaths are covered with beetles, vines, and trees whose flowers reek of carrion and attract scavenging beetles and flesh flies. Certain orchid flowers apparently mimic fungi, luring fungus gnats with their shape and odor.

Some of the showiest flowers in the tropical rain forest are not pollinated by insects but by birds. Hummingbirds are the most important such pollinators, but there are a number of other colorful birds, such as honeycreepers, in the rain forests of tropical America that also feed heavily on nectar. Birds have excellent color vision, and hummingbird flowers are typically bright red or orange. There is no question that these colors are highly attractive to hummingbirds. If you want to get a close look at the little hermits that dwell in the rain forest understory, all you have to do is wear a bright red T-shirt and sit in a patch of sunlight. Sooner or later you will hear a loud buzzing hum and find yourself face to face with a disappointed hummingbird who thought it had come across the mother of all flowers.

Hummingbird flowers are often tubular in shape and they are usually suspended away from branches. Hummingbirds are powerful fliers, able to hover in mid-air as they probe these flowers with their long tongues, and the shape and position of the flowers makes it difficult for other animals to steal the copious nectar. Hummingbird flowers produce a large amount of nectar that is low in nutrients but full of sugar, and these quick fixes provide the active little birds with a great deal of energy. Contrary to what many people believe, hummingbirds do not feed exclusively on nectar. Most hummingbirds spend much of their time hunting for insects and appear to use nectar in much the same way that some of us use coffee. Even though hummingbirds are not strictly dependent on flower nectar, their addiction is strong enough to have resulted in the evolution of distinct floral types that cater to their desire.

If you search for rain forest flowers only during the day, you will miss a great deal. When you step into the tropical night and smell a heavy, cloying perfume reminiscent of jasmine, you are probably near a flower that is pollinated by hawkmoths. Hawkmoth flowers are common on rain forest plants. They tend to be white, which makes them relatively easy to see at night. The most spectacular hawkmoth flowers are seen on night-blooming cacti like *Hylocereus*. These flowers are large, showy, tube-shaped structures with deeply recessed nectaries. The depth of the tubes restricts access to those few hawkmoths that can unfurl a tongue over six inches long. But not all hawkmoths have such long tongues, and long, tubular flowers alone do not define a hawkmoth flower. Bill Haber, a leading student of Neotropical pollination ecology, has shown that while many hawkmoth flowers are not tubular, they all tend to have the copious quantities of nectar required to sustain the energetic flight of these moths. On more than one occasion we have mistaken hawkmoths for hummingbirds as they hovered in front of flowers just before dusk.

Hawkmoths can almost be considered the nocturnal equivalents of hummingbirds, which they rival in their ability to hover and power-surge through the air at high speeds. Hawkmoths and hummingbirds not only share a similar high-energy flight pattern; the flowers they are attracted to are also similar in many respects, both producing large quantities of nectar and tending to have tubular shapes. However, there are significant differences as well— differences which ensure that hawkmoth flowers are not visited by hummingbirds and that hummingbird flowers are not visited by hawkmoths. Hummingbird flowers are usually red rather than white and nonodorous rather than fragrant; they also open during the day rather than at night. These differences tend to segregate the pollinators, although a few day-flying hawkmoths may utilize some hummingbird flowers.

Bat flowers are primarily a tropical phenomenon. This is not surprising considering the abundance and diversity of tropical bats and the fact that they may fly many miles in the course of an evening. Unlike insectivorous bats, whose sophisticated echolocation abilities reduce the need for sharp vision, fruit- and nectar-feeding bats have large, powerful eyes even though they are color-blind. These bats also seem to have a good sense of smell. Accordingly, bat-pollinated flowers tend toward whitish colors, pale greens and creams that may be inconspicuous by day but are easy to see at night. They tend to be large, which also makes them easier to see in the dark. They often have an open shape, with a bushy mass of long, protruding anthers that rub pollen onto the face and chest of the bat when it shoves its mouth and long tongue into the flower in search of nectar. Bat flowers typically produce abundant nectar, which is important for sustaining the high metabolism of a flying mammal. Despite the abundance of sweet nectar, you would never be tempted to sample the flowers the way children love to nip nectar-laden spurs of honeysuckles because bat flowers give off a musty fermented odor that most humans find unappealing.

Although these features make it easy for bats to collect nectar while becoming coated with pollen, they also allow other pollinators access. To restrict the visits of inefficient pollinators, bat flowers tend to open at night. Many last but a single night, wilting and falling in the heat of the morning. As a further concession to bats, many of the trees that are pollinated by bats place their flowers on the bark of the trunk or a large branch, rather than mixed in with the foliage. This condition, known as cauliflory, facilitates nectar-drinking by an airborne bat or allows the bat a firm roost while it probes for nectar. The floral structure greatly increases the chances of successful bat pollination.

The congruence between the behavior of flowers and their pollinators has led students of pollination ecology to speak of the "harmony" between the two groups. But if such harmony exists it is purely of a self-serving sort. The bats are interested only in filling their stomachs, and it is no concern of theirs that they may be doing a favor for the plant. Indeed, a hungry bat may eat the flowers and large quantities of pollen. Some bats are reported to dine exclusively on pollen, and any plant that depends on these species for pollination is clearly willing to pay a steep price for gene dispersal. Selfishness is characteristic of other pollinators. Bees that happen across flowers whose nectaries are too deeply recessed to reach with their tongues will often crawl to the side of the blossom and chew their way to the nectar, depleting and damaging the flower without transferring any pollen. When hummingbirds set up a territory over a patch of the banana-like *Heliconia* plants that occupy light gaps in the rain forest, they pugnaciously evict other visitors and thereby may impede the plant's gene dispersal.

Animals are not the only selfish parties in pollination systems.

The plants are equally self-serving. Some flowers attract their pollinators by deceit. Orchids are masters of this art. Some offer what appear to be nectaries but turn out to be just artful pigments. Others have hairs that resemble pollen-rich anthers but are really a ruse to lure bees where they can be dabbed with the orchid's pollen without being able to pack any away to take back to the nest. Some orchids lure bees into trap blossoms that force them against pollen-bearing structures and pollen receptors without offering any real rewards. Other orchids mimic nectar-bearing flowers, and some even play on the indiscriminate lust of male tachinid flies by mimicking females. When the male attempts to copulate with the pseudofemale, he actually pollinates the orchid. Other orchid flowers flutter in the breeze, producing a movement that male *Centris* bees perceive as a territorial challenge. When they aggressively sally forth, plowing into the presumed intruder, they pick up the orchid's pollen. However, deceptive seductions like these are dependent to some extent on naive pollinators and may not work on an insect that has been duped often enough to learn to avoid the flowers. The majority of flowers, even orchids, must still offer significant rewards if they are to get dependable service.

Most pollinators gain an obvious reward for their efforts. Unless the plant relies on deception, the pollinator gets a nutritious meal from the plant in exchange for the use of its wings. But not all pollinators are motivated by simple hunger, and one of the most fascinating pollination systems in the rain forests of tropical America involves only sex, both on the part of the pollinator and pollinatee.

Bees are important pollinators in the tropics, just as they are in the temperate zones. There is an enormous wealth of bees in the American tropics and a wide range of plants has adapted to pollination by bees. Orchid bees of the subfamily Euglossinae are significant pollinators of many orchids in the rain forests of tropical America. Most orchid bees are handsome beasts, bright with metallic green or blue polishes, or striking with orange and black hairs. Unlike the honeybees with which we are familiar, orchid bees are usually not colonial, and it is the male, rather than the female, that visits and pollinates orchid flowers. The males visit these flowers even though orchids offer no nectar to feed them and they have no use for orchid pollen. The male orchid bees collect fragrances, which they store in special pockets on their hind legs and use for their own sexual ends.

Orchid fragrances are complex chemical mixtures. Calaway Dodson, an orchid biologist who is now director of the Marie Selby Botanical Gardens in Sarasota, Florida, was intrigued by these rich fragrances. His observations of wild orchids in South America reveal a complex relationship between these bees and orchids, but it was difficult to work out the details because orchids flower at their own convenience. You have to be in exactly the right place at precisely the right time to observe the behavior of the bees, and this makes it a tricky system to study. Dodson felt that the rich odors characteristic of bee-pollinated orchids offered both a key to the attractiveness of the orchids and an avenue for studying these relationships at his convenience. He discovered that certain aromatic chemical compounds, such as cineole and methyl salicylate, were the active compounds in the orchid fragrances, and that these simple chemicals attracted orchid bees in droves if he set out a soaked blotter pad. Male orchid bees build up stores of these volatile orchid fragrances in specialized leg pockets. The range of chemicals they are attracted to is broad; one species, *Eufriesia purpurata*, has been observed collecting DDT from the walls of Brazilian houses.

It soon became clear how orchids used these fragrances to specify what bees would be attracted. It was the mix of fragrances that determined what bees would visit a flower. Orchids generally don't attract just a single species of bee, but they do attract a narrow range of the species that might inhabit a forest. Although the benefits of these fragrant attractants to the orchids are obvious enough, it was unclear why the bees found them attractive. They seem to use the fragrances to initiate sexual encounters with female bees. The male orchid bees fly from flower to flower, gathering a bit of fragrance from each one as though trying to mix a powerful potion in their leg pockets. When they hit on the right combination of compounds, they become attractive themselves: other male bees key in on these fragrant males, rather than on the orchids.

While several species of bees might be attracted to an orchid flower, the bees that key in on the fragrant males are other males of the same species, and as more and more show up, the aggregations are characterized by unusual flight patterns and buzzing noises. These swarms often take place in little patches of dappled sunlight in the forest interior, and the loud buzzing and bright flashes of sunlight off metallic bodies apparently draw in the females. A single male evidently can't attract a female, but a group of them can, and these bright, buzzing aggregations attract female orchid bees in much the same way that male orchid bees are attracted to the orchids.

A flower that has access to a specific group of pollinators has only partially solved the problem of long-distance sex. Pollination success also depends on the timing of flower production. Synchronous mass flowering is a common tactic of temperate zone plants. This mass flowering attracts many generalized pollinators, such as flies, moths, beetles, and social bees. The preference of these insects is formed largely by the abundance of a certain flower, weighed against the rewards it offers and the effort required to process the flower. This "Big Bang" approach works well in seasonal environments where there are obvious climatic cues for synchronizing the flowering of individual plants. Although tropical plants can't easily use the cues that temperate zone plants rely on so heavily, such as changes in daylength and temperature, some tropical plants use cues such as changes in rainfall patterns to synchronize their flowering. Synchronous flowering serves other functions in highly seasonal habitats, such as ensuring seed set and germination at times that are favorable; these other functions are much less important in the relatively aseasonal lowland rain forest.

The tropical rain forest has wet and dry periods, but it has pollinators, seed dispersers, and opportunities for germination year round. To capitalize on this year-round availability, many rain forest plants produce a limited number of flowers through much of the year. This limits their attractiveness to a specialized set of pollinators that are able to remember plant locations. The pollinators include butterflies, bees, birds, and bats, which have the capacity and inclination to remember the locations of flowering plants. Once the pollinators discover flowers, they "trapline"— visiting the same plants each day in a milk-run pickup of nectar that guarantees each plant's pollen being widely dispersed. This behavior further guarantees that rare plants will be pollinated once the pollinators have discovered the location of the plants in the vicinity.

The trapline behavior of pollinators and the constant flowering of many plants partially accounts for the monotonous greenness that some visitors to tropical rain forest complain of. These visitors expect to see trees festooned with brilliant orchids and dazzling begonias. There are in fact grand spectacles of flamboyant flowering in the tropical rain forest, but they are rarely evident from the forest floor. From a low-flying plane you might see spectacular tree crowns aflame with flowers, especially during the dry season; from your lowly perspective on the forest floor all you can see of these displays are falling scarlet petals. Individual blossoms may be spectacular in the understory of mature rain forest, but they tend to be scattered about and are often hidden. The grandeur of massed spring wildflowers found in temperate woodlands, the color of summer meadows and fall foliage that dominate the landscape, will not be found in the lowland rain forest. The beauty of the flowers of tropical forests is portioned out, both spatially and seasonally.

To be fully appreciated, the subtle beauty of a rain forest must be seen close up and in detail. The ecological and evolutionary messages conveyed by the flanges, folds, colors, and fragrances of tropical flowers can only be divined by intimate study. The effort will be worthwhile, for the utility of these flowers is as extraordinary as their beauty. The fact that an orchid flower can mimic the sexual behavior of a tachinid fly well enough to fool the flies is almost miraculous. Those who take the time to observe the flowers, or indeed any living thing, close up, will be rewarded in any habitat, but especially so in the tropical rain forest. Seen from the inside, it is a series of small miracles, where intermingled lives have resulted in amazingly specialized co-adaptations, many of which owe much to the creative influence of sexual reproduction.

Chapter *7*

"EAT ME"

> *"Well, I'll eat it," said Alice, "and if it makes*
> *me grow larger, I can reach the key; and if it*
> *makes me grow smaller, I can creep under the*
> *door: so either way I'll get into the garden, and I*
> *don't care which happens!"*
> —LEWIS CARROLL
> Alice's Adventures in Wonderland

A good market in a small town in the wet lowlands of tropical America, greasy with mud and rotting fruit, awash with complex, fermenting pungencies, and crowded with a mix of grunting swine, mangy dogs, and bickering, bellowing shoppers and vendors offers more than a colorful slice of tropical life. The stalls of a fruit vendor, loaded with the common fruits of tropical commerce like pineapples and papayas, will often also sport local fruits rarely seen in North American supermarkets. The closer the vendors are to the forest, both physically and culturally, the richer their offerings will be. These semiwild or wild fruits of the tropical forest, such as spondias, pochotes, granadillas, naranjillas, carbolas, guanabanas, zapotes, pepinos, and scores of other little-known succulences, offer a visual document of the diversity of the Neotropical flora. At the same time, they speak eloquently of the prominent role that frugivory—fruit eating—plays in the lives of Neotropical trees and animals.

Although plants seem to be firmly rooted in place, they must have some means of dispersing their offspring. Some are adapted for colonizing new habitats; these colonizing species are often easily outcompeted by other species, so they must disperse widely in order to find new places to grow. Other plants may persist in old habitats; but young plants must still be able to move far enough away from their parents not to have to compete with them, and to avoid enemies like predators and disease that may accompany their parents. Tropical plants face the same dispersal problems that temperate zone plants do, and plants in both regions show many of the same solutions to the problem of getting around. But in a tropical rain forest the favored solutions are ones seldom used in a temperate mixed deciduous woodland.

Botanists have found that seed dispersal tactics can be lumped into broad classes based on the appearance of the structures used for dispersal. The physical structure of these dispersal devices (known as diaspores), is generally correlated with such variables as the dispersal agent, habitat, and successional stage. Both diaspores and dispersal tactics vary in cost and effectiveness, and evolution must carefully weigh these factors.

The cheapest tactics of seed dispersal employ "free" dispersal agents such as wind and gravity. Wind-carried diaspores are sometimes small. Many orchids have tiny diaspores, and they broadcast millions of dustlike seeds over a wide area. The problem with this method is that small seeds have little room for nutrients. Many orchids are dependent on soil fungus for nutrients when they are young; without the proper fungus, the orchid sprouts will starve. This is one reason why orchid growers often have problems propagating their plants from seed. The seeds germinate, but lacking the proper root fungus, the seedlings wilt and die even though they are bathed in rich fertilizers. Without their fungal symbiotes, these nutrients cannot be utilized.

Not all wind-dispersed seeds are small. Some diaspores that travel on currents of air use plumelike structures to catch the breeze. Most North Americans are familiar with the fluff ball diaspores of the dandelion and milkweed, weedy species whose seeds travel long distances on the breeze. In the tropics of the New World some conspicuous trees employ a similar device. The giant kapok tree encloses its seeds in a wad of soft fluff and this diaspore has proven useful to many Amerinds, who traditionally use it to fletch their blowgun darts. Balsa trees, relatives of the kapok, also use fluffy, wind-carried diaspores to find new openings in the rain forest to colonize.

Certain plants use their own devices to propel their seeds out into the world. Some have developed explosive diaspores that throw their seeds a short distance. Temperate zone habitats show many good examples of this strategy, including plants like witch hazel and touch-me-nots. But the strategy does not disperse the seeds widely, and in the tropical rain forest it is employed primarily by trees whose seeds can germinate and grow in shade. I was once in a rubber plantation in the lowlands of western Ecuador on a rare day when the sun made regular excursions out from behind the clouds. Every time the sun appeared, I heard what sounded like shots ringing out from the trees overhead. The sun was warming up the seed pods, which explosively propelled the walnut-sized seeds as far as thirty feet off.

None of these diaspores is particularly well suited for most plants in a mature rain forest. Only the tallest trees, the high-canopy vines, and the epiphytes are in a position to make use of the wind; there is almost always a breeze stirring in the canopy layer, but the lower reaches of the forest are usually windless. Strong winds are not that unusual in tropical forest regions, yet even when the wind screams above, the air near the forest floor remains remarkably calm. So the understory is not a suitable place for wind-carried diaspores. Explosive diaspores may seem like a good bet for understory plants, but they have never caught on because they generally depend on drying or warming to "set" the trigger. It is the tension produced by differential drying that propels the seeds, and in the continually dank recesses of the rain forest floor this is not a worthwhile strategy.

If cheap, easily available avenues of seed dispersal are denied to plants, the most logical alternative would be hitching a ride with an animal. The best seed dispersers are indeed animals that travel widely and are large enough to carry along many seeds.

Anyone who has taken a late summer walk in a North American meadow is familiar with animal-dispersed seeds. Those nasty hooked burdock burrs that cling to your socks with supernatural intensity are effective diaspores as long as there are large mammals around whose fur will provide a suitable matrix. But there are few large furry mammals in the understory of tropical rain forest, and tenacious, clinging diaspores are rarely encountered in primary forest. Only at the edge of the forest are they likely to show up, and many of these come from plants that have been introduced, inadvertently, from other places that have abundant large mammals, such as the African savannahs.

The rain forests of the American tropics may have few large mammals scurrying around near the ground; however, they house a wealth of wide-ranging birds and mammals that dwell in the treetops. Rain forest plants, especially trees, exploit these creatures to transport their seeds. But rather than using a simple, passive means of attaching the seed to the disperser, many plants have seized upon a strategy that benefits both dispersee and disperser. The rain forest's alternative to wind and hook dispersal is fruit. One major study of diaspore classes in tropical rain forest found that at least half of the trees used a fleshy fruit to disperse their seeds.

Why should a plant need to manufacture a large, nutritious fruit? The cost of producing a huge sapote fruit or a crop of fat figs must be considerable. It would clearly be much simpler and cheaper for the tree to drop its seeds rather than making a nutritious, fleshy envelope for them. However, an infant tree attempting to grow near its parent is subject to severe competition for light and soil, both from its parent and from its siblings, and the parent tree must minimize this wasteful competition. Many seedlings do not do well in deep shade. These plants may require the abundance of light provided by a tree fall or forest edge to survive. Only by dispersing will they find such light gaps. Parent trees also provide a resource base for herbivores and pathogens. Any seedling that tries to grow in the shadow of its parent might have to face high risks of predation and disease. By dispersing, a juvenile tree has a chance to get beyond the cluster of predators and pathogens that may attend its parent.

In order to disperse its seeds effectively, a rain forest tree must seek out mobile animals. But in the rain forest, mobile animals like birds, bats, and monkeys are not overly abundant. To attract these dispersers, a plant must stridently proclaim: "EAT ME!" Its message must be heard above the tangled visual noise of the forest and it must reward its takers well. Some of the most successful solutions to these advertisement-and-reward problems eventually find their way into the fruit stands of the tropical market. The colors and gastronomic qualities of these nutritious fruits say much about the animals they are designed to attract.

Bird fruits are often characterized by bright colors. They may be orange, purple, or yellow when they are ripe, but most are some shade of red. The dominance of red bird-dispersed fruits presents an interesting set of problems. On one level, we can explain why cherries are red by stating that they contain carotenoid and xanthophyll pigments; but this tells us only how cherries happen to be red. An evolutionary biologist, seeking a more fundamental answer, would argue that cherries are red in order to entice birds to disperse the tree's seeds, which lie waiting in the fruit's pit. This explanation leads us to yet another mechanistic problem. Why, out of all the colors available, have so many fruits converged on the color red? Perhaps red is simply the complementary color of the pervasive green background of the forest, making it an easily seen signal for creatures with color vision. A red fruit is a promiscuous lure, offering sweet, nutritious rewards to a broad spectrum of hungry creatures. Birds that feed on these bright sugary fruits tend to be opportunistic omnivores, and although much of their diet consists of fruit, they will feed on insects if fruit is scarce.

I once spent several days nursing a bad cold at a field station in the rain forest of western Ecuador. Each night I plowed through the forest, wet to my waist, and each day I tried to recover. It so happened that there was a large *Castilla* rubber tree in fruit just outside the window of the station, so I occupied myself during my convalescence by watching birds feed on its large orange fruits. In the course of an hour one morning I saw twenty-three species of birds visit the tree to partake of its fruit. They were a varied lot, ranging from colorful little tanagers to large toucans, and some of the birds who showed up and gobbled down the fruit were unexpected. Most of us think of woodpeckers as insect-eating birds, adapted for pounding through wood to get at the fat grubs, but one of the most persistent visitors to the fruiting *Castilla* was the Black-cheeked Woodpecker. There were even a few Band-backed Wrens hungrily wolfing down fruit, along with more conventional fruit eaters like the Orange-fronted Barbet, the Masked Tityra, and several species of tanagers. Although these casual observations were not sufficient to identify the most effective fruit dispersers, they did reveal that there were many possibilities.

In addition to the more or less opportunistic fruit eaters, some species of Neotropical birds appear to be obligate fruit eaters. These birds, which include the oilbird, several species of cotingids, and some trogons, seem to subsist entirely on a diet of fruit. Unlike many other birds that feed heavily on fruit when they are adults but offer their hatchlings a diet of insects, these fruit specialists seem to feed exclusively on fruits throughout their lives. And the fruits they thrive on are not brightly colored or conspicuous.

The obligate frugivorous birds of the Neotropical rain forests seem to be particularly attracted to fruits like wild avocados, which offer more than simple carbohydrates and sugars. These fruits are oily and rich in protein, and in contrast to their sweet, brightly colored counterparts they are usually dull-colored. Many have large seeds (but not nearly as large as those of domesticated avocados) that most birds find difficult to pass through their digestive systems; some fruits may even wrap their rich flesh around poisonous seeds. The frugivorous birds process these fruits by regurgitating the seed intact. This benefits both plant and bird; the plant can dispense with manufacturing a seed coat hard enough to survive passage through the intestines, and the birds benefit because the rich food can be quickly assimilated.

The plants are also able to manufacture seeds of a large size, a useful ability whenever competitive seedlings are at a premium. This investment in a large seed and effective dispersal is characteristic of many large trees of mature rain forest. Under such competitive conditions a few large seeds are worth more than many small, uncompetitive seeds. Even in rain forest, however, there are trees like *Cecropia* and figs that produce fruits with numerous small seeds. These plants are often pioneer species that rely on wide dispersal into open areas such as mudslides or tree falls. They may be epiphytes that must germinate on a sunny stem high in the forest canopy. Competitive ability is less important for these species than a huge seed shadow that increases the plant's chances of getting a seed into an appropriate spot as soon as possible.

The large-seeded species are sometimes said to be "K-strategists," which is ecological jargon indicating that they are adapted for survival and reproduction in an environment where population levels are consistently near the capacity of the habitat. Competition for limited resources may be intense for these species, and it may be difficult for them to grow to maturity. The small-seeded fruits are typical of trees characteristic of early stages of successional change and are known as "r-strategists" for their high fecundity and growth rate. These species do not face intense competition for limited resources, but there is a high premium on rapid colonization of virgin resources.

Riverbanks are often the site of plants with small-seeded fruits, such as *Muntingia*, a small tree that bears fruit year round. The berries of this tree are small, sweet, packed with tiny seeds, and fed upon by many species of birds and bats. Wherever *Muntingia* is common and whenever it is in fruit, the leaves of all the plants along the riverbank will be spattered with its defecated seeds. These fruits are an energy source for many animals and they offer superb animal-watching possibilities.

The small-seeded fruits of figs and sapodillos are eaten by animals ranging from monkeys to bats. They are often roundish green and yellow structures, different from fruits specialized for birds. But there are many exceptions amongst the hundreds of fruits to all of these generalizations. Tropical fruits cannot be lumped into discrete classes of large-seeded K-strategists and small-seeded r-strategists. There is a continuum of strategies, and simple generalizations refer only to the end points.

Arils are a good example of an intermediate tactic along this continuum. Many leguminous trees produce hard-coated seeds about the size of common peas and beans; but instead of wrapping them in a costly thick fruit, they wrap a thin brightly colored nutritious coat around them. This coat is only exposed when the seeds have ripened and hardened and the pods split open to display the bright aril. This attracts hungry birds that remove the aril and toss the tough seed away. Alexander Skutch recorded thirty-one species of birds processing the arilate seeds of a *Dipterodendron*. Arils are also used by understory plants to attract ants. *Calathea*, a relative of the common household prayer plant, coats its seeds with an oily aril. Ants collect the seeds and dump them within the humid, well-turned soil of the ant nest where they can germinate easily. Ant arils and oily structures are the common mode of dispersal of temperate spring wildflowers such as violets, trilliums, columbine, and Dutchman's breeches. Ants are not deterred by their small rewards and low-down location and are thus potentially valuable "throwaway" dispersers in both temperate and tropical understory habitat.

Throwaway dispersal is also used by a number of other rain forest plants in innovative ways. *Anacardium* fruits have an edible stem but their seed coat is toxic. When howler monkeys feed on them, they pull the whole structure from its branch, eat the stem, and throw away the fruit. In much of Latin America the brilliant red and orange cashew stems, juicy and full of Vitamin C, are eaten while the nut is discarded. This may seem wasteful to anyone who has seen the price of cashew nuts, but these fruits must be carefully peeled in order to avoid poisoning. The sap is full of toxins similar to those found in poison ivy; it is much easier to eat the nutritious stems and ignore the potentially dangerous seeds.

Howler monkeys don't have much of a throwing arm and there are better ways to move around a heavy seed. One of the more peculiar sights in tropical rain forests is the monkey pot. These are large structures about the size of a rice bowl, built of a hard, barklike material, and often found lying on the ground. They are heavy and inevitably provoke morbid speculations from visitors, who wonder about their effect on tender human heads, especially when they are seen dangling threateningly from a tall tree. The trees that produce monkey pots are members of the genus *Lecythis*, close relatives of the Brazil nut tree. The monkey pot is not a fruit, but a protective structure that houses an array of tasty morsels attached to the inside tip of each seed. To get at the edible tip, a bat must grab the exposed nut, pull it from its slot in the monkey pot, and rotate the nut to eat the tip. It then discards the nut at some distance from the tree.

Predation and fruit dispersal are inextricably linked. The pigeon that disperses an arillate seed at one moment may sit and carefully crack and digest fig seeds a few minutes later. Unripe seeds must be cased in tough pods or laced with toxins to dissuade overeager dispersers who may become predators if the timing is off. If you bite into an unripe papaya, your mouth will be filled with an acrid white sap laced with meat-tenderizing enzymes. But hungry birds will peck through an unripe papaya in search of seeds to eat. If fruit is scarce, a frugivorous bird may be forced to fly from tree to tree to feed and disperse the seeds en route. But I have watched quetzals perched in a heavily laden wild avocado blithely belch out seed after seed to fall in a pile, doomed, at the base of the parental tree. A fruit tree must inevitably pay a concession in order to be dispersed by animals; a certain amount of seed predation and inefficiency has to be accepted.

Vagaries in disperser abundance mean that alternative dispersers are usually needed. Henry Howe found that only one species of bird, the Masked Tityra, was effective at dispersing the seeds of the large rain forest tree *Casaeria corymbosa*, even though he saw twenty-one other species of fruit-eating birds visit the tree. Presumably this wealth of frugivores buffers the tree against the loss of its main disperser. Highly obligatory dependencies court mutual extinction, since if one partner declines in abundance the other will suffer. But seed-dispersal systems in the tropical forest are buffered; if bats are scarce for some reason, the seeds of the monkey pot tree can be dispersed by rodents. Agoutis and pacas eat many seeds, but if they are abundant the rodents may stash and forget a few.

This is the principle of predator satiation common to many temperate nut trees that rely on rodent dispersal. In the temperate zone a stand of oak or hickory may be dense enough so that when the nuts ripen, the squirrel population will be swamped with a glut of food. Many nuts will be stashed underground, and some of these will be forgotten, or perhaps the stasher will be killed, thus allowing the seeds to sprout the following spring. The effectiveness of this ploy can be greatly enhanced by a phenomenon known as mast fruiting. Nut trees and conifers in temperate forests will often go several years with only a few scattered trees fruiting and then one year virtually all the trees in the forest may fruit synchronously. This produces a huge crop of seeds at irregular intervals. There are not enough seeds available during nonmast years to support large populations of seed eaters, so when a mast year comes around these predators are not numerous enough to severely deplete the nuts. Since there is an abundance of seeds for only one year, most predators cannot build up their numbers sufficiently to do much damage to the crop.

Mast fruiting is a risky tactic for tropical rain forest trees. Temperate zone mast-fruiting trees usually rely on cues related to weather to synchronize the fruiting. Individuals that ignore these cues and deviate from the population produce few offspring because their seeds are sought by many predators in a nonmast year. Perhaps mast fruiting is uncommon in the relatively aseasonal neotropical rain forest because weather fluctuations are not severe enough to act as reliable cues. However, there are some well-known examples of mast fruiting in the tropical rain forest that make this explanation seem inadequate.

The strategy behind mast fruiting is not restricted to plants. Ants and termites often "fruit" synchronously at the beginning of the rainy season. I was once in the upper Amazonian basin along the Rio Napo in eastern Ecuador looking for lizards along the edge of a large forest clearing. It was just after a heavy rain had soaked the forest, so I was somewhat taken aback to see what looked like smoke rising in a little plume from the forest. There were no people in the area, so I decided to go in and take a closer look. A few hundred yards into the forest I found the source of the "smoke." It was a nest of termites, and tens of thousands of winged males and females, the kings and queens of future colonies, were pouring out of the nest entrance, flying straight up into the air. The eruption lasted only about ten minutes, and ended as abruptly as it had started. When I walked out to the forest edge to resume my lizard hunting, the cloud of termites was coming to the ground. They were crawling everywhere, and as I looked back into the forest I saw another plume appear. Shortly after that one ended, yet another appeared.

The behavior of the termites when they descended was fascinating. As soon as they landed, they somehow twisted their bodies and their wings immediately fell off. Males quickly found females and the two would scamper off rapidly, trying to escape the hordes of hungry *Paraponera* ants that were feasting on them. Social wasps like *Polybia occidentalis* call their reserves into duty when such an abundance of prey is available, and workers who normally tend the nest leave it to bring in more meat.

Birds were also feasting on the clouds of termites. Swallows, which normally find their food over the river, were swooping over the forest, and a host of flycatchers were popping up and down from their perches like yo-yos. Despite the carnage, the synchronous emergence of sexual termites reduces the chances of any individual being eaten. Termite colonies are common enough to make this tactic work.

The scarcity of mast fruiting in the Neotropical rain forest is more likely to be related to the high diversity of trees. Mast fruiting works best if a species is common. If there are hundreds of tree species in a forest, it is difficult for any single species to saturate its seed predators. This is one of the costs of being rare, particularly for a nut tree. You can often find piles of palm nuts or sapote seeds beneath an isolated fruiting tree in the forest in which every seed has been opened and killed.

But the tropical rain forest is not a uniformly diverse realm. There are patches of forest—sometimes extensive patches—where a single species of tree predominates. The forests of parts of eastern Panama are dominated by such a species, the cuipo tree. Extreme soil and drainage conditions can result in forests dominated by a few species; flooded swamps may have a single species of palm and sandy beach soil may be thickly populated by calabash trees. In these conditions, synchronized fruiting may satiate seed predators and only a fraction of the seeds will be destroyed. Studies of a Neotropical oak showed that it was liable to go extinct locally unless it occurred in patches large enough to swamp acorn-eating deer and rodents.

Most lowland rain forests in the New World tropics are diverse, and it is not surprising that trees that simply let their fruits go are uncommon. Even small seeded trees usually employ the services of mobile animals because below the parent tree populations of seed-eating lygaeid bugs and *Apterostigma* ants home in on piles of seeds and eat them. A fig tree might be able to disperse its seeds successfully by simply dropping them as long as there were enough peccaries to swallow them up and carry them off before the seed predators got to them. But a single fig tree, or even a few dozen trees, cannot support a peccary troop. And even if there are enough fig trees around, the peccaries may be away rooting in a swamp when the trees need them.

What figs and other rain forest trees can do to disperse their progeny hinges on the abundance of conspecifics in the forest, the social structure and population stability of its dispersal agents, and a host of other factors that are beyond the tree's control. Despite this complexity, the importance of fruit as a dispersal mechanism in the tropical rain forest is surprisingly clear. This is an important ecological concept, but like many ecological ideas it may not have much impact when encountered on the dry pages of a scientific journal. It is in the Neotropical markets and forests —in the taste of papayas and pochotes, the sampling of the bright distilled essences of countless taste trials gone by—that a gut appreciation of frugivory begins.

Chapter 8

BUGS AND DRUGS

All flesh is grass, and all the goodliness thereof
is as the flower of the field.
—ISAIAH 40:6

All life is supported by primary producers. Plants that build elements and small molecules into stem and leaf are at the root of life on this planet. Isaiah was thinking of his flocks when he came upon this wisdom, but an ocelot lapping at the blood of a deer owes its existence to the green transformation of sun and soil into living matter as much as any sheep grazing on grass. This presents us with an enigma. Why should an ocelot bother with the tedium and danger of the hunt? Plants may climb but they don't run. In the haunts of the ocelot, animals as large as tapirs can browse their way to fatness. So why has the ocelot evolved to prefer the toil and risks of carnivory?

Flesh is a concentration of the nutrients contained in plant matter. But meat is more than a simple concentration of minerals; it also acts as a filter, a metabolic distillation that removes many of the toxins that lurk in almost every plant. The ocelot and other carnivores may have opted for a life devoid of salads not only because plants are so watered down but also because they are so poisonous and costly to process.

Ever since the first arthropod raised its mouthparts from the decaying litter of ancient swamp forests and began to gnaw on green, a battle has been waged between plants and herbivores. Some of the armaments in this contest are obvious. Herbivores are equipped with all manner of shredding and grinding implements. Although the spines, thorns, and stinging hairs of cacti, palms, and herbs look bellicose, plants seem in general more passive than animals. This, however, is a misperception on our part.

Our world view is built mainly from sights and sounds rather than from tastes and smells. We are only dimly aware of the vast and potent arsenal of chemical weaponry that resides in the greenery around us. There is little in the outward appearance of vegetation that would lead us to expect its astounding chemical diversity. More than 10,000 different chemical compounds have been isolated in recent years from the tissues of plants. For many years the prevailing view was that these compounds were metabolic waste products. They are usually not substances used in the regular physiology and metabolism of the plant and they frequently are of bizarre and novel chemical composition. They have thus come to be called secondary compounds. Secondary compounds are the active ingredients of many of our drugs, herbs, spices, and fragrances. We have been using secondary compounds in our daily life for longer than humanity's collective memory, but only recently have we begun to appreciate their ecological functions and evolutionary significance.

Plants have evolved secondary compounds primarily to discourage herbivory. These chemical defenses are used in myriad ways, varying according to the nature of predation pressure exerted on the plant and the value of the afflicted part. If the part is valuable, it ought to be well protected. Poppies protect their progeny with a capsule full of opiated sap, and various trees line their underbark circulation systems with strychnine or quinine. If the part is an easily replaced leaf or well-protected root, it may contain no defensive chemicals at all.

The quantity and type of chemicals evolved by the plant will also reflect the predators with which it must contend. Many plants are preyed upon primarily by insects, and they have evolved compounds like rotenone that are toxic to most insects but relatively innocuous to large mammals. Some of these natural insecticides are extremely sophisticated.

A number of plants have deciphered the chemical code that insects use to regulate their growth and development. If you crush a basil leaf, the pungent essential oils that endow this herb with its culinary qualities fill the air. But the odor and taste that we find so delightful are anathema to many insects. These oils chemically mimic insect juvenile hormones, which regulate the insect's development, so an insect that munches on basil will have its life severely disrupted. Compounds like these essential oils may also work to deter other predators; for example, they inhibit the digestive bacteria of ruminant grazers such as horses. The predominance of sage in heavily grazed parts of the American west is probably due to these inhibitory oils. Other plants exposed to both insects and a wide variety of arthropod grazers have opted for more generalized defenses that render them inedible to almost everyone.

The tannins concentrated in oak bark and tea leaves cure leather by binding and complexing with protein to form polymers that are difficult to digest. Our habit of adding cream to coffee is a technique for taking the tannins out of solution; the bitter tannins bind on the milk proteins. Other plants have gone the opposite route and have invented compounds that stimulate protein digestion.

I once thought that a pineapple was just another canned fruit and that meat tenderizer was a white powder that some food conglomerate synthesized and packed in shakers. It was my first contact with a fresh pineapple that led me to make the connection between the two. While traveling in northern Colombia, I found myself in the hot, squalid town of Cienega. The only pleasant aspect was the piles of colossal pineapples at the market. These succulent fruits tasted incomparably better than the processed version I was familiar with, but as I neared the end of my feast I felt my tongue tingle. I was soon spitting blood, my tongue tender and bleeding. In my ignorance and gluttony I had eaten the core of the pineapple, which was packed with papain, the active ingredient of commercial meat tenderizers. Anyone who has eaten a green papaya, the namesake of this enzyme, probably has had a similar experience.

Plants have not always come out ahead of the hungry herbivores.

The same evolutionary pressure that leads to development of secondary plant compounds also selects for counteradaptive responses by the herbivores. For example, the painted daisy *Chrysanthemum coccineum* has been called the Lucretia Borgia of the garden. It has stumbled across the mutations required to manufacture pyrethrum, an insecticide that kills insects by paralyzing them. The substance that commercial sprays rely on for a "quick knockdown" is extracted from the dried petals of this flower.

But pyrethrum will not knock down every insect. Some grasshoppers can eat pyrethrum with impunity since they have evolved enzymes known as mixed-function oxidases that are capable of breaking it down. You might think such an adaptation would spell the end for the painted daisy, yet the battle goes on. The painted daisy has synthesized sesamin, a compound that inhibits mixed-function oxidases. This coevolutionary interaction between the eaten and the eaters continually reshapes the metabolism and behavior of the combatants. Over time there develops a congruence between predator and prey. For example, the only organisms that can eat botulinum, the deadly toxin produced by botulism bacteria, are vultures. Generations of exposure to this hazard have led them to develop effective biochemical defenses against it.

There are limits on what plants can afford to invent. Much of life's basic metabolic machinery is shared by everything from bacteria to humans, and plants are therefore constrained by the problem of self-poisoning. They share this and other constraints with commercial pesticide manufacturers; health risks and costs are important factors in pesticide development, regardless of who manufactures them. The more steps involved in synthesizing a compound, the more it costs. Plants reduce these costs by concentrating the compounds where they are most needed and by recycling them whenever possible. Castor beans (*Rinicus*) continually shunt defensive compounds from older leaves to more productive new ones, saving on both synthesis and raw materials.

Many of the defensive compounds plants rely on are alkaloids that contain nitrogen. Nitrogen is at a premium for a number of plants because they need large quantities of it for growth. Plants that live in nitrogen-deficient soils, such as acid bogs, often lack secondary defensive compounds. There are other situations where plants might choose to use nitrogen for growth rather than defense. Plants that colonize tree falls in the rain forest must grow rapidly in order to compete effectively for light. Pioneer trees in the tropical rain forest often sacrifice defensive compounds for more nitrogen to put into growth. It is not unusual to see a balsa tree *(Ochroma pyramidale)* rapidly growing toward a gap in the canopy, its leaves pocked with holes created by hungry insects. Insects may eat as much as 40 percent of the leaf area, but the balsa keeps on growing. Other pioneer species have come across other defenses in lieu of secondary compounds, often utilizing ants, for example (see Chapter 9).

Plants are sometimes unable to tolerate the loss of leaf material. Some parts of the tropics are dominated by white sand soils. These soils are derived from old beaches and are so coarse and porous that nutrients are leached rapidly away. The plants living in such situations ought to be severely affected by the loss of any of their nutrients to herbivores since the potential for recovering them from the soil is low. Under these conditions plants ought to invest heavily in defenses, even on leaves, despite the costs.

Dan Janzen has used this reasoning to piece together an argument that unifies and explains much of what is known about the unusual ecosystems associated with tropical white sand soils. Visitors to white sand forests have always remarked on the quiet, and that these forests are often barren habitats devoid of animal life. Few birds are seen or heard, probably because insect populations are low in both species and numbers. Insects have found it difficult to cope with the high concentrations of defensive compounds, particularly tannins, in the plants in this type of forest. The raw materials required to produce tannins are primarily sugars, which are created by photosynthesis, rather than nitrogenous compounds, which are scarce in white sand soils. This makes it easier for the trees to pay the costs of defense. These tannin compounds yield highly acidic decomposition products. When they leach into streams, they have the same effect that acid rain has in industrialized temperate areas: they poison the waters. Their brown acidity produces blackwater rivers, the most famous of which is the mighty Rio Negro in Brazil. This river and others like it resemble immense, unending streams of strong tea. They are the aquatic equivalents of desert—and the white sand forests are the entomological and zoological deserts of the humid tropics.

Plants have evolved defenses that may be far more subtle than poisons or spines. The prevailing visual signal you receive during a walk through the rain forest is one of greenness. Wherever you look there are green leaves. But once in a while you will see a colorfully blotched plant, perhaps a *Philodendron* streaked with yellow and white, another aroid flecked with red spots, or a purple-tinted *Coleus* glaring forth from a sunny tree-fall gap. These varicolored plants can inspire two reactions; you might remark on the beauty of their patterns, or you might wonder if perhaps the plant is sick. The chlorophyll that understory plants so desperately need is green. Perhaps these plants have been designed by natural selection to elicit the second reaction. Many of the patterns of brightly colored ornamental plants that occur naturally seem to mimic the symptoms of common nutritional deficiencies—the yellowing of chlorosis or the purple tints of potassium and phosphorus depletion. If a herbivore depends on its vision to assess the nutritional value of a plant, it ought to reject those that appear nutrient-poor.

Plants may also try to dupe butterflies that search visually for host plants on which to lay eggs. Passion vines (*Passiflora cyanea* and perhaps other species) produce stipules that look like fake *Heliconius* butterfly eggs. Since *Heliconius* caterpillars are sometimes cannibalistic, female butterflies should reject plants that appear to be already occupied by someone else's eggs.

The most important ramification of these diverse defensive tactics is that the plants have forced a similar diversification in habits upon herbivores. Some herbivores have opted for extreme specialization, developing the enzymes and behaviors necessary to breach the defenses of a single species of plant. Certain insects, in fact, specialize on a single part of a single species of plant. These specialists gain the considerable advantage of being able to thrive on a plant that few other herbivores can utilize at all, and they thus face little competition. But specialization has its costs. There is a reduced opportunity to shift one's diet to adjust for environmental changes. Anything that affects the host plant also directly affects the herbivore, and if the plant becomes rare so must the herbivore. A generalist, on the other hand, can opportunistically track changes in the abundance of different plants and take advantage of the most abundant ones at any time. The ability to be a generalist often enables a species to become common, and the most abundant species usually enjoy a broad spectrum of plant resources.

A generalized herbivore requires a formidable and adaptable digestive system. Hundreds of potentially toxic compounds have to be rendered harmless. The mixed-function oxidase enzymes appear to be important in dissolving these obstacles. Generalist caterpillars usually have far more mixed-function oxidases in their guts than do specialists. These species become agricultural pests more often than specialists since the mixed-function oxidases also detoxify many insecticides.

Mixed-function oxidase enzymes are inducible. This means that they can synthesize larger quantities of the mixed-function oxidases after they are exposed to a toxin, which saves on the energetic costs of making and maintaining these large molecules when they are not needed. It may also account for the timid, slow feeding behavior reported for herbivorous animals like howler monkeys and rats when they encounter a new food source.

Mixed-function oxidases are not the answer to all, or even most, secondary plant compounds. The mixed-function oxidases are thought to work by converting fat-soluble toxins into water-soluble substances that can be harmlessly excreted. A plant that is rendered palatable by the mixed-function oxidases of a howler monkey may become unpalatable in the dry season because the required excretion rates cannot be met. Mixed-function oxidase activity may also render substances like aflatoxins into even more dangerous forms and yet be totally ineffective on other toxins. One possible way around this dilemma of a diverse diet seems to follow an old adage of Paracelsus, which says that toxicity is purely a matter of dosage. Baird's Tapir (*Tapirus bairdi*) is the largest native herbivore in the forests of the New World tropics and it is known to feed on at least ninety-five species of plants in Costa Rica alone. But when it feeds, it rarely gorges on any single plant. It typically waves its elephantine snout in the air casting about for scents, and strokes the leaves with its snout until it finds one that smells right. The prehensile nose then pulls the leaf mouthward to its masticatory doom and the tapir moves on. This ambulatory nibbling probably minimizes the amount of any single toxin that the tapir must endure and may reduce its need for complex biochemical adaptations.

The same shifting of diet is exhibited by sedentary generalist herbivores such as the leaf-cutting ants (*Atta*). These ants cut leaves and other vegetable matter to cultivate underground fungal gardens. The fungi produce specialized fruiting bodies, which the ants then use for food. In effect, the ants use the fungi as part of their digestive system, and the fungi use the ants as arms, jaws, and dispersal agents. The ants must selectively harvest the forest, masticate the leaves to remove surface waxes, and generally make them palatable for the fungi.

It is surprisingly difficult to grow just about any fungus other than bread mold or mildew. Perhaps this is why the leaf-cutting ants forage so selectively, seeking out only certain parts of certain plants at certain times. Like the tapir, they do not often linger on any single tree. One might interpret this as prudent harvesting that minimizes the chance of destroying a food source; but it might also be a tactic used to avoid chemical backlash by the tree. Many plants, including tomatoes, potatoes, lupines, and clovers, increase sharply in unpalatability soon after being damaged. The chemicals released by cell damage stimulate them to produce compounds that inhibit the digestion of protein. The prudent herbivore must therefore chew a little and then move on. This prudence might be responsible for the *Urania* migrations, one of the most colorful spectacles in the New World tropics.

Urania is a large, day-flying moth about the size of a swallow-tail butterfly, whose form it roughly resembles. Like most moths that are alive by day, *Urania* is brightly colored. Its black and iridescent green pigments, flecked with white and pinks near the tail lobes, rival any butterfly in flamboyance. During the rainy season in hot, lowland areas of Central America, *Urania* can be seen on the move in great numbers. In some years clouds of these moths fly across the landscape in a unidirectional flight that can only be called migratory. But unlike other migratory animals that move to warm areas in the winter, to mating sites, or to feeding grounds, *Urania* seems to have little reason to become a nomad. There is no harsh weather to escape, and its host plant, a vine called *Omphalea*, occurs everywhere that *Urania* is found.

Neal Smith, working at the Smithsonian Tropical Research Institute in Panama, serendipitously hit upon a plausible answer to this mystery. When he was rearing *Urania* caterpillars, he noticed that those that fed on vines that had been repeatedly damaged died. This suggested that *Omphalea* might be reacting the way other plants sometimes do—damage stimulates them to produce toxic secondary compounds. Smith hypothesized that after several generations of *Urania* attack, *Omphalea* vines in an area become unpalatable and this triggers the *Urania* migration. This idea is supported by the fact that migrating *Urania* are in reproductive condition and females lay eggs en route. The theory is of more than anecdotal significance because if it is true, then there must be patches of palatable *Omphalea* scattered among the unpalatable to make the migration worthwhile.

It is already known that individuals within a population of plants vary greatly in palatability and other chemical qualities. Anyone who has eaten wild apples or made maple syrup has surely noticed great individual differences in sweetness among different trees. A consensus is now emerging that subpopulations of a species also differ greatly from each other. The trees on one side of a river or mountain may taste radically different from members of the same species found just on the other side. And when people have looked carefully at the relationships between a plant and its herbivores over some distance, they have found that this has reached a level of specialization and differentiation previously unappreciated. Butterfly species, once thought to feed on several host plants, are now thought to be series of subpopulations, each feeding on one or a few plant species.

This view of the world is far different from an earlier one that portrayed plant and animal species as homogeneous entities spread over a section of the globe. It suggests, rather, that species are patches of individuals, which may differ in their chemistries from one area to another, and, more importantly, that these differences may have an impact on other species. From an ecological point of view, calling two individuals by the same Latin binomial may say little about what these two individuals do. Consider what must have happened when a population of passion vines developed leaf stipules pigmented to mimic *Heliconius* butterfly eggs. This must have had an impact on other passion vine species, which would have been rendered relatively more attractive. It would have affected the tiny parasitic scelionid and trichogrammid wasps that lay their eggs inside the eggs of the butterflies. It might even have had an effect on foliage-gleaning birds that feed on caterpillars. It certainly must have affected the *Heliconius*, and the affected populations have surely evolved differently from populations living on passion vines without this capability.

Plants are not alone in having evolved chemical defenses. Many insects and vertebrates use poisons for protection. The insects are often able to sequester toxins directly from their food plants. The classic example of this strategy is the monarch butterfly, *Danaus plexippus*, which stores the cardiac glycosides in the milkweeds that the caterpillar eats. These toxins render both caterpillar and butterfly unpalatable to birds.

Frogs and toads of the tropical rain forest have frequently traveled the toxic trail. Toad venoms are complex mixtures whose components testify to the evolutionary agents that brought them into being. Some poisons are cardiotoxins—substances that interfere with the heartbeat and even stop it if enough is administered. These compounds, evolved and manufactured by amphibians, closely resemble the substances that *Digitalis* foxgloves produce in their leaves. This is not to say that *Bufo marinus*, a toad that hops around lowland tropical America, has been exposed to the same predators as foxgloves growing in a European meadow. But both have been eaten by vertebrates who share common evolutionary origins and fundamental similarities in their biochemical machinery. What interferes with the heartbeat of a coatimundi will also disturb the cardiac system of an alpine goat.

This sort of evolutionary convergence, when two unrelated sets of organisms develop similar solutions to similar problems, is the Darwinist's delight. It can again be seen in the close resemblance of cacti of the New World and euphorbs of Africa, whose spininess and thick, succulent leaves adapt them for desert life. In looking at these convergences, the evolutionist can take pleasure in perceiving some element of predictability in the paths that life has taken. But this is not to argue, as many students of form and function used to do, that toads and foxgloves have similar poisons because of evolution's constant striving for perfection. The shared ancestry and physiologies of the toad's and foxglove's enemies has narrowed the available set of solutions these creatures could realize in evolving antipredatory chemicals.

Toad venoms also contain bufotenine. Bufotenine owes its strong pharmaceutical potential to its close resemblance to serotonin, a potent mammalian neurotransmitter. Our bodies synthesize serotonin as a regulator of many interconnected neural functions; serotonin maintains the tone of our blood-vessel walls and plays a central role in regulating our sleep cycle by its influence on brain functions. Bufotenine is structurally identical to serotonin in almost every respect except that it has two methyl groups stuck on its tail. It is amazing that the addition of these two methyl groups has such a profound physiological effect. Our bodies easily metabolize serotonin, but its dimethyl analogue is devastating.

Bufotenine, like all of the molecules and enzymes that run life's machinery, has a three-dimensional shape. This enables it to combine, split, and recognize other specifically shaped molecules. Bufotenine is similar enough to serotonin to fit in where serotonin normally would; but its two methyl groups make it just different enough to gum up the molecules designed to make use of it. Thus plants, insects, toads, and other organisms have evolved to make analogues of naturally occurring chemicals as poisons. Neurotransmitters like serotonin are among the best compounds to mimic when producing a poison, and it would be surprising if other organisms besides toads had not evolved the same tactic. They have, and the substances they produce are generally called hallucinogens.

Many people labor under the misconception that hallucinogenic drugs owe their origin and manufacture to clandestine Berkeley chemists. But fungi and plants are hallucinogen chemists par excellence. We humans have only begun to analyze all of the hallucinogens that occur in nature, but we have been using them since long before the days of Haight-Ashbury and the Summer of Love. Indeed, we are hardpressed to think of a human culture that has not used some botanically or mycologically derived hallucinogen, with the possible exception of Eskimos, who live in a florally depauperate environment.

True hallucinogens do not give rise to physical addiction. Their effect is to excite the brain, producing visions and emotional experiences of an intensity far beyond that of everyday experience. Their usage has been most highly developed among the first human dwellers in the Neotropical forests, who have discovered dozens of substances, including the saps of various trees, leguminous beans, cacti, barks of vines and trees, leaves, flowers, and fungi. The richness of the ethnobotany of Neotropical hallucinogens reflects both the high diversity of the plants available for such purposes and the fact that virtually every tribe indigenous to the region uses them to make contact with the spirit world they believe occupies the forest surrounding them.

In this region of the world there has traditionally been a strong pantheistic element in the way people perceive the world. Plants and animals are thought to possess knowledge, and hallucinogens have been the tools used by humans to seek this knowledge. Information about hunting success, illness, and other questions too complex to predict is sought with the aid of secondary plant compounds. Hallucinogens are admirably suited to this task because they generate experiences that feel like insights. Thoreau said: "The man of science studies nature as a dead language. I pray for such inward experience as will make nature significant." The people of the forest have found the tools that make such inward experience possible.

Near the turn of the twentieth century, a young *cauchero* (rubber prospector) named Manuel Córdova-Rios was kidnapped by the Amahuaca people of the upper Amazon forest. His extraordinary story is recounted by the tropical forester F. Bruce Lamb in a book entitled *Wizard of the Upper Amazon*. Córdova lived with the Amahuaca tribe for many years, not only sharing in their daily life but eventually being groomed to become chief. Among the fascinating things he learned was the rich pharmacopeia that these forest people relied on to provide them with insights into their daily life. The following brief passage, describing the effects of one such botanical infusion, gives some idea of how these substances were used:

> There was an almost immediate reaction. As the darkness deepened I became aware of an acute depth of visual perception far beyond anything known to me before. The mighty trees around us took on a deep spiritual quality of obedient benevolence that set the character of the whole scene. As the fire died back down to a glowing coal, the darkness settled over everything. At the same time, my visual powers were so augmented that I could see things that in other circumstances would have been totally invisible to me. This explained how the Indians could travel with ease through the forest and even hunt at night. . . .
>
> The call of an owl, "whooo whooo," floated on the still night air and was answered in the darkness.
>
> "You will learn to see and hear at night as clearly as the owl," was the chief's comment. And I felt that it was true.
>
> With chants and the calls of the various animals, the chief evoked in my visions vivid episodes in the lives of the nocturnal forest animals. The chants, the calls and the visions they brought were all to become part of my own repertory.

The infusion ingested by Manuel Córdova-Rios was prepared from the leaves of the shrub *Psychotria viridis* and the bark of the vine *Banisteriopsis caapi*. This infusion, known variously as *yagé* or *ayahuasca* among many tribes in the upper Amazon basin, contains a variety of chemical compounds that are structurally related to serotonin.

Let us consider the "dead language" concealed in the presence of hallucinogens. We must first assume that they were not put there by the spirits of the forest to enhance communication with humans. Given this assumption (with which most Amazonian Indians would strongly disagree), what can we infer about past evolution and ecology from them?

Why should a stringy *Banisteriopsis* vine manufacture a compound capable of transporting a human into a new world of fantastic visions? From an evolutionary perspective, the interactions between the vine and other creatures is straightforward: plants undoubtedly produce most hallucinogens as defensive compounds that protect them from being eaten by small mammalian herbivores. Thirteen seeds of the morning glory, *Rivea corybosa*, are enough to cause wild hallucinations in an adult human. It is obvious that a single seed ingested by a mouse would have a profound effect—one that would surely exert strong selective pressures on any mouse population. Humans are able to ingest hallucinogenic plants because our large size and ability to store cultural information allows us to control the dosage of these potentially fatal compounds.

As relatively new creatures on the planet, *Homo sapiens* has probably had little effect on the evolution of plant secondary compounds. This is particularly true in the Neotropics, where we are extremely recent arrivals. Despite our lack of participation in the evolutionary processes that led to plant secondary compounds in the rain forests of tropical America, our fundamental biochemical kinship with other inhabitants of the area through time allows us to be both victim and beneficiary of this long, silent, ceaseless history. Human use of hallucinogenic plants is nothing more than an evolutionary epiphenomenon, an accidental and unpredictable result of our common heritage of neurotransmission with the plant's real enemies.

Chapter **9**

CREEPING
SOCIALISTS

*O true believers, take your necessary precautions
against your enemies, and either go forth
to war in separate parties, or go forth
all together in a body.*
—Koran, Chapter 4

A naturalist finds it difficult to separate images of place from images of life. When Aldo Leopold looked into the eyes of a dying wolf, he saw mountains. When a fly fisherman looks at a mountain stream, he sees trout. Every habitat has a dominant animal, or group of animals, that gives it a special meaning to a human observer. This type of dominance cannot be quantified because it depends on the perspective of the viewer, but ecologists can quantify another sort of dominance in stark numerical terms.

From the perspective of nutrient flow, the most important animals are the ones with the greatest combined weight, or biomass, per unit area. This is a straightforward index, though a difficult one to come by in practice—but it gives ecologists only a partial insight into the relative importance of the creatures in a habitat. Some animals whose populations have a high biomass interact with only a few other species of plants and animals, and therefore are less important, in both an ecological and an evolutionary sense, than animals with a lower combined biomass that interact with many other species.

Ants constitute a large part of the animal biomass in many tropical forests. They can easily outweigh all of the vertebrates in a parcel of lowland rain forest, despite the fact that even the largest ants in tropical America are rather small creatures. Ants are far more important than their biomass alone implies, for they touch on the lives of almost everything that lives in the forest. No matter where you step, no matter where you lean, no matter where you sit, you will encounter ants. There are ant nests in the ground, ant nests in the bushes, ant nests in the trees; whenever you disturb their ubiquitous nests, the inhabitants rush forth to defend their homes. In their selfless defense of the colony we get some insight into how their complex societies have allowed them to play a dominant role in the economy of the rain forest.

Colonies of *Atta* ants, also known as leafcutter or parasol ants, may contain over a million individual workers, which puts them among the largest and most complex societies in the world. *Atta* workers from the same colony range in length from less than a fifth of an inch to over an inch. Different-sized workers also have mandibles that differ in proportions. Each size of worker is specialized to do a certain job: the smallest take care of eggs and larvae; the medium-sized ones forage; and the large soldiers defend the nest. All these functions serve the welfare of the queen and the sisterhood of the colony. It was while watching a colony of *Atta* performing their devotions that we observed a dramatic example of rigid pismire pragmatism being applied with a frightening lack of sentimentality.

Atta soldiers are the largest ants in the colony except for the queen. Their allometrically enlarged heads and mandibles leave them unsuited for anything except cleaving flesh and cuticle when the colony is threatened. At other times *Atta* soldiers are remarkably placid and seem to perform no useful tasks for the colony. The ratios of different castes in an *Atta* colony are probably regulated by chemicals produced by the ants, which determine how an egg will be reared. This system of caste regulation has a lag period, and if conditions should suddenly change there may be an overabundance of one caste. From time to time the ratios of the large castes to the smaller castes seem to get out of phase. If food or other resources are scarce, one caste may have to be expended in favor of another. This may have been responsible for the behavior we once observed in a Costa Rican *Atta* colony.

Atta soldiers normally enter and leave the nests along with their fellow workers. When they meet, they briefly confirm their kinship by stroking antennae and exchanging chemical cues. But as we watched a Costa Rican colony in deciduous forest at the beginning of the dry season, suddenly, for no apparent reason, the smaller ants began to respond to the touch of the soldiers in a peculiar manner. After tentative antennal strokings, they grabbed their larger nest mates by an appendage. More workers were attracted to the fray and shortly the soldiers were spread-eagled. The workers then leisurely cut the soldiers to pieces and carted off the remains unceremoniously to the refuse heap. The slaughter was extensive at the entrance to the nest; whenever we looked at the colony, dozens of soldiers were pinned down and being dismembered. The wrecking crew seemed to use cues involving odors specific to certain castes. Only soldiers were butchered and only the small workers did the butchering. When we dangled a leg or other part of a soldier in front of a small worker, it elicited a grasping response long after the soldier had expired.

The most remarkable aspect of this sacrificial scene was not the behavior of the small workers but the behavior of the large soldiers. The soldiers offered no protest even though their giant mandibles and huge muscle-packed heads could have made mincemeat of their executioners. They met their fate passively. Although the scene was horrifying from our perspective, it made biological sense because all of the workers and soldiers in an ant colony are sterile servants of their mother, the queen. The sterile females serve their own genetic ends by promoting the welfare of the colony. If their death benefits the colony by increasing its efficiency, then they are worth more to their genes dead than alive. The large soldiers may have utilized resources better expended on small foraging castes during the lean times of the oncoming dry season, and the colony used a direct approach in pruning its dead weight.

The simpleminded socialism evolved by ants, vespid wasps, termites, and many bees is a life-style that seems particularly well suited to the New World tropics. These groups all reach their

maximum diversity there. Of course the same can be said of many
other groups of organisms, such as flowering plants, freshwater
fishes, frogs, or butterflies; but there is evidence to suggest that
social insects, particularly ants, are numerically better represented
in the tropics than elsewhere. This numerical dominance is immediately obvious to anyone who visits the New World tropics,
yet it is extremely difficult to quantify and document. Researchers
have attempted to measure the abundance of every animal in
patches of rain forest. The sampling techniques these biologists
use are biased against mobile or cryptic burrowing creatures like
ants, but even with these biases, ants have been shown to be the
dominant animals in terms of biomass in tropical rain forest, as
we said earlier. They probably constitute a higher proportion of
animal biomass in these forests than in any temperate zone
habitat.

Neotropical ants also differ from temperate ants in being more
abundant and diverse in forest habitats rather than in the open
areas in which temperate ants thrive. In temperate regions, ants
rely on sunlight to keep them warm and active during cool spring
and autumn days. The dark bodies of most temperate ants soak
up solar energy, which allows them to forage when it is cool. They
sit at home when it is cloudy. The lack of opportunities for solar
heating explains why ants are scarce in the gloom of tropical
cloud forests, even though the average temperature in these
habitats is warmer than that of temperate regions or of alpine
areas higher in tropical mountains.

If you search diligently in tropical American cloud forests between 6,000 and 9,000 feet up the Andes, you might find a
sprinkling of small, lethargic ants. But if you continue your
search higher in the same mountains, as high as 15,000 feet in
the altiplano around Lake Titicaca, ants can be both common
and vigorous. The clear air and burning intensity of the sun in
the high tropical Andes give ants an opportunity to crawl about
vigorously amid the cacti and tussock grasses even when snow
covers the ground. In the tropical lowlands, perpetual warmth
frees the ants from dependence on sunlight, and in these regions
they are active by both day and night, from the uppermost leaf
tips of the tallest canopy trees to the damp dark recesses of the
forest floor.

The impact of this perpetual and prolific pismire activity in the lowland tropical rain forest is immense. Almost every plant and animal that dwells there must consider ants as a prominent factor in its evolutionary and ecological calculus. In one study, Roger Swain found that ants accounted for almost three-quarters of the insect predation in the understory of a Brazilian forest; Bob Jeanne, in a heroic effort that involved sampling from New Hampshire to Amazonia, has shown that ant predation rates are far higher in tropical forests than in temperate forests.

Most ants have fairly generalized tastes. Some may cultivate fungi, others may eat spider eggs or seeds, and some may hunt termites or raid the nests of other ants and wasps; but most utilize a wide range of arthropod protein, sweets, and fats. They patrol the rain forest ceaselessly and relentlessly. Any piece of meat or sugar left on the rain forest floor is quickly discovered, often within minutes. If the bait is large, the ants will lay a chemical trail back to the nest to recruit nest mates to the food source. Speed is essential because other ants may discover the food if the original discoverers tarry. Ants vary in their ability to recruit and defend food sources. Some, such as the *hormiga loca* (crazy ant), *Paratrachina longicornis*, are adept at locating food and recruiting nest mates to carry it off, but they are easily displaced by more aggressive ants such as *Azteca*, who use noxious chemical sprays to drive competitors away. Other ants, such as the tiny thief ants (*Solenopsis* spp.), coat their food with a distasteful secretion that renders it unpalatable to other ant species. This complexity of behavior and the patchy distribution of ants according to nest site preferences produces a complex succession of species at baits. Ants are usually territorial. They blanket and divide the spaces of the forest into a mosaic whose properties change with every step.

For a human naturalist treading the Neotropical rain forest, it is the ubiquity of pugnacious pismires that will most constrain your activity rather than such rarities as poisonous snakes. Sitting on a fallen log is not hazardous because of scorpions or spiders, but because of the chance of inadvertently discovering a colony of *Odontomachus* ants. Scorpions and spiders might be unpleasant surprises, but they are uncommon surprises, whereas *Odontomachus* is likely to lurk under almost every suitable log. These vicious ants will come rushing forth from the log with spring-trap mandibles ready to snap shut on any exposed flesh, their stings primed for a retaliatory injection. If you climb a rain forest tree

you needn't worry much about snakes, but you will ignore ants at
your own peril. One of the most painful nonlethal experiences
a person can endure is the sting of the giant ant *Paraponera
clavata*. These ants, with their glistening black bodies over an inch
long, sport massive hypodermic syringes and large venom reser-
voirs. They call on these weapons with wild abandon when
provoked, and they are easily offended beasts. Unlike the stings of
honeybees and polybiine wasps, the stings of *Paraponera* are not
one-shot affairs.

One night as I was collecting moths at a light trap in the rain
forest of western Ecuador, I felt something drop down the neck
of my shirt and scurry across my shoulder. When I wrestled with
my shirt to find out what it was, the ant became squeezed against
my skin. It drove its stinger into my neck and shoulder flesh four
times in rapid order, and each sting felt as if a red-hot spike was
being driven in. My field of vision went red and I felt woozy. The
shouts and nervous laughter of my companion sounded far away.
After an hour of burning, blinding pain I was left with a sore
back and lymph nodes in my armpit so swollen that I couldn't
move my arm without pain for the next two days. Later, I talked
to an orchid enthusiast who told of sliding down a tree and
plunging his foot into a nest of *Paraponera*. Even now, years later,
sitting in the glow of a wood stove in a deep Ontario winter, this
vision of hordes of vicious black ants swarming up the pants sends
a convulsive shudder of fear and revulsion through me.

As a rule, tropical plants benefit from the presence of ants, at
least from the presence of insectivorous ants. Patrolling ants glean
the foliage, picking up and eating the eggs and larvae of voracious
herbivores. A plant might benefit if it happened to find a way to
increase the visits by these ants to its foliage, and such adaptations
have been made by many plants in the tropical rain forest.

Extrafloral nectaries are one way of ensuring that ants stick
around. Their plodding ways render ants poor pollinators; strong
fliers make the best pollinators. Plants normally bury their nectars
within a complicated floral structure, reserving their sweet rewards
for bees, birds, bats, butterflies, and other winged creatures that
will fly their gametes hither and yon. But ants are as enamored of
the sweet, nutrient-rich nectar as any pollinator. If they discover
an accessible source of such sweetness, they will recruit nest mates
to the site, defend it, and return regularly to harvest it. Some

plants have evolved nectaries that produce a sweet exudate without the protective cloak of the flower's corolla. These extrafloral nectaries may be no more than a simple enlarged pore, perhaps a tiny glandular swelling with a minuscule drop of sweetness oozing forth.

Plants that have evolved such nectaries often place them where and when they require the most protection from herbivores: at the base of flower and leaf buds, or at a crucial time of year. Sweet cherries in the temperate zones, for example, develop sweet exudates when the tent caterpillar invasion is in full swing in early spring, drying up after the danger is past. The plants with these extrafloral nectaries evidently benefit from the presence of ants because the ants drawn to the sweet nectar will also pick off the eggs or larvae of other insects they encounter. Some ants are aggressively protective; these may chase off herbivorous insects, not through any particular love for the plant but simply out of their own territorial self-interest.

The sweet tooth of ants is not necessarily always advantageous to a plant. There are some insects that mimic extrafloral nectaries at a plant's expense. Plant-sucking insects, such as certain aphids and membracid treehoppers, tap into the lifelines of a plant and produce a sweet honeydew exudate as a byproduct. When ants, social wasps, or stingless bees discover a colony of plant-sucking insects secreting sugar-rich fluids, they will tend and defend the parasites just as they would an extrafloral nectary. The ants regard nectar-producing insects with the same dispassionate selfishness they do the plants. They are interested in the sweet nectar, and it makes no difference to the ant whether it is produced by the plant or by an insect eating the plant.

The selfish interests of the ant "protectors" are evident if you are observant. You might see bright red mites parasitizing membracid nymphs while its ant "protectors" stand idly by. The mites are no threat to the ants and the ants do nothing to protect their nectar-producing charges from this danger. But if a potential usurping competitor happens by, the tending ants will peck at it if necessary. The sugar brings out the territorial instinct in these energy-thirsty creatures.

The province of extrafloral exudates is not exclusively tropical, nor are these exudates necessarily aimed at ants. Many common temperate plants employ extrafloral nectaries. The elderberries and sunflowers in a temperate garden are often visited by parasitoid wasps, who sip at the sugars leaking from these plants. Such sugars are known to increase the longevity and density of some of these parasitoid wasps. Since the wasps often parasitize leaf-eating caterpillars, it is likely that these crude extrafloral nectaries reduce the plant's herbivore load.

Plants have no means of regulating who visits their nectaries. Creatures useless or even harmful can use them. The only way a plant can circumvent the potential abuses of such a system is either to abandon it completely or to invest more heavily in refining the system. A few tropical plants have taken this latter path by providing some ants with a set of offerings and inducements to lure them into an obligate partnership, in which both plant and ant are so interdependent that the survival of one depends upon the welfare of the other.

Thomas Belt, who spent considerable time in Ceneral America in the nineteenth century, was the first to call attention to the extreme sophistication of the relationships between certain ants and certain plants of the genus *Acacia*. These plants, called bullhorn acacias, are easily recognized. Their swollen thorns resemble the horns of the zebu-brahma cattle so characteristic of the lowland tropics. The thorns are hollow, and inside them dwell colonies of ants of the genus *Pseudomyrmex*, a group of small, thin-bodied, fleet-footed ants. The bullhorn acacias not only provide these ants with a dwelling; they also supply extrafloral nectaries at the base of leaves as well as pinhead-sized globular orange bodies attached in rows along the edges of young leaves. These nectaries are so distinctive that they have been given their own name—Beltian bodies. They contain all the nutrients required by a colony of acacia ants. Since the ants' needs for food and shelter are provided by the plant, all of their excess energy should be channeled into promoting the welfare of the tree.

To see this self-interested loyalty in action, you need only rustle an acacia tree or poke the leaves with a stick. Ants will come pouring forth from the hollow thorns, and if they chance to get on your skin, you will quickly feel the wrath of their stings. These powerful stings must deter most mammalian grazers, and the constantly patrolling workers remove insect herbivores from the leaves before they can do any damage. There are obvious direct benefits for the plant, but the situation also has an interesting hidden benefit. Most acacias produce nitrogen-rich, cyanide-like defensive compounds to protect themselves from herbivores. However, these compounds can be costly to produce in certain soils; it is far less costly to produce the sweet exudates that ants need, and bullhorn acacias do not need to produce large quantities of these substances.

Pseudomyrmex also remove the climbing vines that threaten bullhorn acacias, and in some cases they may trim away all the vegetation within several yards of a tree. Bullhorn acacias are characteristic of tropical forests with a pronounced dry season, so this clearing activity not only reduces competition but may also reduce the risk of fire damage. Cheating does occur; at least one species of *Pseudomyrmex* and several species of ants in the genus *Crematogaster* will occupy bullhorns and take advantage of the tree without any reciprocity. They are opportunistic parasites on this system.

The sophistication of the ant-acacia system is not a lone miracle of coevolution. It is matched by another ant–plant interaction in the New World tropics. Ants of the genus *Azteca* are common throughout the lowland forests of tropical America. Although the ants themselves are small, they are often conspicuous because of the large, carton-like nests they build on the trunks of large trees. Moraceous trees of the genus *Cecropia* are typical and easily recognizable wherever there are clearings or edges. They thrive on light and exposed soil, and grow rapidly in bright sunlight. The pioneering habits of *Cecropia* require that it invest more heavily in growth than in chemical defenses. Unlike the leaves of many slow-growing tropical rain forest plants, the foliage of *Cecropia* seems to be quite palatable. Sloths relish it, and you will often find the huge palmate *Cecropia* leaves pocked with insect damage.

To circumvent some of this herbivory *Cecropia* plays host to certain species of *Azteca*. The trunk of the *Cecropia* is bamboo-like, with large hollow chambers between the nodes. *Azteca* can enter these hollows through small openings just above the point where leaves branch off. The plant further accommodates the ants by producing specialized structures called trichilia, which in turn produce a nutrient-rich solution that ants thrive on.

The *Cecropia* also produces tiny white capsules about the size of sesame seeds, known as Müllerian bodies (after the nineteenth century German zoologist Fritz Müller, who also gave us the term Müllerian mimicry). The Müllerian bodies are almost half glycogen, a high-energy carbohydrate, a wise choice because *Azteca* are frantic little creatures and *Cecropia* grows in ideal photosynthetic conditions. Even so, these plant offerings are not enough for *Azteca,* which also tend sap-sucking mealy bugs inside the plant's stem. Although the plant invests heavily in the ants, there is reciprocity. The *Azteca* groom the tree, protecting it from herbivorous insects; and if there is a large disturbance, they will come pouring out of the hollow stems in vast numbers to defend their home. Although these little ants lack a sting, they have tough jaws and secrete caustic chemicals that they then rub into the tiny bitemarks.

Cecropia clearly benefits from this relationship, even though it is not dependent on it. *Cecropia* thrive on West Indian islands and in mainland cloud forests where *Azteca* are absent; these species dispense with trichilia and do well without ants, but these habitats lack the intensive herbivore pressure of mainland lowland rain forest. Similarly, *Bixa orellana*, a common tropical shrub whose seed capsules produce the red pigment you see smeared across Amazonian Indians and in rice and tamales in Latin American cooking, has large extrafloral nectaries in the lowlands but loses them at high elevations.

It is the balance between ecological costs and benefits that regulates the nature of the relationships between ants and plants. Ants are courted by plants as an alternative to chemical or mechanical defenses, which under many circumstances are extremely costly to produce. That plants should make use of the abundance of ants in the tropical forest is not particularly remarkable, yet the sophistication of the *Cecropia–Azteca* system is truly amazing. The ecological calculus leading to this adaptation must factor in the costs of chemical defenses, the nutritional needs of ants, and the abundance of both sloths and moths against the aggressiveness and abundance of ants. These factors may vary from place to place and from year to year in a manner that no human ecologist can hope to understand now.

Despite such complexity, the *Cecropia–Azteca* confederation did evolve, an unlikely alliance forged without dialogue, treaty, or entreaty between two parties with no notion of desire or ambition. Natural selection, working for the selfish interests of each party, has resulted in a complex, finely tuned system that benefits both players. These improbable arrangements are perhaps among the most tangible of ways in which to comprehend the tremendous creative potential that resides in chance and the vast expanse of evolutionary time.

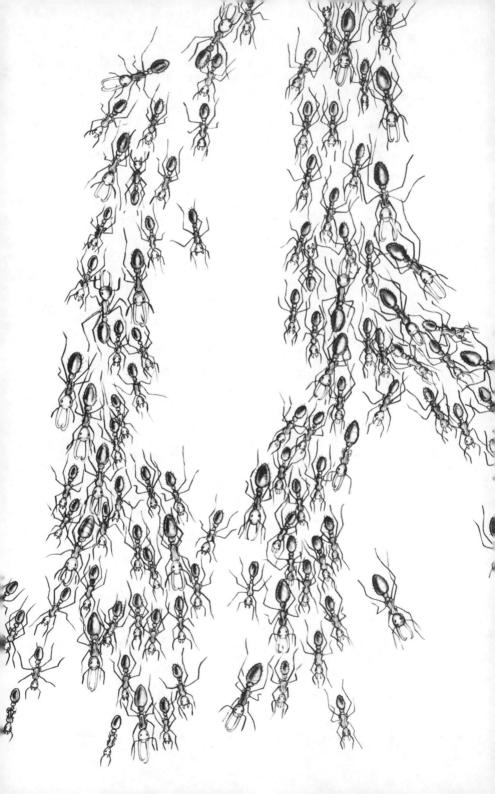

Chapter 10

ARMY ANTS

An army travels on its stomach.
—Napoleon Bonaparte

Terror stalks the floor of the rain forest. The sound of desperate leaps and frantic scuffling heralds its arrival, and a dank musk drifts ahead of the impending violence. Columns of soldiers and hunters advance across the forest floor, shifting and weaving with the zeal of the hunt. They overrun their victims, dismembering them and dragging the carnal booty away. An army ant raid is under way.

There are few sights in the rain forest as awesome as the foraging columns of army ants, but these raids occur on a relatively small scale. Although army ants have played a major role in many old jungle movies and adventure stories, their impact on creatures as large as humans is more metaphorical than physical. Some residents of tropical forests even look forward to their raids, because a brief visit can clear a house of a host of insect pests.

Not all army ants form great raiding columns. Many are secretive subterranean dwellers; but others, such as *Eciton burchelli*, present a spectacle worthy of romantic fiction. Colonies of this species may have hundreds of thousands of adults, which raid by day in massive swarms that have a genuine dramatic visual and ecological impact.

The drama of an *Eciton* raid can best be appreciated by approaching it on an intimate level. If you get down on your hands and knees, you can see details from a foot away that would be lost from a standing position—but you must be cautious. *Eciton,* like most other ants, are chemical beings. Their eyes are mere light detectors, incapable of resolving detail, but the ants have a keen perception of odor and taste. If you breathe on a raiding column, you will excite their taste for flesh and they will start to search for the source. Their poor vision and their reliance on tactile and olfactory stimuli to recognize food means that they are just as willing to attack humans as they are the usual cockroaches, katydids, scorpions, and other miscellany of the forest.

I once showed a particularly healthy raiding column of *Eciton* to a student, who inadvertently set one foot in the middle of a smaller peripheral column. Before she knew it, ants were swarming up her legs, and she got quite a start when she felt them digging away at her flesh. Fortunately, these ants don't have dangerous stings, and large, mobile creatures like college students can easily escape a raiding column with no more to show for the experience than a few dozen small bites.

If you look closely at an *Eciton* raid, you will see ants of many different sizes, although medium-sized workers appear to be the most numerous. When one of these medium-sized army ants comes across a piece of animate flesh, her first reaction is to pinch it firmly with her formidable mandibles and inject it with her venomous sting. As she does so she also releases a pheromone that alerts her sisters, who move in and set about subduing and carving the item into easily transportable chunks. The smallest workers often act as dissecting pins, grasping nearby limbs and twigs with their mandibles and spread-eagling the victim. Medium-sized workers then vivisect the hapless prey, usually at the joints if the victim is an arthropod. Although they occasionally kill small vertebrates in the course of a raid, particularly creatures unable to flee like nestling birds and sleeping frogs, *Eciton* lack the large, shearing mandibles of the African driver ants, and they seem incapable of doing a good job of butchering vertebrates.

The largest army ants in the raiding swarms are the soldiers, who sport outlandish sickle-shaped mandibles. In many parts of tropical America, Indians have found a remarkable use for these soldier ants as practical first aid. The ants are picked up by the body and the jaws are placed over an open cut. The soldier will clamp her mandibles shut, and the Indian promptly twists her head from her body, making an efficient and readily available emergency suture. The huge mandibles of the soldiers are useful only for defense. These ants often amble about in some sort of defensive peripheral activity, although they may also help transport the largest pieces of prey back to the colony, which is more a function of their size than their impressive choppers. The different-sized classes of workers provide the efficiency of specialization required by any large and complex society.

At first glance, anarchy seems to prevail in an *Eciton burchelli* raid. Unlike some army ants, *Eciton burchelli* does not send out neat raiding columns. They are swarm raiders, surging through the forest in great, untidy coalescing columns. These columns shift constantly, dwindling away here and breaking away there. Some workers run forward with prey while others run backward. Collisions and confusion are frequent. Yet somehow the statistics of mass action, the evolutionary programming of individual workers who respond to a simple set of stimuli in a rigidly prescribed manner, results in a complex, predictable behavior.

At night the ants link themselves together with their tarsal claws, forming living nests that protect the queen and immature ants. These bivouacs, which can be as large as a bushel basket, are usually lodged in a sheltered spot in the forest, perhaps inside a hollow log or in the convoluted base of a large buttressed tree. The foraging raids begin each morning, initiated by increasing light intensity. As dawn filters into the forest, the bivouacked workers become restless and start to break apart. When the bivouac dissolves, the workers seem at first to wander without direction. As they mill about, some lay down trail-marking chemicals. Gradually direction emerges from chaos. Perhaps the smooth surface of a log or a game trail offers the colony a path of least resistance, and eventually a large swarming column of workers develops.

The mass of ants may be a foot wide or more, thick with ants that run in both directions. But they are programmed to do more exploratory running forward into new territory, so gradually the column advances. Once the initial inertia is overcome, the column lengthens rapidly, expanding at the rate of a foot a minute. It thins and starts branching. During the course of the day the column will grow into a fan-shaped swarm perhaps 100 feet wide at the front.

The raiding columns shift constantly in both size and position. Most spread across the forest floor, flushing out the insects normally seen only at night—the cockroaches, scorpions, millipedes, katydids, and other arthropods that rest by day under bark and litter. Other columns may climb up trees into the canopy, or descend into the soil via burrows, where they can plunder the nests of wasps, termites, and other ants. These raids continue throughout the day. But when daylight dims, the trails reverse the branching pattern of the morning and coalesce into a main column leading toward a bivouac site. All the prey garnered during the day is transported there to feed the queen and larvae.

The foraging style of the army ant has many advantages, particularly the ability to capture and subdue larger prey that normal ant colonies cannot take advantage of. These larger items of prey are less common and more widely dispersed than smaller pickings, and the creatures that feed on them must be mobile. Predatory ants with fixed nests must settle for smaller colony size, smaller items of prey, less group foraging, or some combination of these factors.

Six hundred thousand army ants can harvest a large number of insects each day. An *Eciton* colony can consume several quarts of arthropods daily from a few hundred square yards of forest, enough to severely deplete local populations. But army ants are not the only insectivores who benefit from these raids. The size of the *Eciton* raiding parties and the fact that they are among the most common of army ants attracts many opportunists intent on collecting the chaff and gleanings left unharvested by the ants.

Some of these camp followers actually insinuate themselves into the ranks of the army itself. Certain wasps, beetles, and millipedes chemically mimic the colony odor of the army ants so that they become indistinguishable from nest mates to the ants. You can see these beetles and millipedes roaming along the columns, never participating in the food gathering but always ready to reap the benefits of the hunt. These social parasites are among the burdens of group living, along with communicable diseases, yet they never seem to become common enough to burden the ant societies that foster them.

Other camp followers are more benign, at least as regards the ants. They work for their living and merely take advantage of the flushing effect of the ant raids. The forest understory lacks an abundance of large grazers to stir up insects, but the army ants excel at this. Thus, many birds and insects follow *Eciton* raids in much the same way that cowbirds and cattle egrets traipse after domestic animals and gulls follow tractors. Bristly tachinid flies perch on leaves above the raid, and when a large grasshopper or katydid leaps to escape the ants, the flies wing after it, hoping to glue an egg to its body. If the fly is successful and the hopper escapes the ants, the fly egg will hatch into a larva that burrows into the flesh of the hopper and consumes it from the inside out.

Not all these camp followers are invertebrates. Perhaps the most conspicuous followers of army ants in the New World tropics are birds. Several species of woodcreepers, cuckoos, and motmots are often found near *Eciton burchelli* raids, and one large family of Neotropical birds (the antbirds, Formicariidae) has many species that seem to forage exclusively with the aid of army ants. There are other birds that may follow raids from time to time, but only a few species have evolved to rely heavily on the ants for stirring up food. Not just any species of army ant will do for these birds. Army ants that raid in thin columns, such as those that specialize in hunting social insects, or nocturnal army ants are rarely followed (although screech owls may sometimes follow nocturnal raiders). Antbirds often travel in flocks, with dozens of individuals of many species taking part. In Amazonia as many as ten species of antbird may follow a single raiding column. The birds constantly chatter and peep as they nab the insects flushed out by army ants, and these characteristic sounds provide an excellent cue for locating the head of the raiding swarm. The birds may have as great an impact on the arthropods of the forest floor as the army ants themselves, as they can take care of those beasts that depend on flight for escaping the ants.

There are also animals that benefit from army ant raids in remarkably oblique fashion. You will often see ithomiid butterflies flapping slowly around in the vicinity of an army ant raid. Some sport the bright patterns and colors that suggest warning coloration and terrible taste, while others are pale and almost transparent. These butterflies are distasteful, probably because of their use of alkaloid-rich Solanaceae as food plants, and they can flit about the raiding columns of ants in full view of the accompanying antbirds. Their distastefulness allows them to make their own use of the chaff of an *Eciton* raid. The first observers who noticed the association between these butterflies and *Eciton* attributed it to chemical confusion. They thought that the odor of the ants might resemble the scents of the butterflies' sexual pheromones or the smell of the butterflies' favorite food plants, both reasonable assumptions. However, two biologists, Tom Ray and Catherine Andrews of Harvard University, took a closer look at the butterflies and found that there was a preponderance of females. Since it is the male butterflies that are normally attracted by sexual scents, and both sexes should be equally attracted to floral odors, both of the previous hypotheses seemed dubious. What Ray and Andrews discovered was that the female butterflies were searching for the nitrogen-rich bird droppings. Many tropical butterflies are long-lived and spend much time in search of food. Presumably this is what the ant-following ithomiids are doing. The odor of the ants is a predictable signal that there will be a trail of antbird dung in the vicinity. The butterflies are actually following the camp followers.

The total effect of this intensive harvest is to lower the arthropod density within the area of the raid severely. The implications of this for the plants, which have been cleaned of pests, and for distasteful insects, which have been freed from competition, have not been studied; and the ecological impact of army ants on the forest economy is still poorly understood. However, the impact of the harvest on the ants themselves is well known.

Napoleon's dictum that an army travels on its stomach is as

true for the ant armies as it is for human armies. *Eciton burchelli* moves according to cycles that reflect the waxing and waning of the collective hunger of the colony and the demands this hunger makes on the local food resources. The colony is periodically nomadic, relocating its bivouac in a new spot each evening and ·raiding fresh territory each day; but it is also periodically stationary, maintaining its bivouac in the same spot night after night. The change from one phase to another is predictable. It is an endogenous rhythm, timed to a physiological clock within the animals, not influenced by weather, moon phase, or astrological sign. This biological clock appears to be located in the larvae of the colony.

Experiments by the late T. C. Schneirla of the American Museum of Natural History showed that removal of the larvae rendered the adult workers lethargic. This makes good sense. Most of the food collected during the raids goes into rearing the larvae. When there are many hungry larvae in a colony, more food is required and the colony must move constantly in order to find fresh hunting grounds to fill these needs. This is the nomadic phase, during which the larvae grow rapidly. When the larvae undergo pupation, there is a considerable decrease in the grocery needs of the colony. Worker ants, who are sexually inactive and don't grow, require only a sparse maintenance allowance. The queen needs considerable food, because this is converted into eggs that will keep the colony going, but there is only a single queen. The food requirements of the colony do not demand that fresh hunting grounds be sought every day, and the colony enters its so-called statary phase, when the bivouac remains in place, functioning more as a field headquarters than a real bivouac.

It is the egg-laying activity of the queen that helps to regulate the cycle. She lays her eggs in great bursts. When the colony enters its statary phase, she quickly becomes inflated with eggs—within a week as many as 60,000 may develop. Compared to the athletic trim of the workers and soldiers, the egg-swollen queen resembles a freak stuffed sausage. At the midpoint of the statary stage she goes into labor, churning out up to 300,000 eggs within a few days. These eggs require a week or so to hatch, and with the awakening hunger of the larvae the colony is forced to begin its nomadic stage once again.

Some biologists have drawn parallels between large individual predatory animals (such as lions, tigers, and bears) and the massive colonies of predatory ants. There is no question that army ants play a major role in the economy of tropical rain forests, and their ecological impact may be similar to that of large individual predators. The evolutionary forces that act on the army ants, however, are clearly more complex than those that influence larger predators.

The evolution of a cyclic reproduction pattern, with all of the eggs laid over a short interval, is particularly important to the army ant life-style. During the egg-laying period, the queen can remain sedentary and devote all of her energies to egg production. The colony, which then consists mostly of nongrowing workers, does not require much food to keep going. The workers can keep the queen stuffed with food without taking it from the mouths of hungry babes and they can do so without seeking virgin hunting territory. When the egg laying is over, the queen's body resumes a more normal shape and she can keep up with her wandering tribe without any assistance. If she laid eggs continuously, she would remain swollen (although perhaps not so much as during the brief oviposition period) and might have difficulty keeping up with the nomadic colony. The colony would also be forced to deal with many different life stages continuously, and the demand for food would be constant. The alternating pattern of nomadic and statary phases is an ecological simplification that makes a large colony of predatory ants possible.

Explaining the cyclic life of *Eciton burchelli* as an adaptation generated by selection for the efficient use of resources is difficult to reconcile with the visual impressions of a raid. Efficiency seems far removed from the chaos of this army without generals. But such chaos has its virtues, chief among them flexibility. What general could direct an army through the complicated maneuvers demanded of subduing a scuttling scorpion in the complex, if Lilliputian, maze of the forest floor? And even if such a general existed, could she simultaneously direct part of her army against a fat caterpillar chewing placidly on a leaf several feet up a small bush? The workers in an army ant raid are free to formulate their own local solutions to these, and other, problems. Some people may find in this a metaphor of human significance. To a naturalist who understands natural selection, it is a dramatic embodiment of the notion that adaptation is not a simple matter of efficiency. All is compromise.

Chapter 11

ARTFUL GUISES

This life's five windows of the soul
Distorts the Heavens from pole to pole
And leads you to believe a lie
When you see with, not thro' the eye.
—WILLIAM BLAKE
"The Everlasting Gospel"

A naturalist's first visit to a tropical rain forest can be both an exhilarating and disappointing experience; the richness of the vegetation may overwhelm the senses at first, but sooner or later the apparent scarcity of animal or insect life will begin to raise questions.

Although large animals may indeed be scarce in many rain forests, smaller creatures lie all around you. Many of them will probably be sitting in plain sight, but they may not be what they appear to be. The tropical rain forest is full of sophisticated visual tricks, played for high stakes by one creature against another. So don't be deceived into thinking that animals are scarce just because you can't see them. Wherever you go in the rain forest, unseen eyes lie hidden in the greenery.

Some of the most beautiful eyes in the tropical rain forest never see. Painted on the hind wings of many moths in rich detail are false eye spots—deep blue spheres countershaded with ebony and highlighted with shiny silver flecks. During the day these eyes lie hidden beneath the soft cover of the moth's wings, and therein lies their value. If you poke around the forest by day with your nose close enough to a tree to smell the lichen and bark, you may find a resting silk moth. Some of these moths, which are well represented in the tropical rain forest, have wing spans as large as your hand, yet they are seldom seen because their mottled fore-wings, painted with blotches and streaks of brown, russet, and tan, render them anonymous on varicolored tropical tree trunks. A sleeping moth this large is a tempting curiosity and few people who spot one can resist nudging it.

Only then is the splendid artistry of the hidden eye revealed. The moth rapidly spreads its forewings, and in place of a cryptic mottled moth, shining bright eyes the size of an owl's suddenly glare forth. Even if you know what to expect, their sudden appearance is surprising. This flashing of bright eyes has the same jolting effect on a foraging bird who might take a tentative exploratory poke at the moth. Experiments have shown that these eye spots startle hungry birds, sometimes to the point of scaring them away. But even if the bird is not frightened away, its brief double-take might be enough to give the moth an opportunity to fly off.

Insects do not stop at simple imitations of disembodied eyes. Certain sphinx moths, whose caterpillars are as large and con-spicuous as small cigars, use a more radical approach. When molested, the caterpillars constrict certain muscles that magically transform their body into an excellent duplicate of the head of a small viper. The enlarged triangular head, prominent eyes, and swaying motion faithfully duplicate the appearance of the real thing. This must have at least the same impact on birds and lizards as simple eye spots.

Startle displays are employed by a wide variety of insects, rang-ing from moths and butterflies to planthoppers and beetles. They respond to a prod or a poke with eye spots or a colorful flash before making their exit. This startle defense is seen in insects from temperate areas, but it is in the tropics that the device gains its widest currency. Flashing is not limited to insects in tropical America. There are frogs with bright patches of color hidden beneath their folded legs, which suddenly flash forth when they leap to safety. There are even frogs with eyelike patterns hidden in the groin who raise their hind end when confronted with danger, to reveal large, snakelike eyes.

It may be that the increased diversity of tropical life simply offers more examples of visually oriented startle defenses, but we think that their commonness probably reflects a real increase in the amount of visual predation small tropical insects suffer from birds, mammals, reptiles, and amphibians. Regardless of the causes behind the abundance of false eyes and bright flash colors, the artistic effects wrought by predators who see with rather than thro' their eyes are most richly manifest in such areas.

A startle defense must surprise a predator in order to be effective. It is the unexpected that alarms in nature, and most creatures that employ a startle defense use it as a secondary tactic. Their prime defense is simple invisibility.

It is often difficult to see animals of any kind in the tropical rain forest. Many species, of course, are exceedingly shy and will always manage to keep several steps ahead of you. Others are nocturnal, hiding themselves in hollow tree trunks or rolled-up leaves where they can't be seen by prying daytime eyes. But there are a good many more creatures, particularly insects and reptiles, who sit or lie in plain sight most of the day yet are rarely seen by any but the most observant of naturalists.

Superb sticklike phasmids and geometrid caterpillars go so far as to duplicate the bud scars and bark texture of the twigs on which they feed and hide. Brassolid butterflies and katydids can look like leaves in all stages of life and decay, from the fresh blush of new growth to dead brown leaves scattered amid the litter. Insects that resemble dead leaves are incredible in the fidelity and fine detail with which their bodies reproduce the spots and blisters of fungal decay and the network structure of leaf veins. Katydids that live in the wettest forests, particularly those in the cloud forests, are coated with green extrusions that are almost indistinguishable from the lichens and mosses carpeting the trees. Some caterpillars are conspicuous because they feed on glossy foliage during the day, yet they make no effort to blend in with their surroundings. Instead, they resemble something every bird knows and ignores—a bird dropping.

The cryptic achievements of many rain forest creatures are best appreciated in their natural habitat. Most good nature photographers go to pains to isolate their subjects, to make them easily visible; while this serves a useful illustrative purpose, it distorts the functional meaning of their appearance. A butterfly whose wings are adorned with paisley swirls and sensuously waving bands of color may look striking when seen against the white background of an insect collection tray or the plain background of a good photograph, but in its natural context of lichen-coated tree trunks the same butterfly is an unobstrusive wallflower. Butterflies, of course, must fly, and when they do, they inevitably call attention to themselves. But some tropical butterflies remain inconspicuous even in flight; many ithomiid butterflies flutter slowly through the forest on transparent wings rimmed in black and gray, a scheme that blends well with the dusky light of the dim forest understory. Higher-flying relatives found in clearings and the sun-flecked mid-canopy zones have dark wings splotched with bright yellows, whites, and oranges, which blend remarkably well with their sun-dappled environment.

In order to cope with such cryptic prey, birds have evolved remarkably sharp vision; avian visual acuity is on the order of eight times greater than our own. But bird brains are not adept at processing the massive quantities of information their eyes are capable of registering. A foraging bird typically brings to its nest a collection of insects that differs in composition from the available pool of choices in the environment. This suggests that it somehow selects particular prey items from a visually complex environment. In order to forage effectively, birds filter their visual perceptions through a behavioral mechanism known as the search image. A foraging bird will respond only to a circumscribed set of cues, such as specific colors, patterns, and shapes, thereby focusing its attention on a relatively narrow set of targets. This allows the bird to forage efficiently without becoming lost and confused in the morass of detail its eyes can feed to its brain.

The principle behind search imaging is simple and has implications in our own lives, for example, when we go out to hunt wild strawberries. While we poke around on hands and knees, our eyes receive impressions of intermingled leaf colors, grasses and twigs, and perhaps a passing bird or two; but an efficient picker responds only to the brief flashes of red that signal a ripe strawberry. Irrelevant detail is ignored, and search-imaging strawberry pickers do much better than daydreamers who let their eyes linger on everything in sight. Birds that form search images for particular items, be they berries or insects, similarly filter out extraneous detail. Although this strategy implies that they ignore many edibles, they gain in the long run by concentrating on a limited spectrum of prey, which they locate with great efficiency.

Search imaging may reduce a bird's investment in food processing as well as in searching. Some prey require handling techniques that involve learning where to peck, how hard to peck, whether to anticipate a hop or not, and whether a set of tough wings must be removed to get at a tasty abdomen. A bird that learns how to handle these items efficiently has a great advantage over a naive competitor, and these behavioral specializations can greatly enhance the efficiency of a search image. Not only can the bird search effectively for prey; it can also handle the prey skillfully and efficiently once it has been found.

Search imaging seems to be a highly efficient way of foraging, but it is not perfect. The trade-off that comes with a search image is a lack of opportunism. The avian search images that have been studied are narrow: most birds seem to incorporate the image of only one or two insect forms at any one time. A foraging bird may not be able to take immediate advantage of a sudden surfeit of food if it fails to match its search image, and an abundance of easily available prey might be ignored. But the behavioral specialization of search imaging is not as restrictive as genetic specialization. These behavioral specializations enable a bird to learn how to locate and process prey with an efficiency that outpaces a nonspecialist, while still allowing for the behavioral and ecological plasticity that strict genetic specialization excludes. If a particular type of prey falls in abundance, a search-imaging bird can experiment with new images until it discovers another abundant and palatable species to focus on, while a predator locked in genetically to a particular type of prey may suffer when its prey declines.

The simpleminded search imaging of birds may explain some of the bizarre forms that rain forest insects have evolved. There are moths with weirdly twisted wings, with hairlike tufts sprouting from the wings, and with large cuts apparently bitten into their wings. Some moths rest in strangely contorted positions, holding their abdomens in unusual asymmetrical poses. Some biologists might regard these as byproducts of random evolutionary processes, but certain of these eccentricities must have a disruptive effect on the aerodynamics of the moths that exhibit them and therefore must have some useful function. Perhaps their unusual shapes remove these moths from the search images of foraging birds, who key in on the conventional triangular resting posture. Visual predators with search imaging may also drive organisms like frogs and lizards to evolve diverse aspects, which might account for some of the folds and protuberances that have no apparent function in courtship and species recognition. When confronted by a simple-minded but visually sophisticated predator, an unusual appearance alone may be an effective defense.

Some of the wondrous and unique forms of tropical life may thus have evolved as responses to search-imaging predators. Visually hunting predators may be responsible for the great diversity of forms that rain forest animals exhibit. But this is not the only effect they have had. Just as birds can form search images of desirable prey, they can also learn to avoid images that they associate with unpleasant experiences.

Insects that feed on poison-laden plants often sequester these toxins in their own bodies and become toxic to birds. Rather than attempt to hide away, they advertise their toxicity by calling attention to themselves. Distasteful insects are typically adorned in bold and contrasting colors: brilliant reds against blacks, yellows, and oranges that stand out against the greenery in bold geometric patterns easily impressed upon the mind. These conspicuous-looking insects often seem to flaunt themselves even more by their brazen behavior. Unlike most animals in the tropical rain forest, some of these brightly patterned little beasts make no attempt to remain out of sight of potential predators. They walk about and mass together in places where only a blind predator could fail to notice them. The behavior and appearance of these creatures contrasts sharply with that of their palatable relatives.

Most rain forest frogs are nocturnal. During the day they seek shelter in damp places, inside rolled-up leaves, hollow trees, or under leaf litter. They emerge after dark to feed and mate, and in the darkness they have little to fear from visually hunting predators. Frogs must be tasty morsels indeed; with few exceptions they are inoffensive creatures bearing neither strong teeth nor long claws with which to defend themselves. But some frogs and toads have managed to evolve effective chemical defenses. Their skin glands produce defensive toxins instead of simple moisture. Although many of the frogs that have evolved these defensive secretions are nocturnal or relatively inconspicuous diurnal creatures, the species with the most powerful skin toxins fit neither of these anuran stereotypes.

The poison-arrow frogs of the genera *Dendrobates* and *Phyllobates* are conspicuous denizens of tropical American rain forests. They walk about boldly on the forest floor, and if your eye is not drawn immediately to their bright patterns of red, yellow, or orange in the gloom of the forest, the males calling loudly from exposed perches will force you to take notice. Clearly, these little frogs have little to fear, and their behavior and appearance seem calculated to draw attention from potential predators rather than keep them out of harm's way.

The toxic punch that these frogs pack is truly formidable. A species recently discovered in western Colombia. *Phyllobates terribilis*, carries enough toxin in its small skin to kill a thousand people if it enters the bloodstream through an open wound. This poison is not quite so lethal if it is swallowed, but it still must be a powerful deterrent to any potential predator. Perhaps the most significant predators of these deadly Colombian frogs are the native Chocó Indians. These forest people, who inhabit what may be the wettest rain forest on earth, utilize three species of dendrobatid frogs for poisoning their blowgun darts. Anthropologists observing the preparation of the darts have noted that the Indians capture the frogs by hand and either slowly roast them over a fire or impale them on a stick to make them release their poison. But these observations were made on tribal groups who used either *Phyllobates aurotaenia* or *Phyllobates bicolor* for the poison. The tribal groups who used *Phyllobates terribilis* were very much aware of the greater toxicity of this species, long before it was studied scientifically by Charles Myers of the American Museum of Natural History and John Daly of the National Institutes of Health. The forest people used leaves to protect their hands when they captured these frogs for poison extraction and they simply rubbed the blowgun darts over the back of the frog.

Natural selection works primarily on individuals. Many people therefore believe that an individual must survive contact with its predator if warning coloration is to evolve. While it is certainly true that an animal that gets eaten and provides a learning experience for a naive predator does not benefit directly, other individuals in the same population, who may share many of the same genes, may benefit and pass on the genetic legacy. This type of kin selection may drive the early stages of the evolution of warning coloration; individual selection is probably an important factor in the process, but it is difficult to postulate how it can account for the very first stages. If a prey population is composed of poisonous or unpalatable individuals, accentuation of search-image cues already in use should enhance an individual prey's chances of survival. And in many instances a naive predator can perceive the noxious quality of its prey before it kills it.

Given enough of an incentive, predators may evolve to avoid certain types of prey instinctively. The Turquoise-browed Motmot of the Central American rain forest is a strikingly handsome bird that feeds on a variety of insects and reptiles, including snakes. Young motmots exhibit exploratory behavior when they are shown possible prey. Ornithologist Susan Smith presented young motmots with wooden sticks painted in various color patterns and found that they pecked at all but one. The stick they avoided was painted with alternating red and yellow rings—a pattern similar to that of the deadly coral snakes of tropical America. This apparently innate aversion to a specific pattern is highly adaptive. If a young bird pecked at such a pattern in nature, it might receive an indelible learning experience, but it would be the last lesson that bird could learn. Coral snakes do not offer opportunities for learning, and selection of the most rigorous kind has favored those individuals with an innate avoidance for this particular pattern.

Coral snakes are not the only snakes in tropical America that boast a pattern of red and yellow rings. There are also a number of unrelated snakes, some completely harmless and some with relatively weak venom and inefficient fangs. If the motmots are genetically programmed to avoid the coral snake pattern, these other snakes will benefit from their close resemblance to the deadly coral snakes. Henry Bates, the British naturalist who wandered through Amazonia during the nineteenth century, was the first to realize that some animals might try, in an evolutionary sense, to mimic unpalatable or undesirable creatures so as to reduce their own risk of being eaten. Bates believed that unpalatability might explain why unrelated butterflies often looked so similar. Palatable insects will benefit if they evolve to resemble conspicuous, unpalatable species that are avoided by birds. These edible mimics take advantage of a predator's ability to associate conspicuous warning patterns with foul taste or healthy stings, and they needn't bother with evolving these defenses themselves. Batesian mimicry, as this duplicity has come to be known, is widespread in the insect world and must in turn have been partially responsible for honing the fine eye of the birds.

If a Batesian mimic becomes common enough, it becomes advantageous for a predator to learn to distinguish it from its unpalatable model. Unless the predator is genetically programmed to avoid the undesirable model, it will also pay the model to evolve away from its mimics because naive birds who first develop a taste for a palatable mimic might then pursue, and perhaps kill, the noxious model before it learns to avoid them. Batesian mimicry is thus an unstable triangle, which changes constantly according to the relative abundances of models and mimics and to the ability of the predator to discern between them.

The warning coloration that a distasteful species evolves to keep predators at a distance can be shared with other distasteful species. This spreads the cost of educating the predators and increases the chances of survival of similar-looking unpalatable individuals. This phenomenon, in which unpalatable species come to resemble other unpalatable species, is known as Müllerian mimicry. It is named after Fritz Müller, who first recognized it in the butterflies he collected in Brazil not too long after Bates's sojourn. It is the reason why some groups of unpalatable species, such as ithomiid butterflies and stinging wasps, become remarkably uniform in shape and coloration even though dozens of species with different ecologies are involved. There will be strong selection for a rare unpalatable species to mimic a more common one. If both species are distasteful, then individuals of both species benefit from looking alike.

Some insects have evolved into gaudy composite mimics that appear to involve both Batesian and Müllerian elements. Ctenuchid moth caterpillars feed on plants rich in poisonous alkaloids, and even after they have emerged from their cocoons they are unpalatable to most birds. This may account for their gaudy coloration and habit of flying about in broad daylight, unlike most other moths, who are inactive until the cloak of darkness protects them. But ctenuchids have not settled on just any conspicuous warning coloration. The smoky wings and black bodies of some ctenuchids resemble the fierce-stinging *Parachartergus* social wasps, and the brightly banded abdomens of others resemble formidable *Polistes* or *Stelopolybia* paper wasps. The hind legs of many ctenuchids also have patches of scales that flare out to resemble the rear legs of leaf-footed coreid bugs. These coreids are equipped with potent caustic sprays that can blind a predator. Although the moths are distasteful, they lack the aggressive capabilities of both wasps and coreids, yet they doubtlessly benefit from their resemblance.

The same evolutionary forces probably generate the herds of brightly colored caterpillars and stink bugs you find clustered on rain forest vegetation. These masses of brightly colored immature insects are equipped with potent chemical weaponry. Living in a group means more competition among individuals, but each individual is less likely to be eaten by a predator. A group of brightly colored unpalatable insects on a conspicuous perch offers a more powerful visual warning than any individual could muster. Not all clustering caterpillars are unpalatable, however. Some caterpillars feed at night in the tree crowns, yet descend onto the trunks at dawn and cluster in the dim light at the base of the tree during the day. This suggests that they may be avoiding foliage-gleaning insectivorous birds. Why should they cluster during the day rather than secretively dispersing as anonymous individuals? Their selfish herds may be formed to reduce predation by non-visual predators such as ants and parasitoid wasps and flies. Any disturbance of any individual in the cluster sets off a peculiar chain reaction of twitching, flailing caterpillars, which may dissuade potential predators from taking a bite.

Mimicry is not restricted to avoiding predators. Certain insects combine Batesian qualities with aggressive mimicry. Many mantispids—predatory relatives of the delicate lacewings—mimic social wasps. This presumably affords them protection from insectivorous birds. Their resemblance to nectar-feeding wasps may also give them a predatory advantage. As they sit around flowers, mimicking the nectar-feeding wasps who normally do not disturb other visitors to the flower, the wasplike mantispids are able to lash out and seize flower-visiting flies to fill their own stomachs.

Nor is mimicry restricted to the visual realm, particularly when the predators are other insects. I once studied a large staphylinid beetle that visited the baits I had set out to attract dung scarabs. Unlike the beetles, the staphylinids showed no special interest in the dung. They usually sat on understory vegetation far from the bait; but in contrast to the scarabs, which sat idle in the same places, the long, sleek staphylinids vigorously waved their abdomens while extruding a series of hairs from the tip. They also gave off the odor of ordure, a behavior I first interpreted as pheromonal mate calling. But one morning as I followed a beetle through the understory, it alighted, waved its foetid tail, and a fly buzzed down onto the leaf, presumably to investigate the source of the smell. The staphylinid immediately lunged at it, its mandibles agape, but the fly flew away unscathed.

This piqued my curiosity, so I took two clean vials and placed a staphylinid tail tip in one. I set the vials down side by side and sat back to watch. The first skipper butterfly that came along headed immediately for the vial with the staphylinid tail and began probing with its long proboscis for the odorous riches. Clearly, the predatory staphylinid was using its dung-imitating odor to lure in potential prey.

Mimetic deceptions may foil birds and insects who use simple foraging tactics, but there are other, more discriminating predators in the tropical rain forest. If you watch foraging primates, such as a group of white-faced monkeys, you will see them turn, probe, and poke their potential prey with an inventiveness and curiosity singularly lacking in birds. Insectivorous monkeys feed on many different kinds of insects. It seems unlikely that most insect masquerades and charades would be convincing to such calculating consumers. White-faced monkeys in Costa Rica can surmount such formidable and complex defenses as those of the stinging *Pseudomyrmex* ants that occupy the swollen thorns of some acacia trees. Although the adult ants are not especially savory to the monkeys, the succulent larvae that live protected inside the hollow thorns are. It is not practical to clamber through the tree because the ants will swarm out, viciously stinging any vertebrate flesh they come into contact with. The monkeys solve the problem by dangling from a nearby tree and breaking off single branches of the ant-laden tree. They still get stung, but only by a few ants at a time—this is a price they seem willing to pay to get at the larvae.

Monkeys can see both with and thro' their eyes, and there are insects that seem to reflect the agency of such cerebral predators in their defense behaviors. Arboreal wasps, which share the forest canopy with monkeys, employ a graded series of threats when they perceive the limb vibrations that signify an approaching verte-brate. *Synoeca*, a large, metallic blue-black social wasp, builds a carton nest that is full of wrinkled undulations resembling those of a grossly enlarged rippled potato chip. When these wasps are first annoyed, they scrape their abdomens across the ripples, creat-ing a raspy noise that is amplified by the acoustical properties of the largely hollow nest. If the disturbance continues, the wasps become more agitated and the rasping turns into a distinct chugging rhythm reminiscent of a steam locomotive getting started. They begin to emerge from the nest, but simply crawl excitedly over the surface, flipping their wings and curving their abdomens in a sinister fashion. If that fails to scare off the cause of the disturbance, buzzing workers take to the air and loop threateningly around the nest. Only then do the wasps begin their actual attack. The warnings they presented should have allowed any predator time to decide just how badly it wanted the nest.

Other social wasps use variants of this graded warning system, which seems to be directed primarily toward perceptive, calculat-ing foes. Monkeys apparently make these calculations. John Ter-borgh of Princeton University, who has been studying monkey foraging in the Madre de Dios region of Amazonian Peru, observed the behavior of monkeys approaching a wasp net. They came up cautiously, chattering excitedly, until a large and particularly bold male leapt in the nest and wrenched away a piece of the comb, fleeing through the treetops as fast as he could to escape the irate wasps. For a few stings he gained a fistful of succulent wasp larvae.

The role of primates in molding the appearance of tropical in-sects has probably been slight. Most of the duplicitous artistry of rain forest insects seems to have been commissioned by natural selection in response to the demands made by the keen-eyed forest fowl. The human consequences of this are sometimes vexing. Appearances that may act as warning for birds may be appealing to a curious human naturalist. The long, silky white hairs of some megalopygid caterpillars almost beg to be touched; but if you do so, thousands of tiny urticating hairs will pierce your skin, carrying with them a potent venom. The intense, fiery pain of such an encounter can lead to unconsciousness, and at the least it will leave an itching, tender sore that may linger for weeks. This is clearly a potent learning experience, although one not readily transferable from birds to people.

It is no simple task to unravel the messages that rain forest creatures hold in their appearance. Many things are not what they seem to be, and certain messages have different meanings to different receivers. A naturalist in the tropical rain forests of America is inevitably a stranger; the messages are intended for creatures more attuned to their subtlety. The naturalist can try to unravel them, but it requires more than thoughtful eyes alone to understand the richness of these artful guises and moldy disguises.

Chapter 12

SOUTHBOUND

> *In America we get food to eat,*
> *Don't have to run through the jungle and*
> *scuff up our feet . . .*
> *Ain't no lions and tigers,*
> *Ain't no mom-ba snakes,*
> *Just the sweet watermelon and the*
> *buckwheat cakes.*
> —RANDY NEWMAN
> "Sail Away"

One of the most beautiful city parks in New England is, strangely enough, a cemetery. The Mount Auburn Cemetery in Cambridge, Massachusetts, is the oldest garden cemetery in the United States and includes many illustrious names among its permanent residents. Each spring its carefully landscaped hills and dales burst into flower, turning the cemetery into an island of color and fragrance amid the busy streets of metropolitan Boston. Mount Auburn Cemetery in early May lacks the somber ambience of most cemeteries, and people paying respects to departed ancestors then are confronted with a surprising scene. Everywhere you look, scattered over and around the tombstones and vegetation, are people, and few appear to be lamenting the passing of loved ones. Their attention is focused not on the silent graves below but on the vibrant life overhead, where flocks of brightly colored birds are flitting through the trees, feeding heavily as they pass on the way to their breeding grounds.

Massachusetts may have the highest concentration of birders in the world; on a warm Sunday morning in May at the height of the spring migration, it sometimes seems as though every one of them is at Mount Auburn Cemetery. Spring songbird migrations in the United States have been studied for many decades, and at places like the cemetery the sequences of arrival and departure of the common species are well known. Yet there are always surprises, and it is the occasional rarity or migrant out of place that adds an element of uncertainty and anticipation to each visit. The hope of seeing something different, as much as the joy of seeing old acquaintances, both human and avian, is what attracts experienced birders to the cemetery day after day year after year.

Mount Auburn Cemetery does not look much like a rain forest, and no one who has lived through a New England winter would ever mistake its climate for tropical, but the spectacle of the spring migration always makes us think of the tropics. Birding the spring migration shares some of the same characteristics as birding the rain forests of tropical America. Of course, there is no comparing the diversity of birdlife in a tropical forest with that of any habitat in temperate latitudes. A typical patch of lowland rain forest in tropical America is home for 200 or more species of birds, and exceptional areas in the upper Amazon basin in Ecuador and Peru may have over 500 species. Only a few dozen species are involved in the spring migration at Mount Auburn, so it certainly isn't the diversity of birdlife there that recalls the tropics. Rather, it is the bright colors of the birds, the mixed aggregations of species foraging together through the trees, and the chances of seeing something unexpected and unusual that offer a Mount Auburn birder a hint of the birdlife of the tropical rain forest.

The migrant birds that funnel up the flyways of North America and pass through the cemetery each spring represent more than a simple analogy to the tropical forests. The colorful warblers and tanagers and the drab flycatchers that breed in the northern woods and enliven our springs and summers are in fact residents of the tropics for much of their lives. Many of the birds that find themselves in Mount Auburn Cemetery in early May have just arrived from the rain forests of tropical America, for that is where many species spend the long months between breeding seasons. For most of its adult life the black and orange Blackburnian Warbler that calls from a spruce tree in the New Hampshire woods has more ecological interactions with trogons and antbirds than it does with grouse or cardinals. Although we normally think of them as residents of North America who winter to the south, it is our North American bias that makes us regard them this way.

For many years, ornithologists regarded migratory birds as "invaders" or "interlopers" in tropical habitats. They assumed that these birds were temperate zone species because they breed in North America. Reproduction is the most critical biological function, and it is during the breeding season that animals tend to face the most important ecological and evolutionary challenges. Ornithologists traditionally focused their attention on these birds when they were on their temperate zone breeding grounds, paying them less heed when they moved south for the winter. This makes some sense biologically; but there were other less defensible grounds for regarding migrants as temperate species who go south during the winter and merely kill time there waiting for the spring. When an ornithologist from the United States commits time and money to studying birds in an exotic tropical locale he or she may not be enthusiastic about studying a migrant species that could be watched close to home. It was easier to regard them as being functionally distinct from resident tropical species; this way they could be conveniently ignored when studying tropical bird communities.

This view is rapidly changing. A recent book published by the National Zoological Park and the Smithsonian Institution Press, *Migrant Birds in the Neotropics: Ecology, Behavior, Distribution, and Conservation*, reflects the dramatic shift in ecologists' view of migratory birds. It has become clear that migratory birds do have a significant impact on the birdlife of many tropical forests. Even so, some of the old biases persist, and the ecologists most adamant about considering migratory birds as integral parts of tropical bird faunas tend to live in the tropics. The ability to monitor events from season to season and from year to year gives these resident naturalists a perspective that few temperate zone–based tropical ecologists can share.

Migratory birds comprise a large part of our temperate birdlife. Almost a quarter of the species that breed in North America are migratory, and many of these migrants spend a considerable part of their lives in the tropics. Although such migrations are a common phenomenon, discussed almost casually in biology classes and among birders, they are truly wondrous journeys. The birds travel thousands of miles, often at night with nothing but the stars to guide them, and many species cross open ocean for hundreds of miles without pausing to rest. A tiny hummingbird perched on the shores of the Yucatan must have enough energy stored in its body to sustain a flight that will carry it across the Gulf of Mexico, else it will fall unnoticed into the sea. There have to be compelling reasons why these frail little birds will subject themselves to these long and costly moves.

Many migratory birds feed primarily on resources—such as insects, small animals, and even fruit and nectar—that are not available during a cold northern winter. Since birds have never evolved the strategy of hibernation, they cannot avoid their metabolic needs. An insectivorous bird has little choice but to move when its prey becomes scarce in the fall. Most North American birders probably assume that these migratory birds go south for the winter simply because there is no food available in the north. This may be true, but it does not explain what these birds gain by migrating. If their preferred prey is available year round in tropical climates, what advantage could there be in going north in the first place?

There is no single simple answer to this question, but one major factor involves the availability of prey. Contrary to what you might expect, however, the critical factor is not so much the wintertime availability of prey in the tropics as the summertime abundance of prey in the temperate zone. This argument makes sense if you think of the migrants as tropical birds.

When most of us think of spring, we think of warmer weather, longer evenings, and the flush of green that replaces the cold, gray lifelessness of winter. Insects that have overwintered as diapausing eggs suddenly hatch with the warmth of spring to chomp away on the new plant growth. Marshes and wetlands also explode with activity in the spring, and there is an abundance of prey for aquatic birds.

The sudden burst of life that characterizes springtime in North America is largely a temperate zone phenomenon. Lowland tropical rain forests are not subject to the seasonal changes in climate that stimulate such bursts of productivity. Temperatures are constant throughout the year, and although rainfall may vary from season to season, there is always enough to keep most of the vegetation green and thriving. This doesn't mean that insects and other potential bird foods don't undergo annual cycles of scarcity and abundance. Many tropical organisms vary greatly in abundance through the year. Although populations of different insect species may fluctuate widely and regularly, they are not synchronized to the same extent that temperate zone cycles are. Peaks and valleys for individual species in the tropical rain forest may overlap broadly.

There are tropical habitats that exhibit flushes of productivity. These flushes are not correlated with fluctuations in daylength and temperature as they are in the temperate zone, but with the arrival of the rains. In tropical lowlands that experience pronounced wet and dry seasons, there is a flush of productivity associated with the advent of the wet season and this is accompanied by a burst of breeding activity by resident birds. The burst of productivity has a major impact on avian breeding cycles in deciduous tropical habitats, but it doesn't match the opportunities that await a migrant who ventures northward into spring.

In the tropics, days and nights are of uniform length regardless of season and regardless of habitat. On the equator, daylength is constant; even at the fringes of the tropics, the difference between the longest day of the year and the shortest might be measured in minutes rather than hours. Most birds hunt their prey in the light of day, and it is obvious that there is more time available for them to hunt in a long summer day in North America than in the strict twelve-hour regime of the equatorial zones. Many migratory birds breed in latitudes where there are eighteen hours or more of daylight during the period when young are being raised. This should allow parents to feed about half again as many young at a time as they could in the unvarying days of the tropics.

A naturalist might see one major flaw in this argument. The activity of prey organisms is not constant throughout the day. There are peaks and valleys in the daily patterns of insect abundance; many insects are most active early in the morning and late in the afternoon. During the heat of the day they may be difficult to find. Even though there may be eighteen hours of daylight available for a bird to stalk insects in, the majority of the insects may be available for only a few hours near dawn and dusk when the midday heat and breezes are gone and the air is still and cool. If birds depend on the hours of subdued daylight for finding most of their prey, then surely there is no real difference in hunting time between the tropics and the temperate zones. After all, the sun rises and sets only once a day no matter where you live.

This is a perceptive argument, but we can counter it with the fact that tropical dawns and dusks are unlike temperate dawns and dusks. One thing that we always miss when we spend the northern summertime in equatorial regions is the lingering glow of a summer sunset. A special pleasure of life in temperate latitudes is the gradual transition from daylight to darkness, a period that sees much activity by both animals and man. In the tropics there is no gradual transition from dark to light and from light to dark; the sun rises and sets with alarming haste. So birds that feed on invertebrates in the temperate summer may have even more effective hunting time available than the difference in daylength alone implies.

The long days of the northern summers and the flush of productivity seem to allow migrant birds to raise more young each year than their tropical relatives. David Lack, the late director of the Edward Gray Institute in England, has shown that temperate birds lay more eggs at any one time than related tropical species. He also showed that within the tropics those species that breed in the more seasonal deciduous forests and savannahs had slightly larger clutches than those species that breed in rain forest. This indicates that the flush of productivity probably plays a role in determining how many young a pair can raise. However, the differences between temperate and tropical breeders was much greater, suggesting that the increase in daylength and hunting time may be more important than the flush of activity.

The evolutionary advantage of breeding in the temperate zone thus seems clear: birds that have more available food and more time to hunt can raise more young at a time. However, the smaller clutch size of tropical forest birds may be offset by their ability to breed several times each year. The relatively benign rain forest climate may not offer sudden flushes of prey to stimulate nesting activity, but it does provide a relatively constant supply of prey throughout the year, so that birds may be able to start nesting at any time. Even when this is taken into account, tropical breeders may not be as fecund as their migratory relatives. Lack ascribed the differences in clutch size between temperate and tropical breeders to differences in foraging time and prey availability. But there are other factors that may also have played an important role in the evolution of clutch size.

Alexander Skutch's studies of the life histories of tropical birds in Costa Rica indicate that the nests of tropical forest birds suffer severely from predation. Most of the species he has investigated have an alarmingly low rate of fledging chicks, and nest after nest may fail completely. Moreover, this seems to be true regardless of where the eggs are laid. In the temperate zone, birds that lay their eggs in open nests may suffer from high predation rates as well, while birds that lay their eggs in holes are more secure from predation. The choice of nesting sites doesn't seem to make much difference in the tropical rain forest, however. Tropical forests play host to a wealth of creatures that relish eggs and vulnerable nestlings. Although we tend to think of toucans as fruit-eating birds, they are accomplished nest robbers as well. Their long bills allow them to probe deep within even the most protective of nests, and their appetite for eggs and nestlings is formidable. Monkeys, opossums, raccoons, and kinkajous are likewise adept at reaching into nest holes and extracting the contents.

Birds and mammals are not the only raiders of tropical bird nests. Snakes also prowl through the trees in search of easy prey, and these limbless reptiles seemed to strike an angry chord in Skutch's soul, as evidenced in this passage from *A Naturalist on a Tropical Farm:*

> It crams itself with animal life that is often warm and vibrant, to prolong an existence in which we detect no joy and no emotion. It reveals the depths to which evolution can sink when it takes the downward path and strips animals to the irreducible minimum able to perpetuate a predatory life in its naked horror.

Although we don't share this interpretation of the feeding adaptations of snakes, we're sure that tropical birds would agree with Skutch. Most snakes in the temperate zone spend their time on the ground, although there are a few species that wander through trees and bushes periodically. In a tropical rain forest, many species of snakes spend most of their life without rubbing their bellies against the ground. Some are too small to endanger bird eggs and nestlings, and these species are often specialized to eat the frogs and lizards that abound in the trees. But there are larger tree-dwelling snakes in the tropics, including rat snakes, pit vipers, and boas, that wax happily on a diet of nestling birds and are not easily deterred by the protestations of the parents.

Skutch's data concerning the high mortality rates of tropical forest birds have been called into question by some ecologists. They argue that the data that have been used to demonstrate high rates of nest failure come from unnatural habitats—small, isolated patches of forest that may harbor an unnaturally high density of both birds and nest predators. Population densities of forest animals are often much higher in these isolated patches than in continuous tracts, a fact that can be put to good use if you want to see a lot of rain forest birdlife on a brief visit. If both birds and nest predators are unnaturally common, you might expect to see higher rates of nest failure. There is some validity to this argument, but we think that Skutch's observations reflect a valid generalization. Although the rates of nest failure he observed may be unnaturally high, tropical forest birds must face more risks from predation than their temperate zone relatives because there are far more species of potential predators.

Bird nests are notoriously difficult to find in the tropical rain forest. Indeed, the nests of many common species are still unknown, despite the efforts of many accomplished tropical naturalists. The best strategy small birds have for avoiding nest predation is avoiding nest predators, and by making their nests difficult to find they stand a better chance of successfully rearing a clutch. When nests are found, they often turn out to be small and inconspicuous—sometimes no more than a simple, well-hidden ramp upon which the eggs are laid—or they may be structures that both hide and protect the eggs and young. Many tropical birds nest in holes—some carve them into trees, some dig them into steep earth banks, and some even construct elaborate little mud houses.

The crypticity of these nests is usually accompanied by circumspect parental behavior. The parents will often sit completely still on the nest, even if it is jostled, hoping that you will not notice them and go away. If a nest is discovered by a predator, an entire clutch will probably be lost, so it makes sense for the parents to wait until the last possible moment to flush and give away the location of the nest.

The small clutch sizes of rain forest birds may therefore be the result of several evolutionary pressures. Small clutches are easier to conceal from predators because the nests can be smaller and less conspicuous and the parents do not have to visit the nesting site as frequently. They also needn't feed their young as frequently because there are fewer hungry maws to fill, which further reduces the chances of their leading a predator to the nest. Small clutch size might thus be highly advantageous for a bird that breeds in a tropical rain forest where predators abound.

In addition to avoiding predation, small clutch sizes may have evolved in response to the pattern of resource availability in the rain forest environment. Food may be always available to forest birds, but it may never be present in large quantities, and parents may have to spend a considerable amount of time tending to the needs of even a few hungry youngsters. Further constraints could have been imposed by the relatively short hunting period available to a strictly diurnal forager in tropical latitudes. Even if predation were not a problem, these tropical forest birds probably could not raise as many young as a bird nesting in the temperate zone springtime.

Small clutch sizes may make it difficult for rain forest birds to produce many offspring in any given year, but this is not necessarily a disadvantage. Banding studies have shown that many small forest birds are extremely long-lived once they reach maturity, and they may be able to nest year after year. The social structure of a typical resident bird seems to reduce the pressure to breed successfully each year. Males and females remain together throughout the year and appear to establish permanent pair bonds. Even if a clutch should fail one year, the same pair can try again the following one. This is significant from an evolutionary perspective, because the reproductive output from this one pair can be spread out over many clutches.

Permanent pair bonds may be related to the resource base of the tropical forest because pairs of forest birds tend to establish territories that they defend from other members of the same species. This suggests that their population densities are related to the average productivity of the environment, implying in turn that populations of forest birds may be at or near the carrying capacity of the environment. If this is the case, producing large numbers of offspring each year might be wasteful, because the chances of their being able to locate and defend a suitable territory would be slim indeed. Regardless of the causes that underlie this behavior, the year-round territoriality of forest birds has a significant effect on the distribution of birds within a forest. Individuals of the same species tend to associate as pairs or small family groups scattered widely through the forest. This social structure results in the interesting paradox of the large, mixed-species foraging groups that are so characteristic of tropical rain forests.

A tropical birder may spend hours walking through an apparently birdless rain forest, only to come upon a sudden flurry of activity. Tanagers, woodcreepers, gnatcatchers, and a host of other small, insectivorous birds will be found foraging together in a single tree, their chirps and whistles calling attention to their progress through the forest. The birds never sit still; they flit constantly in and out of view among the leaves and epiphytes, and the flock never seems to linger very long in any one tree.

These mixed-species foraging flocks pose a real challenge to a birder new to the tropics. You have to be able to make immediate identifications of each species or else try to keep track of the field marks of dozens of unfamiliar species so that you can identify them later. If you depend on a field guide, you may be able to identify only two or three species before the flock has disappeared from sight. It may seem hard to reconcile the size of these flocks with the strong territorial propensities of many tropical forest birds, but after you have seen a number of flocks the paradox will begin to resolve itself. Even though flocks may contain dozens of individuals, rarely will they include more than a pair of any single species. The territoriality of many forest birds extends only to members of the same species, and the territories of many non-competing species overlap broadly. The mixed-species foraging flocks may be nothing more than an aggregation of all the local leaseholders, and the structure of the flocks may be set as much by the territorial behavior of individual species as by any group cohesiveness.

Mixed-species foraging flocks confer many advantages on their members, but the two most significant are probably increased foraging efficiency and increased protection from predation. Prey can be flushed from hiding places more easily and areas of local prey abundance can be exploited more thoroughly. The many watchful eyes of a flock also reduce the chances of a sneak predator attack, and the constant bustle and activity of a large flock may confuse some predators. Certain types of predators may also find it more difficult to locate flocks than individuals, because the flocks are so widely scattered in the forest.

Given these advantages, you might expect that migrant species would be especially prone to seek out these mixed-species foraging flocks. By joining such a flock, they would be able to take advantage of the resident species' knowledge of an area, both in regard to prey concentrations and predator dangers. But as anyone who has spent time looking at these foraging flocks is well aware, migrants are rarely part of the group scene in tropical forests.

George Powell, a biologist with the United States Fish and Wildlife Service, studied mixed-species foraging flocks in the rain forests of lower Central America, an area where about forty species of migrants spend the winter. Only seven of these species regularly joined resident foraging flocks in the mature rain forest, and within these flocks they made up but a small fraction of the individuals. Migrants were more conspicuous members of resident flocks in drier, more open forests; in some highland areas they made up almost half of the individuals in certain flocks. What accounts for the apparent reluctance of migrant birds to join resident mixed-species foraging flocks in lowland rain forests?

The answer to this question may be reflected in the social structure of the migrants. Migratory birds, in contrast to rain forest residents, typically lack permanent pair bonds. Males and females establish temporary relationships that last for only a single season on their northern breeding grounds. The pair bonds established during the breeding season soon dissolve, and while these birds migrate, individuals are free to come and go as they please. The same casual relationships hold when the migrants reach their tropical wintering grounds. There are a few migrants that establish winter territories in the tropics, but these are the exception, and interestingly enough they are often the same species that regularly participate in mixed-species foraging flocks. Migrant species seem to have opted for an entirely different ecological strategy from their stay-at-home relatives, and this difference in ecology may explain why they are willing to risk the rigors of a long annual migration.

Perhaps migrants are gamblers; to be good gamblers they must be opportunistic. Their evolutionary strategy involves an element of risk. By undertaking long migrations, they take advantage of strong seasonal flushes of productivity and long days in which to forage. They can tend large clutches of eggs, and if successful, they will produce more fledglings each year than they could have done had they bred in the tropics. Many of the young they fledge, of course, may fall victim to the rigors of the lengthy migrations; but this strategy has obviously paid off in the long run. The permanent residents of the tropical rain forest, by contrast, are a conservative lot; they depend on a strategy that keeps them close to home. By becoming intimately familiar with a specific area, and guarding it jealously against conspecific interlopers, they can extract their livelihood from a relatively stable environment.

In their tropical wintering grounds the migrants retain their opportunistic natures. With a few exceptions, they do not tie themselves to one place by maintaining territories. The residents may be locked into a system, prevented from taking advantage of unexpected bounties by their rigid territorial behavior, while the migrants are free to come and go as they will, exploiting temporary and seasonal abundances of prey in the tropics that may be denied the residents.

The evolution of migratory behavior is exceedingly complex, having evolved independently many different times. The patterns we have described, and the explanations we have provided, are generalized, and there are many exceptions. Migrants may behave differently on wintering grounds in southern Mexico than they do in Costa Rica, and even the same individual migrants may interact differently with different resident bird faunas along their migratory route. Confusing matters even more are the many short-term migrants that live in tropical rain forests. There are a number of species that migrate within the tropics, breeding in lowland rain forest but spending part of the year foraging in cloud forests.

These differences affirm the notion that the great diversity of tropical nature holds many secrets; the more we learn, the more apparent our ignorance becomes. We still have a great deal to learn about the ecology and evolution of bird migration, but we are convinced that our central theme will hold true: from both an ecological and an evolutionary perspective, migrant birds are integral parts of tropical nature. Their breeding patterns and feeding ecology cannot be studied without following them to their tropical haunts, and the ecology of the rain forest residents cannot be fully understood without examining the impact of the migrants. We must look beyond our temperate zone prejudices and study the migrants in their tropical habitats along with the residents.

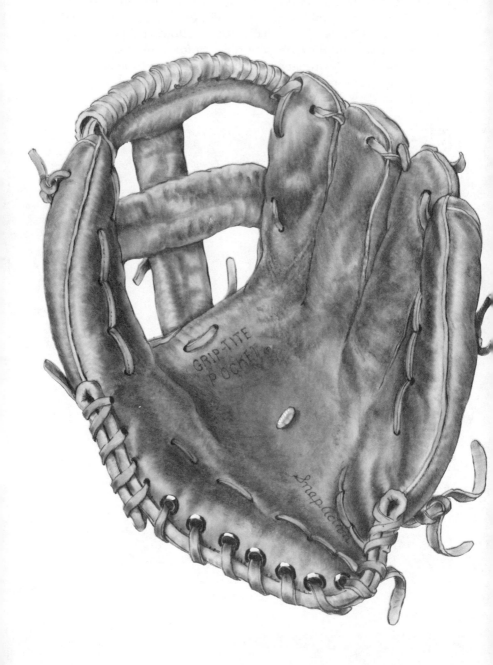

Chapter 13

JERRY'S MAGGOT

Edible: *Good to eat and wholesome to digest, as
a worm to a toad, a toad to a snake, a snake
to a pig, a pig to a man, and a man to a worm.*
—Ambrose Bierce
The Devil's Dictionary

For those of us who dwell in large cities, direct interactions with
other species may be limited to encounters with dogs and cats
(and even then we tend to treat them as conspecifics) and occasional battles with cockroaches. Modern urban life has pushed us
to a distant final link in a disrupted ecosystem. We live our lives
far removed from the food chains that support us, sitting atop a
trophic pyramid we never really become a part of.

Our limited interactions with other species force on us a form
of ecological myopia. The message of interconnectedness has never
penetrated deeply into our society, and even those of us who accept it intellectually may fail to appreciate how complicated some
of these relationships are. College biology texts often gloss over
interspecific interactions, offering simplified discussions of predation, competition, mutualism, and little else. But there are still

places and occasions when an urban North American can step back into a food chain and experience firsthand the ecological relationships between himself and other species. Our friend Jerry Coyne had such an experience on his first visit to the tropical forests of Central America.

Jerry is a biologist. At the time, he was a graduate student at Harvard's Museum of Comparative Zoology. Well versed in evolutionary logic, genetical theory, Ivy League ecology, and the use of biometrical tools, he was also aware that his actual experience with living creatures was "limited to unexciting fruit flies crawling feebly around food-filled glass tubes." Working in the Museum of Comparative Zoology had done little to change that. The Museum was no longer what it had been in the days of its founder, the celebrated Swiss naturalist Louis Agassiz, whose constant exhortation to "study Nature, not books" was practiced by all. Jerry's biological interactions continued to be with fruit flies in a crowded, sterile lab, and the only animals he saw, aside from his fellow graduate students and the ubiquitous dogs of Cambridge, were the stuffed mammals that resided in the display cases between his office and the Pepsi machine. Finally, after a winter and spring of listening to some of us urge him to get out of the lab, he enrolled in a field course in tropical ecology. Soon he was jetting to Costa Rica, determined to experience for himself the riches of tropical nature.

Jerry's introduction to the tropics was a revelation. It not only confirmed his misgivings about his previous training but changed his entire approach to his science. No longer would he trust "the naive and simple generalizations about nature produced by so-called theoretical ecologists," as he put it, and no longer would he search for slick hypotheses while glossing over the rich natural historical details of life. But he came away with more than these intellectual revelations.

A few weeks before Jerry was due to return to the Museum, his head began to itch. This was hardly remarkable. Skin fungus, chigger and mosquito bites, and a wealth of other pruriginous rot are the lot of field biologists in the lowland tropics, as he and his fellow students were by then well aware. Their field station was next to a large marsh, and hordes of mosquitoes descended on them as they listened to lectures after dinner. At first, Jerry assumed that the itch on his scalp was a mosquito bite, as indeed it was. But unlike the usual mosquito bite, this one did not subside. It grew larger, forming a small mound, and besides scratching Jerry began to worry. After several days of private fretting he sought help. One of his fellow students, a medical entomologist, agreed to examine the wound. Her diagnosis sent a chill of fear through poor Jerry. Poking out of a tiny hole in his scalp was a wiggling insect spiracle. A hideous little botfly maggot was living inside the skin on his head and eating his flesh! This intimacy with nature was a little too much for Jerry, and he ran around in circles crying for the removal of the maggot.

Unfortunately, removal of a botfly maggot is no simple task. This botfly (*Dermatobia hominis*) has existed as an unwanted guest in the skins of mammals and birds for countless generations. Its larvae have evolved two anal hooks that hold them firmly in their meaty burrow. If you pull gently on the larva, these hooks dig in deeper and bind it tightly to your flesh. If you pull harder, the maggot will eventually burst, leaving part of its body inside the host, which can lead to an infection far more dangerous to the host than the original bot. Botfly larvae secrete an antibiotic into their burrow, a tactic that prevents competing bacteria and fungi from tainting their food. A single bot in a nonvital organ thus poses little danger to an adult human, aside from mild physical discomfort and possible psychological trauma.

Occasionally a bot sets up residence in a particularly tender or private patch of flesh that cries out for immediate removal. In Costa Rica the locals used to use a plant called the *matatorsalo* (bot-killer) to kill the embedded larva. The acrid white sap of this milkweed kills the larva, but the task of removing the corpse remains. The most appropriate course of action then is a deft slice of a sterile scalpel. But surgeons are few and scattered in most tropical forests, and under these conditions many unwilling botfly hosts choose the meat cure.

This treatment, which is far from perfect, takes advantage of the biology of the botfly larva. The maggots are air-breathers and must maintain contact with the air through their respiratory spiracle, a snorkel-like tube that they poke through the host's skin. If you sandwich a piece of soft, raw meat over this airhole tightly enough, the larva must eventually leave its hole and burrow up through the meat in search of fresh air. When this happens, both meat and botfly are discarded. One of the students in Jerry's course afflicted with a bot in the buttock did this successfully. But the dense mat of hair that was Jerry's pride and joy would have to be shaved off in order for this to work, and toiling in the sweaty tropical heat with a patch of raw meat strapped atop his head was not something he relished. Faced with such a choice, Jerry decided to live and let live for the time being, and to seek professional help when he returned to Harvard.

After his initial bout of hysterical revulsion, Jerry learned to accept his guest. It was relatively painless most of the time. Only when the larva twisted would it cause sharp twinges of pain. Swimming made the larva squirm, presumably a reaction to having its air supply cut off temporarily, and Jerry felt this as a grating against his skull. These inconveniences were not enough to blind him to the wonder of it all. The bot was taking Jerry's "own body substance" and rendering it into more botfly flesh. This transmogrification of one creature into another is a miracle easily observed, but difficult to experience. Sudden death at the jaws of a large carnivore or the brief bite of a flea do not provide one the opportunity to reflect on the transmutative nature of predation and parasitism. But for the minor expense of a few milligrams of flesh, Jerry could both contemplate and feel the process at his leisure. He was inside a food chain, rather than at its end. Jerry grew fond of his bot and the bot grew fat on Jerry.

When Jerry returned to New England, his bot had produced a goose egg–sized swelling on his head. It hurt more and he immediately sought medical advice at the Harvard Health Services clinic. Although he was quickly surrounded by a crowd of physicians and nurses, none of them had seen a botfly before and they regarded Jerry more as a medical curiosity than a suffering patient. Chagrined, he abandoned thoughts of a medical solution and decided to let nature take its course. Despite the discomfort, the bot continued to provide some pleasure. Jerry took great delight in the looks of horror he could produce by telling acquaintances of his guest as he dramatically brushed aside his hair.

While sitting in the bleachers at Fenway Park one evening watching the Red Sox fall prey to the Yankees, Jerry felt the beginning of the end. Protruding from the goose egg atop his scalp was a quarter inch of botfly larva. Over the course of the evening this protrusion grew, and eventually the bristly, inch-long larva fell free. Jerry prepared a glass jar with sterilized sand to act as a nursery for his pupating bot, but despite his tender ministrations the larva dried out and died before it could encase itself in a pupal sheath.

The saga of Jerry's maggot began long before Jerry came along. It started with an egg, or more precisely, with a means of getting an egg onto a suitable host. Botflies should be stealthy in order to parasitize dextrous, perceptive animals like birds, monkeys, and humans. But adult botflies are large, day-flying creatures that are easy to see and hear and easy to avoid. Botfly species that parasitize rodents glue their eggs to the root hairs of plants that stick out along the sides of rodent burrows. When a rodent walks by, its body heat causes the eggs to hatch; the larvae wriggle onto the animal's fur, and thence into its flesh.

Dermatobia solves the problem of egg placement with a remarkable adaptation. An egg-laden female captures a female mosquito, glues her fertile eggs onto the mosquito, and then releases her. The smaller, sneakier, night-flying mosquito is well suited for feeding on a dextrous and perceptive animal like a human. When the mosquito begins her meal, the body heat of the host triggers the hatching of the botfly egg, and the tiny larva falls off its carrier and burrows into the human or animal host. It is hard to imagine a more surreptitious strategy than this oviposition by proxy—an adaptation that evolutionary biologists could never anticipate.

The intermediate evolutionary steps that led to such egg-laying behavior are baffling. Indeed, it is a good example of the type of "perfection" of sophisticated adaptations that troubled Darwin in the *Origin of Species*. If we assume that the ancestral condition of the botfly was to deposit its eggs directly on the host, or even on grass or leaves, the number of steps between this and oviposition via mosquito is difficult to contemplate. It is not enough to grab any small fly, because this would be wasteful. The botfly must be able to discriminate between suitable vectors and unsuitable ones, and this discrimination must be sophisticated because *Dermatobia* usually uses mosquitoes of the genus *Psorophora* as egg carriers. The recognition cue may be simple; but even if this is the case, the transitional stages necessary to evolve the mechanism would not be apparent.

You might wonder why this sort of oviposition by proxy is confined to the lowland tropics and has not evolved in or spread to the northern temperate zone. Boreal and alpine habitats are unrivaled for the voracity of their mosquitoes. Our most vivid memories of clouds of bloodthirsty mosquitoes and biting flies come not from the tropics (although we have spent many hellish evenings in clouds of mosquitoes in mangrove swamps), but from pastoral New England woods and idyllic Rocky Mountain meadows. Perhaps the issue pivots around the dexterity of their mammalian prey. In boreal areas, dextrous animals like monkeys, kinkajous, and coatimundis do not exist. Except for humans and raccoons, most of the larger mammals in North America are rather clumsy, at least in the sense of manual dexterity. Moose, deer, bear, coyotes, and their ilk do not manipulate their food and they keep all four feet on the ground most of the time. Northern biting flies thus exhibit no subtlety in their approach because no hand or paw will rise to crush them.

Temperate zone mosquitoes whine a direct, noisy approach, and their landing and bite are easily detected. But consider a typical rain forest mosquito. She rarely lands on you if you are moving, and you hear her only in the quiet of night after conversation has ended and you are drifting off to sleep. Her landing is soft, even tentative, and if you move she flies off and bides her time. Her bite is gentle when it comes, a delicate touch that is rarely felt. She is careful; she is sneaky.

Of course, both the temperate latitudes and the tropics support many mosquitoes, and some species don't fit these generalizations. But it seems to us that the general stealthiness of tropical mosquitoes owes something to having evolved in concert with dextrous mammalian hosts. And this stealthiness provides a plausible explanation why *Dermatobia hominis* is a tropical creature. In the northern temperate zone where most warm meals walk on all fours, a botfly doesn't have to rely on cumbersome reproductive adaptations. With a little persistence, it can avoid swishing tails and eventually home in on its target to lay its eggs. There is no advantage in seeking out a mosquito to do this work, and botflies and warble flies in North America lay their eggs directly onto their hosts.

The interaction between *Dermatobia hominis* and its host is complicated in terms of the mechanics of oviposition, but the ecological relationship between Jerry and his bot was quite straightforward. The bot gained and Jerry lost. This is parasitism, and it fits easily into the classification scheme of interspecific interactions that can be found in most textbooks. The chart below is typical of such classifications, where the effect of one species on another is given a sign indicating positive (+), negative (—), or neutral (0) associations:

SPECIES A	SPECIES B	
+	—	parasitism or predation
+	0	commensalism
+	+	mutualism

Parasitism and predation are both pretty clear; the predator or parasite gains and the prey or host obviously loses. Equally clear are those situations where both species gain, as in mutualistic interactions. A good example would be the trees and fungal mycorrhizae discussed in Chapter 2. Commensalistic interactions, in which one species gains without having any effect on the other, are perhaps less obvious, although algae growing on a tree trunk might be one example. But this simple scheme, like most such schemes in nature, has its shortcomings. Things are not always so simple, especially in the tropics, where the vast number of species can lead to complex interactions. There the lines distinguishing parasitism from mutualism and commensalism can twist and turn with byzantine complexity, and the nature of these relationships can become hazy indeed.

One of the best examples of the complexity of ecological interactions in the tropics and the hazy intergradations linking parasitism with mutualism also happens to involve botflies. Another type of parasite plays a major role in this particular web of interactions, although this other parasite does not actually enter the body of its host.

There are a number of birds that engage in what ornithologists call brood parasitism. This habit has evolved independently seven different times, and brood parasites can be found in both temperate and tropical regions. Brood parasites lay their eggs in the nests of other species, which then raise the parasite's young at the expense of their own offspring. Such parasitism seems particularly odious to most human observers, and even some biologists regard the phenomenon with moral indignation. This is easy to understand. Brood parasites are often larger than their foster parents, and there is something about watching a small foster parent feeding a monstrous, greedy nestling that strikes the same indignant chord in our sensibilities that seeing congressmen voting themselves tax breaks does. And if this weren't bad enough, some brood parasites use reprehensible tactics to ensure their own well-being. The young of the European Cuckoo shove the rightful eggs out of the nest before they hatch, and hatchling African honeyguides stab their nest mates to death with a specially modified tooth.

The brood parasite in the system we will describe is the Giant Cowbird (*Scaphidura oryzivora*), a member of the oriole family. Its breeding habits are similar to those of the Brown-headed Cowbird of temperate North America. The female cowbird first locates the nest of a host species. Then, when the time is right, usually just after the host female has deposited her eggs, she sneaks in and lays her egg or eggs in the nest. Hatchling cowbirds are well suited for their lives as parasites. They develop rapidly and they are aggressive. Baby Giant Cowbirds hatch a week or so before their legitimate nest mates; they also develop much more quickly. Their eyes open within forty-eight hours of hatching, while those of the host nestlings may not open for six to nine days. Unlike the cuckoos and honeyguides, cowbirds do not dispose of their nest mates, but their rapid development gives them a head start over the nest's rightful inhabitants, and they are able to usurp a major share of the food brought to the nest by the parents.

The parasite clearly gains, as its total reproductive effort consists only of finding a suitable host nest and dropping its eggs. It need never bother with raising young, an activity which normally requires a considerable expenditure of risk and effort. The situation is also obviously an enormous evolutionary disadvantage for the duped foster parents, who raise the cowbirds to the detriment of their own offspring. Or is it?

Neal Smith of the Smithsonian Tropical Research Institute studied the relationship between the Giant Cowbird and its host species in Panama. The title of his study, "On the Advantages of Being Parasitized," immediately suggests that something counter-intuitive is about to be revealed.

Unlike the Brown-headed Cowbird of North America, which is nonchalant over whom it entrusts its offspring to, the Giant Cowbird selects a particular type of foster parent. There are four such host species in Panama: the Chestnut-headed Oropendola (*Zarhynchus wagleri*), the Montezuma Oropendola (*Gymnostinops montezuma*), the Crested Oropendola (*Psarocolius decumanus*), and the Yellow-rumped Cacique (*Cacicus cela*). These four species nest in colonies, and their large, intricately woven pendulant nests are one of the characteristic sights in tropical forests. The nests are usually clustered in the canopy of a single tree, often a very tall one with an open, spreading canopy, and the trees are frequently found along clearings and riverbanks.

Smith discovered a complex set of interactions between the cowbirds and oropendolas. In some colonies the parasitic cowbirds were sneaky; they skulked around the oropendola nests and stealthily deposited an egg or two when the host females departed. The eggs they laid resembled the eggs of the oropendolas, an adaptation well known in other brood parasites. This is the type of behavior characteristic of brood parasites, and it is to their advantage to be as sneaky as possible. But not all cowbirds behaved in such a fashion. The cowbirds that hung around some oropendola colonies were nothing short of brazen. These female cowbirds were aggressive and often drove off the nesting oropendolas so they could lay their eggs at their own convenience. Rather than lay just an egg or two like their stealthy sisters, these females laid several eggs at a time, as many as five in a single oropendola nest. And their eggs did not at all resemble those of the hosts.

Smith was intrigued by this audacious behavior on the part of a bird that should be sneaky. And he was even more intrigued by the behavior of the oropendola hosts. In those colonies where the sneaky cowbirds laid their eggs, the oropendolas were picky. If they found an egg in their nest that didn't look right, they shoved it out. This behavior, and the stealthiness of the cowbirds, made it obvious that the cowbirds were unwelcome in those colonies. But in the colonies with the brazen cowbirds, the oropendolas just didn't care about foreign eggs in their nests. Even though the cowbird eggs didn't resemble their own eggs, they let them remain, and they didn't even seem to mind getting chased out of their nests so the cowbirds could lay.

Smith eventually found the reason for this peculiar behavioral dichotomy. Oropendolas and caciques are not the only creatures that live in colonial nest sites in these large emergent trees. Such trees are also a favored site for colonies of a number of social wasps in the genera *Polybia, Stelopolybia, Protopolybia,* and *Brachygastra,* as well as for various species of meliponine bees. The colonies of these wasps and bees are large, sometimes running to tens of thousands of adults in each nest. The wasps are equipped with potent barbed stings that deliver a nasty venom, and the meliponine bees bite and rub irritating mandibular secretions into the skin and eyes of any creature foolish enough to venture too close to their nests. Both wasps and bees respond with alacrity to any disturbance, but they seem to be most sensitive to such signals as vigorous shaking of the nests and foreign odors like sweat. Once disturbed, these highly social insects use alarm pheromones to alert their sisters of danger and call them to defend the nest.

The association of oropendola nesting colonies with social insects has some obvious benefits for the birds. As long as they can avoid the wrath of the insects, they are protected from numerous potential predators. There are many animals that roam the canopy who would delight in a meal of bird eggs—mammals like opossums, raccoons, kinkajous, and white-faced monkeys relish both eggs and nestlings, and would no doubt enjoy wasp and bee larvae given the opportunity. By defending themselves against these predators, the wasps and bees also afford protection to their more vulnerable neighbors. In addition, the birds are protected from predators like snakes, which would not be interested in the wasp or bee larvae because they would trigger the insects' response by their movement through the canopy. Oropendolas are not the only Neotropical birds who have stumbled on the benefits of aggressive hymenopteran neighbors; some trogons actually build their nests inside wasp nests.

Smith discovered that proximity to a bee or wasp nest afforded the oropendolas respite from a plague of botflies. Botflies of the genus *Philornis* were common parasites on nestling oropendolas where wasps and bees were absent, and unlike Jerry's relatively benign guest, *Philornis* could devastate their hosts. A single botfly larva could severely debilitate a little bird in the nest, and seven such larvae were enough to kill the nestlings. But in some unknown way the presence of aggressive wasps and bees kept the botflies at bay. If the oropendolas built their nests too far from the wasp or bee nests, botfly larvae might show up in nestlings; but if the bird nests were close to the wasps and bees, there were no botflies.

The association between oropendola colonies and insect colonies is not perfect. In some trees where oropendola colonies are found, there are few if any aggressive wasps or bees. In these trees the birds build their nests on the periphery of the crown, on thin branches that a predator would have trouble negotiating. Although this may afford the birds protection from nest-robbing mammals and reptiles, the botflies are undeterred, and many of the nestlings succumb to their infestations.

Smith found that some of the oropendolas and caciques who had nests in these beeless and waspless trees were able to raise their young without being plagued by botflies. What made these nests interesting was the presence of parasitic Giant Cowbird nestlings. In nests that lacked the brood parasite and were not located in trees with wasps or bees, the botflies infested the hatchling oropendolas and caciques and few survived to leave the nest. It appeared as though the presence of cowbirds was somehow salutary; in some way these parasitic birds seemed to benefit their hosts.

Smith studied the behavior of the nestling cowbirds for some clues to this puzzle. The precocity and aggressiveness of the hatchling cowbird, which gives these brood parasites a head start on the rightful inhabitants of the nest, actually works to the benefit of the host species in the absence of protective wasps and bees. Whenever a cowbird nestling sees a botfly or botfly larva, it responds with a quick peck and a satisfied swallow. They eat these dangerous parasites before they can infest the helpless oropendolas, and in this way benefit their hosts.

Whether we call a cowbird a parasite or a mutualist with respect to the oropendolas thus depends on the abundance and distribution of wasps, bees, and botflies. A shift in the abundance of these insects can have profound effects on the nature of the cowbird-oropendola relationship.

The wasps that help defend oropendola nests also help protect other organisms. In some cases it seems to be a straightforward commensalistic relationship. Large decticine katydids roost during the day in foliage next to wasp nests and are protected from the same type of predators that might invade the oropendola nests. There is even a species of social wasp that relies on this strategy, but in this case the advantages may suddenly turn into liabilities.

The Central American wasp *Mischocytarrus immarginatus* is a delicate creature as wasps go. The adults, which are slender and patterned in black and yellow stripes, are rather docile and their colonies rarely contain more than a few dozen individuals in an open platform of exposed brood cells. You can often touch a *Mischocyttarus* colony without eliciting a defensive reaction. A wasp with this placid disposition and fragile nest is obviously no match for a hungry opossum. Most species of *Mischocyttarus* build their frail nests in inaccessible cavities under the lip of a stream bank or far out on the tip of a palm frond. But *Mischocyttarus immarginatus* has found an alternative defensive ploy. This species usually builds its nests in the company of another species of social wasp, one with more aggressive adults and with larger colonies. Often it chooses a member of the *Polybia occidentalis* group, who build large, conspicuous, globular or cylindrical paper nests in bushes and on cacti and tree limbs. These aggressive neighbors undoubtedly help protect the timid *Mischocyttarus immarginatus* in much the same way that other polybiine wasps help protect the oropendolas.

This would appear to be a cost-free adaptation by *Mischocyttarus* to the problem of mammalian predation, a clear example of a commensalistic relationship. And so it is during the wet season. But *Mischocyttarus immarginatus* is most abundant in the dry forests of Guanacaste Province in northwestern Costa Rica, where there is a long and pronounced dry season. The forest here drops its leaves during this season, exposing the *Polybia occidentalis* nests, which are very conspicuous because of their size and shape. The thousands of fat larvae in these exposed nests become increasingly desirable as populations of many other insects decline, and a variety of birds, both large and small, soon begin to raid the nests. Red-throated Caracaras and kites will brave the stings of the adult wasps and smash the *Polybia* nests into fragments to devour the grubs.

The onslaught comes quickly; it is not unusual to find half of the *Polybia* nests in a given area destroyed within two weeks. The *Mischocyttarus immarginatus* nests are destroyed along with the *Polybia* nests. There are always a few solitary *Mischocyttarus immarginatus* nests around, and not all of the *Polybia* nests fall prey to birds during the dry season, so the system persists and *Mischocyttarus immarginatus* continues to seek the seasonal advantages of an aggressive neighbor. But the delicacy of this arrangement is easily seen, and a slight lengthening of the dry season might suddenly shift the balance, making it more profitable for *Mischocyttarus immarginatus* to seek sheltered nest sites like most other species of *Mischocyttarus*.

The simple passage from night to day can also alter the ecological relationships between two species. During the day, tropical dung scarab beetles face stiff competition from a variety of flies for a scarce resource. The flies often possess a keen sense of smell that enables them to detect and locate a fresh dung pile rapidly. They are generally the first insects to arrive, and they lay eggs that hatch rapidly into voracious larvae. These eggs contaminate the dung for the beetles that arrive later because the fly maggots grow fast enough to starve out the beetle larvae. But some dung beetles have accepted the aid of another creature to help reduce competition with flies.

If you look closely at adult dung scarabs, you will sometimes see lumps on the limbs and underside, waxy little globules that are in fact a living, shifting blanket of mites. The abundance of these mites might lead you to believe that the beetles are suffering a slow, itchy, bleeding death—an impression particularly vivid if you happen to be suffering from an infestation of chiggers at the time. But this is not necessarily the case. Many of these mites are merely hitchhikers; when the beetle arrives at a pile of dung, the mites scamper off to scour the surface of the heap, feeding on whatever eggs and larvae they find. More often than not these eggs turn out to be those of flies. Studies done on this same phenomenon in the northern temperate zone demonstrate clearly that mites greatly increase the beetle's ability to compete with flies.

In the temperate zone most dung beetles are diurnal, but in the warm tropics there are many species of nocturnal dung-eating scarabs. These large, relatively clumsy beetles fall easy prey to birds and large lizards during the day, and perhaps they have become nocturnal to avoid such predation. Also, many tropical mammals are nocturnal, so perhaps availability of food may have pushed these beetles to be active at night. Whatever the cause, these nocturnal scarabs face less competition from dung-eating flies. Without the flies, the hitchhiking mites become a liability rather than an asset, and a relationship that is mutually beneficial during the day suddenly becomes one-sided at night. Nothing is known of the biology of the mites that infest nocturnal dung scarabs, but we doubt that they confer the same advantages to a night-feeding scarab as they do to a day-feeding one, and it is possible that they actually interfere with the beetle's activities. The daytime mutualist may thus become a nighttime parasite.

These interspecific associations reveal something of the complexity of the tropics. There is little doubt that such complexities are more prevalent in the tropics than in the temperate zones, but the dynamic and patchy qualities of the living world are characteristic of all habitats. Such relationships resist textbook labeling and mental pigeonholing, forcing one to consider the particular and the peculiar. An appreciation of the unique is to us the essence of natural history, and although we must call on general principles to help explain what we see, we consider the real world, with all of its messiness and confusion, far more interesting than any neat theory or model. William Blake's claim that "to generalize is to be an idiot" does have a ring of truth. Perhaps those souls who seek order in the structure of life can find some solace in the fact that we have deliberately sought out complicated relationships to make our point. Straightforward types of symbioses are common; yet even these simple relationships are changing as natural selection works on all involved. The "endless forms" that Darwin's vision brought forth from a static world are not just the limbs and colors of individuals, but the rich and still dimly understood relationships that thread among them.

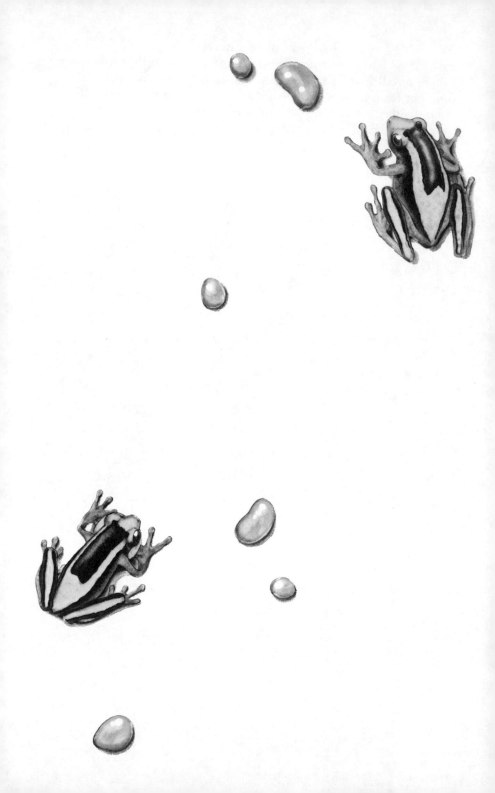

Chapter 14

SINGING
IN THE RAIN

*I like the look of frogs, and their outlook, and
especially the way they get together in wet places
on warm nights and sing about sex.*
— Archie Carr
The Windward Road

Everyone likes frogs. It sometimes seems as though they are
becoming inescapable icons of popular culture, their green counte-
nances peering out cheerfully from television, T-shirts, coffee mugs,
and a host of other artifacts of modern life. Frogs are cute. Their
charm is hard to resist and they have somehow escaped the revulsion that greets many other lower tetrapods.

Although they may appear cute to most human eyes, frogs are
truly peculiar creatures; it would have been almost impossible for
biologists to predict the morphology of frogs if they didn't already
exist. Frogs are vertebrates, undoubtedly evolved from an ordinary-
looking ancestor, but now they typically have heads as long as
their vertebral columns, hind limbs four times the length of their
bodies, and no ribs to support their dangling innards. Although
most of us can distinguish among frogs with generally smooth

skins and long legs, tree frogs, with large adhesive toepads, and toads, which have warty skins and relatively squat bodies, frogs and toads all look more like each other than they do any other creature, their bizarre general form placing constraints on their appearance. But if your only exposure to anurans has been in North America or Europe, the variations that have been built around this basic plan in tropical America are astounding.

Frogs find warm wet nights idyllic, and warm wet nights are typical of tropical rain forests. The songs of frogs give tropical nights a special air. When we are in the rain forest, we like nothing better than to step out after dinner with a full stomach and a headlamp loaded with fresh batteries. A jaunt through a Neo-tropical rain forest on a misty, drizzly night reveals many surprises to a curious naturalist. As your torch plays over the vegetation, it will pause here and there on frogs. Some might be adhering to vertical tree trunks, others might be grasping delicate twigs, and others again might be sitting placidly on the damp surfaces of *Philodendron* leaves. There they will remain, glued to their perches by the blinding light, and if you're careful you can approach them for a closer look.

Although many Neotropical frogs are drably cloaked in shades of brown, gray, and olive, you will often come across one that is different. It might be dull brown, ordinary enough at first glance, but with spectacular cobalt blue eyes providing an unexpected touch of brightness. It might be a green and orange beast with spindly legs and protuberant red eyes with catlike vertical pupils. Perhaps it will be a delicate bright yellow creature splotched with red and blue. These colorful little beasts are elegant indeed, and their large heads and bulging eyes imbue them with character.

Some Neotropical frogs will stretch your credulity beyond its limit, resembling as they do the creations of an alien biology. Picture a drab brown beast perhaps three inches long grasping a thin branch at eye level in the forest understory. The first thing you notice is its enormous head, which has upturned fins at the back of the skull and looks like a huge, roughly textured helmet. This head dwarfs the animal's emaciated body, the bones of which are clearly outlined under its loose skin. The limbs are likewise thin, and the animal resembles a living skeleton with a huge bony helmet. At the touch of your hand it utters a strange noise and opens its cavernous mouth, revealing a striking white jaw lining and a vivid orange tongue. The jaws clamp shut on your unwary finger and you feel the prickle of little teeth while a large tusk on the lower jaw punctures your skin. Is this really a frog?

The appearance of some of the frogs you might encounter on a night walk in a tropical rain forest is no less astonishing than their variety and abundance. In certain parts of the New World tropics, particularly along the flanks of the Andes in the upper Amazon basin, there are enough frogs to satisfy the dreams of any anurophile. Thousands congregate around small forest ponds after heavy rains, and the combined choruses of many different species can sound like a cross between a motorcycle race and a sheet-metal shop. Even deep within the forest, far from any pond, stream, or puddle, the chirps and barks of other species can be heard high in the canopy or on the litter-covered forest floor. In the upper Amazon basin in eastern Ecuador as many as eighty species of frogs may live within sight and sound of each other, a richness of species in a single square mile that rivals that of the entire North American continent.

The rain forests of tropical America are not a uniform realm in which frogs are always conspicuous elements. Individual frogs can be rare even in places that are home to a wealth of species. In part of the Amazon basin where many species are known to be present, weeks of long night searches may turn up just a few frogs. When I search for frogs in the Amazonian rain forest of Ecuador, I expect to find a dozen or two frogs for every hour I spend wandering through the forest. But Ron Heyer and Ron Crombie, colleagues at the Smithsonian who have searched for frogs in the Brazilian Amazon, may find only one or two frogs for every hour they spend searching. Sometimes the scarcity of frogs is temporary, and heavy rains may suddenly reveal their true abundance. Sometimes they may be patchily abundant, so that when you stumble on the right place you will find them in large numbers. But in many places they are genuinely rare, and the reasons for this are poorly understood.

Many tropical lowland rivers, particularly in the vast Amazonian plains, undergo a regular cycle of rising and falling water levels. If you visit the forest on these floodplains during the time of low water, the understory looks much like any other patch of rain forest. But if you visit this same forest six months later, when the river is at its annual neap, the forest floor may lie under 30 feet of water. With the rising waters come fish, and predatory fish find few easier targets than polliwogs. In the tropics, frogs and fish seem largely incompatible; wherever there are many fish, you will find few species of frogs breeding. Perhaps this seasonal inundation is part of the reason why frogs are scarce in some places that otherwise seem ideal.

Temperate zone frogs are rarely found in numbers except when they breed, and some of the most abundant North American species seem to vanish once they leave their nuptial ponds. All across eastern North America, countless million male spring peepers fill the marshes each spring with their lustful peeps, but once their business is over they disappear into the summer haze. Other North American frogs, like the common and widespread bullfrog, spend their entire lives along the shores of lakes and ponds, and even when not breeding they are almost always found within a few feet of the water's edge. Toads are an exception to the generally close association of anurans and water in temperate North America. Although they breed in water, they are often encountered well away from it, patrolling gardens and golf courses as well as woods and fields, when conditions are right. But they are rarely found in numbers except at their nuptial ponds.

Relatively few frogs are found in permanent marshes or along the shores of large lakes in the rain forests of tropical America. Given the wealth of the rain forest frog fauna, comparatively few species are found in these eminently froggy-looking swamps and backwaters. This pattern has an obvious cause. Any permanent body of water in the tropics plays host to a rich fish community that poses grave dangers to a slow-swimming tadpole, and most tropical frogs avoid laying their eggs in these places for this reason. The aquatic environment is harsh for a tadpole, surely among nature's most inoffensive of creatures. These clumsy little globs of soft flesh offer a tempting target to a wide variety of predators. It is not surprising that most tropical frogs prefer to lay their eggs where voracious fish and predatory aquatic insects pose a minimal threat.

Even the wettest tropical rain forests exhibit variations in rainfall, a pattern and rhythm that may be subtle but that is clearly understood by its residents. Ponds and puddles come and go. often in regular cycles, and such temporary pools are the favored breeding ground of many tropical frogs. This is also true of many temperate zone frogs, particularly smaller species that undergo a fairly short developmental period. There are fewer predators in these vernal ponds, for dangerous creatures like fish cannot easily survive evaporation; yet the temporary pools can be rich in detritus and algae and will provide abundant food for a lazy herbivore.

Temperate zone frogs that breed in vernal pools follow a predictable cycle. Males arrive before the females, stake out territories along the banks, and fill the air with song. Females follow shortly thereafter, and after a perfunctory courtship, mating takes place as the eggs are deposited in the water. The adults may linger a while, but once their business is taken care of, they are free to depart, leaving their eggs to hatch and develop as they will. The eggs hatch in due course, and the little tadpoles begin a precarious existence, which in a temporary pond may turn out to be a race against the wind and the sun. Development must be completed before the habitat dries up, or an entire year's reproductive effort will be lost.

Temporary pools spring up overnight in the deserts of the American southwest after heavy thunderstorms, and these pools may persist long enough for some frogs to carry out a complete aquatic development. Spadefoot toads dwell in these arid lands, showing up in tremendous numbers when their breeding ponds fill. These anurans have an exceptionally rapid development; only a few weeks may elapse between the arrival of the adults and the emergence of the toadlets.

There are temporary ponds that fill with surprising speed even in tropical rain forest. We have watched shallow depressions turn into large pools overnight, and some of these pools persist for weeks or months before they disappear. The burst of anuran activity that follows the appearance of a tropical pond, particularly in the drier, more seasonal forests, is astounding. A multitude of amorous frogs of many different species suddenly appears, eager to lay their eggs where there are no predatory fish to threaten their young. In the heat of their ardor they seem to lose track of time. Most frogs are nocturnal and their songs are usually heard only at night. But when the ponds are young and the frogs are eager, the din of screeching frogs can continue all day long. This raucous chorus of peeps, grunts, trills, rattles, and rumbles carries for hundreds of yards. If the winds are calm, you can sometimes hear them from a mile away.

When I first saw a tropical pond fill, it was not the quick arrival of the frogs that surprised me, but the immediate appearance of large tadpoles with hind limb buds. I was familiar with the rapid development of the spadefoot toad and other desert anurans, but it was hard to believe that so much development could have been compressed into a few hours. Yet the fat tadpoles swimming lazily around seemed to be undeniable proof that this had occurred. The pond was never connected to permanent water that could have been the source of the tadpoles; the only other conclusion I could draw was that the tadpoles had sprouted forth from the mud. My two alternatives were equally untenable: either the tadpoles grew with supercharged speed or they popped spontaneously from the primordial ooze.

Fortunately, we do not have to resort to the supernatural to explain this phenomenon. The clues that give it away are found weeks before the onset of the rainy season. From time to time I had heard frogs calling from the depression that eventually became the pond, but casual searches never revealed the identity of the caller. They called during the day, yet whenever I got too close, they became silent and I couldn't pinpoint their location. Finally, after determining to solve the mystery of the phantom callers, I cleared the undergrowth from an area where I consistently heard them and sat back to wait for their chorus to resume. When they did so, the songs came from the middle of the cleared area, but they were coming from below the ground. Careful scraping revealed a little hole in the ground, and in this hole was an ordinary-looking frog that goes under the name *Leptodactylus ventri-maculatus*.

The male *Leptodactylus* constructs his burrow in a damp hollow that will become a pond when the rains fill it. He begins calling from the burrow well before the onset of the rains. When a female shows up, mating takes place in the privacy of the burrow. The male whips the mucus from his skin into a thick foam with his strong hind legs, and in this foam the eggs are laid. The eggs are few in number, but they are large and comparatively well yolked. Even though the eggs lack some of the protective membranes that reptiles and birds have, there is little danger of their drying out. The dense foam protects them from desiccation, and since the nest lies in a damp depression it never gets dry to begin with. In the warm, wet recesses of their foam-lined burrow, the eggs hatch and the tadpoles grow. When the rains finally fill the depression with water, the growing tadpoles, fat from nourishment from their yolks, are liberated from their protective cocoons and complete their development like any normal polliwog while other frogs are just getting started.

This pattern of reproduction is itself remarkable, but it also represents a possible transitional state in the evolution of another type of life cycle. We do not mean to imply that it is an incomplete and unfinished version of another life cycle. It is highly adaptive in itself, a strategy that gives individuals a competitive head start in temporary tropical ponds and ensures reproductive success even if the pond dries quickly. By calling it a transitional state, we simply point out that other evolutionary lineages may have passed through similar states, and that the transition from a conventional amphibian life history to an unusual one need not have been accomplished in one fell swoop.

Ron Heyer has described one possible avenue that frogs may have traveled to free themselves of an aquatic breeding site. Frogs of the genus *Leptodactylus* are widespread in tropical America, and the life history exhibited by *Leptodactylus ventrimaculatus* is only one of many exhibited by the group. Some species lay their eggs in foam masses that float on the surface of the water. Others place their eggs in foam in shallow depressions and cavities near shore, where rising water carries the tadpoles to the place in which they will develop. Others like *Leptodactylus ventrimaculatus*, lay their eggs in an incubating chamber on land before there is any water at all. Some species that lay their eggs in these incubating chambers forego a free-living tadpole stage and emerge from their foam-filled chambers as perfectly formed froglets. With increasing independence from water, fewer eggs are laid but more yolk is put into each. This increases the frog's investment in each egg, but it also enhances each egg's chances of survival.

Heyer's scenario of liberation is based on a group of frogs generally associated with drier and more seasonal tropical habitats, although it has many representatives in rain forest. With these frogs, independence from water may have been mostly a response to the dangers of desiccation. You might not think that a frog that lives in rain forest would have to worry much about desiccation, but other factors may have encouraged them to leave the water. Competition with other tadpoles may have been such a factor.

With many different species trying to utilize the same limited resource base, the race would seem to go with the quick, because they
would be able to complete their development while there was still
an abundance of food. Predation from aquatic polliwogivores was
almost certainly a major incentive. Even in temporary ponds there
are many creatures that find tadpoles tasty. Water bugs, the naiads
of damselflies, and even some species of tadpoles eagerly feed on
the eggs and tadpoles of frogs. These creatures do not show up in
numbers immediately, so there is almost always a period of relative
safety early in the life of each temporary pool.

Temperate zone naturalists are used to thinking of frogs as
semiaquatic creatures, or at least as animals that have a close
association with water at some point in their life. Heyer's transitional states lead to an independence from water. In the rain
forests of the New World tropics you will find large aggregations
of frogs at small temporary ponds and you will find a few species
only along forest creeks; but a perceptive temperate zone naturalist will also be surprised by the number of frogs found far from
these normal amphibian breeding sites. Although many Neotropical frogs exhibit a more or less conventional amphibian life
history, with aquatic tadpoles and terrestrial or arboreal adults, a
significant number of them have what a temperate zone naturalist
would consider aberrant life histories.

Frogs are, after all, members of the class Amphibia, and anyone
who has taken introductory biology knows that this name refers to
their life history. Amphibians are denizens of two worlds. Their
eggs are laid in water, where they eventually hatch into fishlike
tadpoles. As time passes they sprout limbs, lose their gills, and
eventually become frogs, free to pursue their adulthood on land
or in water. However, the aquatic polliwogs so beloved of children
in northern temperate latitudes are by no means the only path a
developing frog can take. The frogs of the Neotropical rain forests
exhibit a remarkable set of adaptations that belie the simple picture of amphibian life histories found in most textbooks and make
an open-minded naturalist wonder what a normal amphibian life
history really is.

Martha Crump, now of the University of Florida, studied the
breeding habits of the frog fauna at Santa Cecilia in the upper
Amazon basin of eastern Ecuador for her doctoral dissertation. Of
the eighty-one species of frogs that she found, only thirty-two

exhibited a "normal" anuran life history. The rest exhibited, to varying degrees, independence from an aquatic environment. One species laid its eggs in water-filled cavities in trees, ensuring a private haven within which its tadpoles could grow. Some simply deposited their eggs on leaves overhanging ponds and streams; this protected the eggs from aquatic predators, but the tadpoles still carried out most of their development in the water. Some species matched the transitional stages that Heyer described, laying their eggs in foam nests on and near the water. But the most important aberrant life history is known as direct development, a strategy followed by sixteen species in Crump's study area.

Direct development is nothing spectacular or bizarre if you are a lizard or snake, but it is a decidedly unfroglike way to go about making babies. Direct development means that development takes place entirely within the egg. There are no free-living tadpoles, and the baby frog that emerges from the egg is a fully formed miniature replica of its parents. Frogs that exhibit this life history typically lay only a few eggs at a time, perhaps a dozen or less, but each egg is large and is provided with an abundant yolk supply. The developing embryo must sustain itself on this parentally supplied food source, and the investment of energy a female frog must make can be considerable despite the small number of eggs.

Direct development is relatively unusual in frogs, yet it has evolved independently in several groups. Even though it is limited to a few groups, all of them tropical, one of these groups is a dominant element in the rain forest frog fauna of the New World tropics. The leptodactylid frog genus *Eleutherodactylus*, with over 400 known species, is the largest genus of vertebrates. Most of these are found in Central and South America, and a single patch of rain forest along the flanks of the Andes in Colombia or Ecuador may have as many as twenty species of *Eleutherodactylus*. The reproductive behavior of all the species has not been studied, but so far as anyone knows, all *Eleutherodactylus* undergo direct development.

Although *Eleutherodactylus* have divorced themselves completely from standing water, their eggs lack the shells and membranes that protect embryos from drying out. In order to develop, their eggs must be deposited in moist places, and the litter zone of a tropical rain forest offers such a damp haven. This part of the forest is almost always saturated with moisture, so that delicate amphibian eggs normally will not dry out. Most *Eleutherodactylus* simply lay their eggs in a damp hollow and abandon them; but some species appear to remain close by. One Puerto Rican species takes direct development to its extreme and bears living young, dispensing entirely with the egg.

Direct development is remarkable enough in a frog, yet there are tropical American frogs that take this process even further. Instead of abandoning their eggs, as most *Eleutherodactylus* are wont to do, these anurans hold onto their eggs as development proceeds.

The helmeted apparition we described earlier in this chapter is known as *Hemiphractus*. It is one of a number of marsupial frogs found in the New World tropics. The name "marsupial" is perhaps misleading because the brood pouch is located not on the underside of the female, but on her back. In some marsupial frogs the pouch is not a pouch at all, but simply a cup-shaped depression or swollen soft skin that holds the eggs in place. It is not important where the pouch is located or what shape it takes because its significance lies in its function, which is to provide a protective environment for the development of the young.

Most marsupial frogs are in the genus *Gastrotheca*, and the forty or more species exhibit a range of parental investment and care that begins where most *Eleutherodactylus* leave off. Some *Gastrotheca*, particularly those species that dwell high above the treeline in the Andes, carry the developing eggs in their pouch until the tadpoles are well advanced. They then release the large tadpoles into puddles or creeks to complete their development. Although this is not direct development, such strategy affords an important advantage to a high elevation frog. It is cold high in the Andes— a point driven home forcefully if you have shivered through a snowstorm in an Andean pass directly on the equator. Developmental processes are strongly dependent on temperature, and a continually cold environment is not conducive to rapid growth and development. This is particularly true for aquatic creatures because water does not warm as rapidly as air, and at high elevations in the tropics the water is always cold. By retaining the eggs and tadpoles in their bodies as long as possible and keeping them out of the cold water, Andean *Gastrothecas* greatly accelerate the development of their young.

Marsupial frogs also inhabit the rain forests, where they are among the most elusive of prey for the tropical frog hunter. The lowland *Gastrothecas* are often handsome beasts, large and with distinguished-looking flaps of skin over their eyes. They are a real prize to find, not because they are rare but because they rarely venture where herpetologists tread. We have spent many months at a field station in the rain forest of western Ecuador, diligently hunting for frogs almost every night. One of the species that has eluded us is a *Gastrotheca*. We hear them calling, a loud barking noise, every time we go out, but the noise always comes from the tops of the trees 100 feet above our heads. They rarely descend from their treetop abodes, for unlike most tree frogs, they do not have to meet along ponds and streams to breed.

The marsupial frogs that inhabit the lowland rain forests do their highland kin one better. Development of the eggs takes place entirely in the protective pouch of the mother. The lowland *Gastrothecas* lay fewer eggs than their Andean relatives, but each egg undoubtedly has a greater chance of hatching. The eggs are large, and the young frogs do not emerge until they are miniatures of the parents. By carrying their eggs under a flap of skin that keeps them moist, adult *Gastrothecas* do not need to leave their homes in the forest canopy. The young seem to come down from time to time. (Several friends have found them at the field station, much to our frustration. When you pride yourself on your ability as a frog hunter, it is a terrible blow to have a friend find a rarity that has eluded you.)

The brood pouches of *Gastrotheca* may qualify as parental care; it is a passive care, however, that involves no special behaviors. As long as the mother stays alive and damp, her young will survive. One does not think of frogs and toads as dutiful parents. You will never find a leopard frog tending its eggs or a cricket frog nurturing its young. The frogs and toads we are familiar with lay large numbers of eggs, which they abandon to fate after they have mated. This frees them for more personal concerns, like filling their stomachs, staying damp, and avoiding predators. By laying lots of eggs, no single one of which involves a great investment of energy and nutrients (although the total clutch investment may be high), our typical temperate zone frog accepts the high mortality rates associated with abandonment.

This is the pattern most of us are familiar with and the one we learned in introductory college biology. It should come as no surprise that this is not always the case in the rain forests of tropical America. As tropical frogs become weaned from aquatic breeding sites, their eggs tend to grow larger and fewer. They can afford to invest more into each egg because the eggs do not face the overwhelming dangers that aquatic eggs face. If they invest heavily enough, it might be advantageous for them to stick around and watch over the eggs to make sure that they survive. This post-laying behavior is parental care, and in the rain forests of the New World tropics an observant naturalist can see a remarkable range of anuran parental devotion.

Small streams deep in the interior of tropical forests are the haunts of the delicate little tree frogs of the family Centrolenidae. As many as four or five species may breed along a single creek in a lowland rain forest in Central America or northwestern South America. Most of the species in this family deposit their eggs on twigs or leaves overhanging small streams. These eggs hatch into tadpoles that fall into the water below and complete their development in the normal anuran fashion. This method of depositing eggs offers protection from the aquatic predators—the voracious fish, freshwater prawns, and aquatic beetles—that abound in even the smallest tropical streams. Although some centrolenids lose interest in their eggs once they are laid, other species keep a watchful eye on them until they hatch.

Adult centrolenids are unprepossessing creatures. Most lowland species are an inch or so long when fully grown, and their slender limbs and transparent skin imbue them with a delicacy that is hard to describe. You can clearly see the minute beating heart of some species through the skin on the chest. They lack the skin toxins that certain frogs use for defense; it seems almost ludicrous that some of these fragile creatures actually attempt to defend their eggs. Although these delicate frogs would offer little deterrent to a hungry snake or bird, snakes and birds are not the principal predators of centrolenid eggs.

Centrolenid eggs fall prey instead to a variety of small insects, ranging from small wasps to katydids to fruit flies. There are even fruit flies that appear to be specialized to feed on these eggs, and the egg clutches of centrolenids that do not tend their eggs are frequently victimized by these small ovivores. Roy McDiarmid of the U.S. Fish and Wildlife Laboratories noticed that centrolenids that guard their eggs have a characteristic dorsal pattern that closely resembles the appearance of their egg clutches, and males of these species remain near their eggs both day and night. If a small insect comes along, the male frog can either startle it away or eat it, and the eggs are protected from their most dangerous predators. Other species may stay near their eggs during the night while they are active, but retire to hidden alcoves during the day, when they cannot guard the clutch from diurnal predators.

Perhaps the ultimate in parental care in frogs is shown by members of the family Dendrobatidae, a group of about seventy-five species found only in tropical America. The parental concern that some of these frogs show is remarkable to behold. They lay small clutches of large eggs, which they deposit in damp leaf litter in the gloom of the forest floor. But unlike the direct-developing *Eleutherodactylus*, who deposit and then abandon their eggs in similar situations, dendrobatids do not have direct development. They keep a close watch on their terrestrial eggs. In some species the males tend the eggs and in other species the females stand watch. When the tadpoles hatch, the attending parent shows up and the little tadpoles squirm their way onto the parent's back. The parent then carries the tadpoles around for varying periods. Dendrobatids live on the ground in rain forest where humidity is always high, so the tadpoles don't suffer from their exposure to air as they are carried piggyback around the understory. Some dendrobatids, particularly species in the genera *Dendrobates* and *Phyllobates*, have extremely toxic skin poisons and bright warning coloration, so that predators quickly learn to avoid them. In these species, the hitchhiking tadpoles are safe from many predators even though they themselves might not have any chemical defenses.

Some dendrobatids are less solicitous of their little tadpoles than others. Species in the genus *Colostethus*, which are dull-colored and lack powerful skin toxins, are probably the most anxious to discharge their parental obligations. Their hitchhiking young are doubtless a burden that makes them more vulnerable to predation. They simply carry their charges to a convenient creek, where they abandon them with typical froglike callousness.

Some species of *Dendrobates* take their parental responsibilities more seriously. Although they are creatures of the forest floor, rarely climbing more than a few centimeters onto leaves or stumps in the course of their normal activity, *Dendrobates* are occasionally found climbing high into the rain forest canopy. These little ground-dwelling frogs make the arduous climb into the trees with their tadpoles clinging to their backs. They look for tank bromeliads—those epiphytic oases in the canopy that hold little pools of water—to provide a safe haven for their tadpoles. They deposit their precious charges in these pools and the tadpoles continue their development in a private aquarium high up in the canopy, well out of the reach of dangerous fishes.

Tank bromeliads don't hold much water and they may not be capable of supplying enough food to raise an entire clutch of *Dendrobates* tadpoles. Moreover, they are not completely safe. Giant damselflies also lay their eggs in bromeliad tanks, and their predatory naiads relish the juicy tadpoles. But *Dendrobates* has evolved a behavior that reduces the danger of losing an entire clutch to the vagaries of a strange bromeliad. Rather than dump all of her babies in one place, the patient mother makes sure that her tadpoles are scattered among different bromeliads. This could be a tricky process if she had to peer into every bromeliad axil to ensure that a tadpole hadn't already been left there, particularly since she normally backs into the little pocket. But if there is a tadpole present, it makes itself known. The sight of an approaching frog, or perhaps the trembling of the bromeliad leaf, alerts the tadpole, which begins a strange dance. Instead of swimming about in a tadpole-like manner, the *Dendrobates* tadpole aims its head toward the center of the bromeliad, holds itself rigid, and rapidly vibrates the tip of its tail. Even though the mother frog can't see the tadpole when she backs in, she can feel it. If a tadpole is already there, she will move on to another. By making sure that she doesn't place all of her eggs in one basket she further ensures the ultimate success of her costly investment.

But the truly remarkable thing about *Dendrobates* is that the parental obligations do not end here, at least in some species. After a female *Dendrobates* has carefully deposited her charges, no more than one to each axil in a bromeliad, she does not abandon the tadpoles to their fate. She returns to the world of the forest floor where she feeds and does other froglike things, but periodically she interrupts her daily routine to make the long climb back up to the bromeliads where she left her tadpoles. Once again she backs into the bromeliad, only this time, if she feels the tadpole's tattling tail tip, she does not scamper out. Instead, she deposits several eggs. She is not trying to crowd out her offspring, for these eggs are not fertile: the nutrient-rich bags of protein are food for her tadpoles, which will depend on these nutritive eggs to augment the scarce food supply of the isolated bromeliad tanks. Experiments with captive animals show that the tadpoles will die if they do not get an egg supplement, and people who have raised them successfully often feed the tadpoles little pieces of chopped-up chicken egg.

This careful tending of young is not the sort of behavior most people expect of "lower" animals. Scientists, of course, are careful not to anthropomorphize and attempt to explain such complex behaviors in terms of parental investment, survivorship, and natural selection. But it is hard not to admire, however secretly, the apparent willfulness of a little frog who goes to so much effort to raise her young.

Chapter *15*

NIGHT WALKS

> *It got darker. I thought; and thought in my mind moved with a kind of sluggish stealthiness, as if it was being watched by bitter and sadistic eyes. . . . I thought of a man with bright blond hair who was afraid and didn't quite know what he was afraid of, who was sensitive enough to know that something was wrong, and too vain or too dull to guess what it was that was wrong.*
> —RAYMOND CHANDLER
> Farewell, My Lovely

The streets of a large America city and the interior of a tropical rain forest might seem to have little in common, even though both are regarded as jungles in the eyes of many. Yet they share at least one common denominator: an ability to induce vague unease, if not outright fear, in the souls of those who venture out alone after dark. Whether these feelings are justified or not matters little; few are those who can step out alone for a walk in either habitat without feeling edgy about what might be lurking in the darkness.

Although the risks may be exaggerated, dangerous creatures do inhabit these places, and tension, which puts a fine edge on your senses and makes you more aware of your environment, can be highly adaptive. Even the most urbanized and ecologically un-sophisticated soul feels a sense of trepidation when he or she ventures into the bowels of New York late at night. The hollow click of leather heels on concrete, an innocuous sound that goes unnoticed during the day, will send shivers of fear down your spine if you hear it late at night in a dim, empty New York City subway station. These brief interludes of heightened perception give the citybound naturalist profound insight into the souls of wild animals, who face similar dangers all the time and must pay constant heed to subtle cues from their environment.

I have never been embarrassed to admit that similar feelings seep into my consciousness whenever I set foot into tropical rain forest at night. The night forest is an alien place for creatures as. tied to the light as we are, and I can never get over the feeling that we humans simply don't belong there. But for a naturalist interested in the mysteries of tropical rain forest, the heightened perceptions so unwittingly gained have a beneficial effect. This slight apprehension, this tingle of residual fear about things that go bump in the night, forces our senses to focus more sharply. Scents, sounds, and obscure shapes that we would never notice during the day become the objects of careful scrutiny after dark. These heightened sensitivities and focused perceptions open up new worlds for the tropical naturalist.

A walk through tropical rain forest at night is an experience to savor, a sensual journey that shouldn't be rushed. There is much to see and hear, and if you walk too quickly much will be missed. The interior of a tropical forest is almost always still. In the blackness of night it takes on an existence of its own, charged with mystery and pulsing with the beat of unseen life. Standing in the middle of tropical rain forest on a moonless night without a flashlight on is an experience that is undeniably organic, but it always makes me feel a bit claustrophobic after a few minutes. This feeling subsides once I switch my lamps on, but it never disappears entirely. Although I know that the chances of anything untoward happening to me are slim, there is a residual unease that thousands of hours spent in the blackness of the rain forest night have failed to completely dispel.

You mustn't become so absorbed in what you see that you become disoriented. The understory of mature rain forest is open enough and the trails are faint enough so that it can easily develop into a bewildering maze at night. Trees look much the same near ground level after dark and there are few landmarks to use as guides. Creeks may be scarce, particularly if the forest is on level ground, and they may meander so much that they are almost impossible to follow. None of these problems poses any serious dangers, and a little care normally prevents any unpleasant situations. But if you find yourself in unfamiliar territory and the trails are difficult to follow, you might want to rely on the old Amahuaca trick of breaking an understory plant at waist level every twenty paces or so.

Naturalists accustomed to the swarms of night-flying mosquitoes in North America are apprehensive about night walks in tropical rain forest. Surprisingly enough, it is rare to encounter hordes of mosquitoes. Now and then one may whine by your ears and attempt to probe through your shirt, but rarely will you find the clouds of mosquitoes in rain forest that you regularly encounter on evening walks in the Rockies or suburban New England. Awesome swarms of these beasts are not entirely absent from the tropics, but these masses of bloodthirsty insects are normally found in seasonally flooded rain forest or in deciduous tropical forest. Mature upland rain forest offers them few havens; permanent water is inhabited by schools of larvae-eating insects and fish, and uninhabited puddles and temporary pools are relatively scarce. Since there is often a scarcity of mammalian prey for adult mosquitoes and most feed on only one type of blood (reptile, bird, or mammal), this might limit the number of mosquitoes that would otherwise torment human intruders. We have found that mosquitoes are most abundant in areas near human habitation, but it is difficult to tell whether this is due to greater food availability or more breeding sites. In any case, temperate zone naturalists are often pleasantly surprised by the low numbers of noxious insects in some tropical American rain forests.

A night walk through the rain forest offers many surprises. The sudden explosion of branches overhead can startle even the calmest naturalist, and the eerie mewings that often accompany these noises send chills up the spine of the uninitiated. When the torch beam is directed up into the canopy, pairs of bright orange coals pierce the blackness, staring down unblinkingly at the intruders below. Despite their horrific appearance, these seemingly disembodied eyes are attached to a relatively innocuous beast, the honey bear or kinkajou. These tropical relatives of the raccoon rarely venture to the ground; the strange glow of their eyes does not emanate from within, but is merely the reflection of the light from your forehead.

Unearthly balls of fire turn up in other places in the forest night. In the rain forest of the upper Amazon basin in eastern Ecuador lies a peculiar lake whose waters are soupy green with nutrients. This lake has a high fish population and on these fish lives one of the largest predatory animals in the New World tropics, the black caiman. By day these great alligator-like beasts lie far back in the weeds and tangle that line the shore of the lake. You search for them at night, when they leave their sanctuaries to cruise the open lake, their golfball-sized eyes glowing brilliant orange in the light of a powerful searchlight. In most of the Amazon the black caiman has been hunted almost to extinction; but in this lake, far up one of the Amazon's tributaries where hide hunters probably never thought to search, there still remains a large population. Everywhere we looked one night their shining eyes stared back at us, and we were grateful for the substantial metal boat we were cruising about in.

Many nocturnal creatures possess a reflective layer in the eye that allows them to take full advantage of what little light there is. In vertebrates this reflective coating is called the tapetum, and it lies just behind the retina. Whatever light enters the eye hits the visual sensors in the retina twice, once as it passes through them and again when it is reflected off the tapetum. These reflective layers are tiny tinted mirrors, and if you wear a bright lamp on your forehead they throw the light directly back into your eyes. If you hold a flashlight in your hand while you scan the canopy, these glowing eyes will not be nearly so apparent because the angle of reflection from the little mirrors is narrow and the brightest glow will be seen if the light is held right along your line of vision. An experienced tropical naturalist can often identify an animal instantly on the basis of its eyeshine alone. Color, size, and position are the keys to such quick field identifications. Many spiders have green or blue shines, while those of vertebrates are usually orange or red. But sometimes there are surprises.

Not long after seeing the black caimans, I was poking along a small, clear river in the forest near Puyo in Ecuador on a warm, drizzly night. I was looking for centrolenid frogs, those delicate little beasts that call from the leaves that cover small streams.

My lamp was turned upward as I worked my way downstream along the riverbed. I reached a point where the creek deepened and slowed, and the quiet babble of shallow moving water was replaced by the sounds of my shuffling through waist-deep water. I looked down to see if the water was getting any deeper, and there not 3 feet in front of me, glowing out of a deep pool, was a pair of bright orange eyes. There was no place to run, and I couldn't move quickly in any case because I was waist-deep in the stream. As I sloshed my way quickly ashore, I kept imagining the rip of sharp teeth in my all too tender legs. There was no reason to be afraid—the only caiman likely to be in such a small creek was one of the dwarf species of *Paleosuchus*—but fear is hard to reason with. When I looked back into the pool after reaching the safety of land, I discovered, much to my chagrin and relief, that the glowing eyes were not those of a caiman but a large, succulent freshwater prawn of the genus *Macrobrachium*.

Some animals of the night have dispensed almost entirely with vision as a means of orientation and feeding. Creatures that hunt by night depend on a variety of sensory channels, most of which we can only dimly appreciate. Since much of our contact with other species is visual and we depend heavily on sound for communication with other members of our species, these are the senses we are most familiar with and that we most dread losing. Our reliance on these two major channels of contact with the world around us is the heritage of our primate ancestry; in this respect, we stand apart from most other mammals. Most living species of primates are diurnal, and it is safe to assume that we have evolved from a long line of day-active creatures. But the majority of living mammals are active chiefly at night, and in this environment sight is not the most useful of senses.

Sound is an important part of the tropical night. It is one of the first things you become aware of once it is dark. But contrary to the expectations of those people whose impressions of rain forest were formed by Tarzan movies, the sounds of the tropical night are not constant. Rarely do you encounter huge choruses of frogs in tropical rain forest. The dense breeding aggregations of frogs and toads responsible for deafening choruses are characteristic of dryer habitats in the tropics. The frogs of the wet forest are more subtle; their aggregations are often small, and they may not wish to call as much attention to their presence as their temperate zone cousins do because of the wealth of predators that prowl the forest night.

A. Stanley Rand of the Smithsonian Tropical Research Institute in Panama has been studying the vocalizations of a common Central American frog, *Physalaemus pustulosus*, for many years. Male *Physalaemus* have a varied repertoire of songs, consisting of combinations of whines and chucking noises. Rand and his co-workers discovered that the chucking noises were preferred by cruising females, but that males do not necessarily produce the sounds the females want to hear when it comes time to mate. Ardent male *Physalaemus* sing a simple plaintive whining song when they advertise for mates; and they resort to the more complex and desirable calls when another male comes on the scene. The chucking noises that the females preferred were used mostly for territorial displays with other males, forcing the females to settle for the second-best song. This might seem strange, because the logic of natural selection should favor males singing the songs females most wanted to hear. This would no doubt be the case if ripe female *Physalaemus* were the only creatures attracted by the chucking of lovestruck males. Herpetologists, for example, often track their prey by tracing the calls of unseen frogs, and it is no accident that a disproportionate number of male frogs find their way into museum collections. But there are natural predators as well who cue in on these sounds.

Merlin Tuttle of the Milwaukee Public Museum and Michael Ryan of the Smithsonian Tropical Research Institute recently discovered a nocturnal predator that locates its anuran prey just like a diligent herpetologist. In the forests of Central America lives a bat, *Trachops cirrhosus*, who listens for the song of *Physalaemus* and sweeps in on the preoccupied male as he sings for a mate. The male frogs, as is so often the case, are faced with a profound evolutionary choice: the songs most attractive to a ripe female are the songs most likely to attract a hungry bat. So the males have struck a balance between reproductive fitness and simple survival.

The sonar senses of bats are well known to most people, but those of us who live outside the tropics have incomplete notions of bats' other characteristics. We have such a small and conservative selection here in North America. Aside from two nectar- and pollen-eating species that barely enter the extreme southwestern United States, all of our bats fit a stereotype, being small, nocturnal, and feeding primarily on insects. It is in the tropics that bats reach their fullest flower, and in the tropics of the New World many bats do not behave in what most temperate zone naturalists would consider a batlike manner.

Neotropical forest bats are primarily nocturnal, but aside from this they are a remarkably diverse group of animals. This diversity is best seen in the range of feeding specializations they exhibit. Although most tropical bats are like their temperate cousins, feeding chiefly on insects caught on the wing, some have more unusual dietary requirements. There are many species of nectar-feeding bats—enough so that numerous forest trees have become specialized for bat pollination—and there are a number of meat-eating specialists. In addition to the frog-loving *Trachops*, the giant predatory *Vampyrum* feeds on sleeping birds and lizards, and bats of the genus *Noctilio* feed on fish that they scoop up from the surface of placid pools. But most unusual of all are those species that feed on blood.

There are vampires in the New World tropics. They emerge at night from dark corners and flutter through the forest searching for a victim. Crucifixes have no effect on them, but they rarely constitute much of a threat to human populations; sound window screens or tough mosquito netting will supply enough protection. Their effect on livestock, however, can be severe, and in many places in Central and South America they are serious pests.

There are several species of vampires, all small bats of the genus *Desmodus*. They are not as crude as their counterparts on the movie screen, nor are they as cruel and indiscriminate in their effect as the real Count Dracula. They are stealthy creatures, depending on a quiet approach and delicate incision to accomplish their mission. The front teeth of *Desmodus* have evolved into efficient slicing tools, capable of effortlessly slicing off a thin layer of skin. Their saliva contains a variety of anticoagulants, and as they perch gently on their sleeping victim, the blood flows freely from the shallow cut. The bats lap away at the stream, and when they have had their fill, they fly away, leaving behind their characteristic bloody signs. Their approach and attack must be gentle lest the sleeping victim should awaken and shake them loose.

There is little doubt that the most feared creatures in the tropical rain forest are snakes. The fear that most visitors show is equaled, if not exceeded, by locals, but we believe the danger is greatly exaggerated. It is true that many species of venomous snakes inhabit the rain forests of the New World tropics. Night is a good time for seeing snakes in the tropics, yet venomous snakes comprise a relatively small percentage of both individuals and species of tropical snakes, and snakes of any kind are not often encountered in rain forest. Much of our time in the lowland tropics has been spent searching for these reptiles, and even with diligent effort I rarely find more than one or two a day. The discovery of a bushmaster or coral snake is cause for surprise, not because they pose a serious danger to normal field work but because they are animals of great scracity and sinister beauty.

One group of venomous New World snakes possesses a remarkable adaptation for hunting at night. The long forked tongue that all snakes have is a marvelous device that allows them to taste their environment. Most diurnal snakes have good vision, and they use their sensitive chemical detection system primarily to guide their love lives. In nocturnal snakes, this sensory channel can become important for detecting prey that can't be seen. But such a system has disadvantages. If the prey moves quickly, a predator that depends on chemical cues may not be able to keep up with it. There is an inherent time lag in processing information along this channel because chemical cues linger and are not well suited for determining the exact position of moving prey. The pit vipers —a group of venomous snakes that inhabits Asia and the New World—have a special sensory organ in a pit between their eyes and nose that is sensitive to infrared radiation. These snakes can use long-lasting chemical cues to track their food, and once they draw close, they can detect their warm-blooded prey's exact location by the heat of its body, enabling them to strike at the prey and kill it.

North Americans are familiar with pit vipers because several species are widespread across the United States and southern Canada. These are the rattlesnakes, water moccasins, and copperheads. Only the rattlesnake gets into the tropics of Central and South America, and there it tends to dwell in dry habitats. The rain forests are inhabited by a host of tropical pit vipers, ranging from small tree-dwelling species to the massive bushmaster.

Several years ago, a group of volunteer field assistants from Earthwatch was assisting me with ecological studies of amphibians and reptiles in the Ecuadorian rain forest, research which involved a considerable amount of night work. My volunteers did not relish the night sessions at first because they were worried about the snakes. A surprising number of people interested in natural history are afraid of these limbless reptiles, and I even know a herpetologist or two who are frozen into rigid immobility at the sight of one. It usually takes some coaxing for me to lure nonbiologists out after dark, and part of this coaxing involves a long discussion on the rarity of venomous snakes, punctuated by repeated assurances that the chances of running across one are virtually nonexistent. I tell them that many experienced tropical herpetologists have yet to see their first bushmaster, and this seems to ease whatever doubts remain. But the key word here is "virtually," and the real world is made up of such improbable events.

My team saw only a few snakes during the first nights of field work, all of them nonvenomous, and my assistants soon relaxed, evincing great enthusiasm for the tropical nights. By the last night of work they had seen enough snakes so that fear had been replaced by curiosity, so I was not altogether surprised when I heard one of the volunteers announce that she had found a big snake coiled up in a corner of the study area. I walked over, but just a few feet from the snake I stopped dead in my tracks. The snake was a bushmaster, the largest venomous snake in the New World, and the specimen coiled in front of me was easily eight feet long. It was a magnificent creature, its arm-thick coils a burnished copper with dark brown markings. After taking some photographs of the beast, I casually told the group what it was and then got set to resume our sampling of the study plot. I still like to believe that my volunteers refused to complete the last night of sampling because they were so struck with awe by their rare find that anything else would have been anticlimactic.

Although many rain forest snakes are active at night, the night-walking naturalist is less likely to tread on one accidentally than someone who roams during the day. The narrow beam of light emanating from the headlamp mounted on your forehead will force you to concentrate intently on the small illuminated part of the forest. Each leaf must be carefully examined, each glint of distant reflection investigated. The somber shades of brown and green, the dappling of sunlight and shadow, the generally confusing riot of shapes and patterns that dominate the forest by day are reduced to an inky backdrop at night. Creatures that hide effectively by day as they sleep in the visual confusion of the forest go about their business at night, where they are often revealed against conspicuously incongruous backgrounds in the harsh light of the torch.

The dead-leaf katydids and walking sticks that sit still by day, blending into the melange of leaves and twigs, become a conspicuous feature of the nighttime rain forest menagerie. They meander through the foliage, feeding boldly on green leaves, free from the piercing acuity of avian eyes. They must also feel the freedom offered by the damp cloak of darkness. The air of the rain forest floor is at its coolest and dampest at night. Both walking sticks, with their peculiar pencil-like bodies, and dead-leaf katydids, with their compressed, leaflike bodies, have high surface-to-volume ratios and are especially vulnerable to desiccation when they molt. Insects have a layer of integument that protects them from drying out, but growing insects must shed this rigid sheath as their bodies expand. A new layer forms below the old, and eventually the hard outer layer splits open and the insect crawls out of its tight old skin. The new skin takes several hours to harden and become impervious to water loss; during this period of hardening the insect loses its protective coloration and is vulnerable to predation. It is also subject to desiccation, and most walking sticks and katydids therefore molt at night, when visual predators are few and the air is at its dampest.

There are many groups of animals that are active by day but have relatives that are active at night. A familiar example are the butterflies and moths. There are also many insect groups that are exclusively diurnal except in the warm, wet rain forests. Social wasps are typically active only during the day, but hornets of the genus *Apoica* roam the rain forest night in search of insect prey. Many groups of nocturnal ants replace their diurnal relatives once the sun has set. Time is a resource that can be divided by potentially competing species, and the day is sliced up and shared by species that are dominant at different hours. But since many biologists cease their investigations after the supper hour, remarkably little is known of how rain forest animals carve up the nighttime hours. When I studied the activity of the dung-eating scarab beetles, I found that different genera had peaks of activity at different times, both through the day and through the night. In these beetles, night activity is far greater than day activity, and this seems to be true for many other animal groups. It may well be that the world of the night in tropical rain forest is as rich in wide-awake species as is the world of the day. It is only our own species' ingrained activity cycle that keeps us from documenting the evidence more fully.

This is a world we find endlessly fascinating. It is a place so alien to creatures of the day like ourselves that it never becomes familiar and comfortable, no matter how much time we spend there. It is not the darkness alone that causes our unease. We never feel the same way at night in most temperate zone habitats, where the dangers are few and well understood. Our constant slight discomfort, stirred by a residual fear over which we have no control, makes us feel closer to the creatures that must live out their entire lives there.

Chapter 16

THE ETERNAL TROPICS

The top of Mount Everest is marine sandstone.
—JOHN MCPHEE
Basin and Range

As we have repeatedly emphasized, there is no terrestrial habitat on earth that compares with lowland tropical rain forest in its richness of life. Most temperate zone habitats have certain species of plants and animals that are common and distinctive and that give each habitat a recognizable integrity. Such is not the case in the lowland tropical rain forest. Virtually every tree you walk by will be different—they may look alike near the ground, but they are distinct species—and high up in these trees you will see a huge variety of vines and epiphytes. As you begin to notice the animals, you will soon realize that almost everything you see is different. This, more than any iconic indicator species, characterizes the tropical rain forest environment. It is one of the ironies of tropical rain forest that common species are rare and rare species are common.

What is responsible for this great diversity of life? How can such a great number of species coexist in a small patch of forest? Even in the most fecund habitat, resources are limited. One of the central dogmas of modern ecological theory is that species can coexist in a state of equilibrium only if they use different sets of resources. If species overlap too much in their use of resources, competition will cause some to flourish and others to suffer extinction. If a tropical rain forest contains ten times as many species as a temperate woodland, either tropical rain forests have a wider resource base, and are thus capable of holding more species, or the species that inhabit tropical rain forests are more specialized ecologically, allowing them to divide resources ever more finely. These explanations are not mutually exclusive, and they may act in concert to allow a large number of competing species to live together in apparent harmony.

On an ecological time scale, the tropical rain forest is often said to be a predictable and stable environment, and ecologists have long pointed out that stability makes it possible for species to specialize on an ever narrower set of resources. Different species of seed-eating bruchid beetles in the tropical rain forest may each feed exclusively on the seeds of a single species of tree. Such narrow specialization is rarely seen in the temperate zones, but it may be common in certain types of tropical rain forest organisms. Such narrow specialization has reinforced the notion of the tropical rain forest as a stable and predictable environment. This stereotype of the ancient, unchanging tropics is reinforced by accounts of the tropics that stress the tedious monotony of its climate, the lack of our familiar seasons, the unvarying daylength through the year, and the perpetual warmth and humidity. But this leaves us with a perplexing paradox. Long-term stability may help explain the maintenance of tropical diversity; yet it does so by ignoring the evolutionary origins of the diversity.

Consider how new species are thought to originate. When most people think of the origin of new species, they think of Charles Darwin, but despite the title of his most famous work, Darwin never really addressed the question of how so many different species came into being. The concept of natural selection that he and Alfred Russel Wallace originated calls on the differential reproductive success of variable individuals within a population to explain how an evolutionary lineage can change through time.

As these lineages change, new species may indeed appear, but such new species emerge from the ashes of the old, one at a time. Natural selection alone does not explain how so many different species came to be. Acceptance of a general explanation for the multiplication of new species came many years after Darwin and Wallace. Although there is still considerable controversy about the exact mechanisms that create a multiplication of species, one model is generally accepted as being the most important. This is a process known as geographic, or allopatric, speciation. Surprisingly, the concept of geographic speciation was first laid out by Leopold von Buch in 1825, more than a quarter of a century before the publication of the *Origin of Species*.

Geographic speciation is a fairly straightforward mechanism. Populations become geographically separated from one another so that there is no longer any direct genetic connection among individuals in the isolated populations. Isolation can come about in many ways: a species may colonize a remote island; a large island may partially sink, creating an archipelago that strands populations on each island; mountain ranges may come up, separating lowland species on either side; or rivers may change course, separating populations on either bank. Through time these geographically isolated populations may change and diverge, perhaps in response to natural selection molding adaptations to local environmental changes, or perhaps simply as a result of random, nonadaptive genetic drift.

If these isolated populations should come back into contact, several things can take place. If divergence among the isolated populations has been minimal, they will reestablish the common breeding pool that existed before isolation. They may retain some of their adaptations to local ecological conditions or some of their randomly evolved characteristics, but these characters will grade gradually into one another across a wide zone of contact. If divergence in isolation has proceeded further when contact is reestablished, the populations may retain their separate genetic identities. There may be some mixing along a narrow zone where they come into contact, or they may come into direct contact with no signs of interbreeding.

When divergent populations reach the point where they can no longer interbreed, they are said to be reproductively isolated and are considered to be distinct species. When these species come into contact, one may prove competitively superior to the other and gradually erode its range, perhaps to the point of extinction. If the competitive abilities of each species depend on special adaptations they have made to certain ecological conditions, each may occupy exclusive geographic ranges with little or no overlap. If the new species have diverged ecologically as well as genetically, they may be able to coexist, and the ranges may overlap broadly while the species maintain their genetic integrity.

There is no single moment when you can say isolated populations have become new species. Speciation is a process that can be studied at any point, and often it will not be possible to determine which populations are distinct species and which are not, particularly if they remain isolated from one another. There is no way you can make rigid definitions along a continuum; but this does not mean that reproductively isolated species are hazy abstractions existing only in the minds of evolutionary biologists. Species exist as discrete, discontinuous units in the natural world if you are a naturalist studying a given place at a given time. The 500 species of birds that may inhabit a patch of Peruvian rain forest are each independent evolutionary lines, with their own histories, ecologies, and behaviors. With exceedingly rare exceptions, they breed only among themselves, and they are discrete natural units in any sense you care to examine them. The problems in any definition of a species arise when we examine populations spread out over time and space.

Biologists will be quick to point out that there are many unresolved questions regarding the exact processes that underlie geographic speciation, and some biologists insist that there are other important ways in which new species can arise. Botanists in particular find fault with certain aspects of geographic speciation, because new species of plants can arise in ways that are, for the most part, denied to animals. Despite the continuing controversy about the relative importance of geographic speciation, few biologists would deny that this model is an important one, and most would agree that it is the single most important mode by which new species evolve.

The contradiction between the idea of ancient, unchanging tropical rain forests and the basic tenet of geographical speciation, isolation, should be apparent. If the tropical rain forest is so stable, how did all of its species originate? The uplift of mountains, the rise and fall of the Central American isthmus, and shifting river channels could account for some isolation. But such events could not explain many of the distribution patterns observed in tropical plants and animals, nor could they account for the huge numbers of species. How could there be enough geographical isolation to account for the wealth of species in this diverse habitat?

Naturalists have long been aware of the significance of climatic change in the evolution of temperate zone plants and animals. Pleistocene cycles of glaciation, for example, have had an obvious and wide-ranging impact on the flora and fauna of North America and Europe. The advances of the glaciers have helped isolate many populations, and when these glaciers retreated, isolated populations could reestablish contact. Everyone assumed that these cycles of glaciation affected only the temperate zones, but this narrow viewpoint has since been shown to be incorrect.

The hard evidence for climatic shifts in the tropics has come from pollen samples. Pollen is produced with lavish excess by many plants, particularly those that are wind-pollinated. Much of it finds its way into streams, which carry the pollen away and eventually deposit the grains at the bottom of lakes and ponds. Pollen is durable and easily fossilized; as it accumulates on the bottom of lakes, it forms a record of some of the dominant plants in the surrounding region. Paleobotanists can identify the plants that fossil pollen came from, and by making inferences with living species, they can determine whether the fossil pollen is from a plant characteristic of a hot, dry climate or a cool, wet climate. By comparing the proportions of different pollen types in a sample of fossil, they can make deductions about past climates. Since pollen accumulates on lakebeds, a core sample that cuts through the accumulation provides a chronological window into past climates.

Core samples taken from lakes in different regions of tropical America have demonstrated regular cycles of climatic change even deep within the tropics, cycles that seem to correlate with Pleistocene glacial cycles in the temperate zones. During the periods when the glaciers advanced across North America, the tropics became cooler and drier; although the tropical characteristics of uniformity of temperature and daylength remained unchanged, the average temperatures dropped. When the northern glaciers retreated, it was warmer and wetter in the tropics.

The climatic changes coinciding with Pleistocene glaciation were subtle in the tropics, and great sheets of ice never bisected the Amazon rain forest, yet they seem to have had a major impact on tropical rain forest plants and animals. Minor shifts in temperature and rainfall can have a major effect on plants and animals unaccustomed to variable environments: a slight reduction in average annual rainfall or a slight change in the seasonality of this rainfall can have profound effects on rain forest vegetation. The forest itself buffers some variation in average rainfall. The canopy keeps the air near the ground relatively cool, and the temperature difference between cool air near the ground and warm, moisture-laden air higher up promotes rainfall. The trees also protect the understory vegetation, and most of the animals who live near the ground, from water stress. Without tree cover, the ground heats up from the intense tropical sun, and warm, moisture-laden air flowing over warmer, drier air will not release rain. As the large trees that provide cover die, the forest might not be able to regenerate itself if the overall climate has become cooler and drier.

During the cool, dry periods of the Pleistocene, while glaciers moved down North America and Europe, several things happened in the American tropics. Tropical mountains became effectively higher. This was not due to any rapid uplifting of the mountain masses, but to the cooling of the climate, which shifted vegetation formations to lower elevations. Cloud forest and páramo were lower and more continuous than they are today and therefore less isolated than they are now. In the tropical lowlands the situation was reversed; the drier climates that prevailed during the cool periods resulted in the contraction of lowland rain forest. Instead of vast, unbroken expanses of forest, there were remnant patches confined to areas where the rainfall remained high enough to support them. These isolated patches acted as refuges for rain forest–adapted plants and animals, and within these enclaves divergence could have taken place. When the climate changed to a warm, wet phase, the montane habitats shifted upward: the páramos and cloud forest were broken up and isolated, and the lowland rain forests again became continuous tracts. Populations confined to the páramos could then have diverged in isolation, while the plants and animals in lowland rain forest came back into contact. These alternating cycles of cool, dry climates and warm, wet climates occurred several times during the Pleistocene.

The isolated patches of forest left during the dry periods were probably confined to the same general regions during each period —places that today share certain significant features. Most of these supposed refuges are clustered near upland regions, which tend to have higher rainfall because of the cooling effect of air rising over tropical mountains. These refuges match up surprisingly well with what are now the wettest sections of tropical rain forest. Moreover, the locations of many of the refuges correspond remarkably well with the distribution of certain plants and animals. Some of these regions have been called centers of endemism because so many distinctive plant and animal species are restricted to them. Moreover, if you look at the distribution of closely related species, you will often find that they do not overlap in distribution. Each species in these groups of closely related species has an exclusive range, and these ranges often coincide neatly with the centers of endemism and the supposed Pleistocene refuges.

The refuge theory of tropical diversification was first developed by R. E. Moreau, a British ornithologist interested in the distribution of African birds. He realized that the cycles of climatic change just beginning to be recognized by African geographers and geologists could have important effects on the evolution of birds restricted to specific habitats. Contraction of these habitats could isolate populations, and this isolation could provide the basis for geographic speciation. Jurgen Haffer, a petroleum geologist with a passion for ornithology, soon thereafter found evidence for similar climatic fluctuations in tropical America, and realized that the refuge model explained some of the peculiar distributions of Amazonian rain forest birds. At about the same time, Paulo Vanzolini and Ernest Williams came to the same general conclusions using a different type of evidence. Rather than examining the distribution patterns of many different species, they studied a single species of Amazonian forest lizard. This lizard showed signs of having diverged within isolated forest refuges, although the speciation process had not proceeded to the point where distinct species had evolved. Nonetheless, the resulting pattern of divergence corresponded well with a theory of forest refuges.

The refuge theory has rapidly gained adherents among biologists who study specific groups of plants and animals in the New World tropics, but it is still not completely accepted by the biologistic community as a whole. Some critics argue that the periods of isolation, which were on the order of tens of thousands of years, were not long enough to allow speciation to take place. The emphasis on Pleistocene events, which accounts for less than 2 million years of our most recent history, ignores much of the diversity we see in the New World tropics. Sophisticated biochemical and immunological studies have suggested that many very closely related species diverged more than 3 or 4 million years ago, long before the postulated Pleistocene cycles took place. Other critics have argued that the refuge theory of diversification does not explain the true extent of tropical diversity. Pleistocene cycles of forest contraction and expansion may explain the distribution of certain species, but they cannot account for the immense number of species that can be found in any patch of tropical rain forest. Another problem with the refuge theory is that some of the distribution patterns used as evidence supporting the theory have alternative explanations, causes that seem to make sense in light of modern ecological conditions.

These criticisms all have some validity, and it's doubtful whether Pleistocene refuges can explain most of the diversity of tropical rain forest biotas. But despite the criticisms, the refuge theory is an elegant way of explaining how an apparently stable habitat can be broken up to provide the geographical isolation needed for new species to originate. Long-term habitat stability, which helps promote ecological fine-tuning and increased specialization, and the disruption and isolation so important for generating new species, are not mutually exclusive conditions because the habitat can remain more or less unchanged while its boundaries shift with changes in climate.

The theory of Pleistocene forest refuges has stimulated interest in the dynamics of evolution in the tropics, and for this reason alone its development has been of inestimable significance. Even if the periods of isolation during the past few million years cannot account for the great diversity of tropical life, the recognition of these cycles of contraction and expansion has effectively destroyed the old image of the unchanging tropics. The dynamics of evolution in the tropical rain forest are no less significant than those in the temperate regions, and these rich tropical habitats can no longer be regarded as evolutionary backwaters where old and archaic forms of life persist simply because life is easy. Disturbance and change have played a significant role in the evolution of tropical diversity, just as they have in our harsher latitudes; the multitude of species that we find in tropical rain forest are eloquent testimony to these cycles of change. The diversity of life in the rain forests of the New World tropics bespeaks the intricacies and complexities that evolution has created on a constantly changing planet.

Chapter _17_

PARADISE LOST?

> *It is really deplorable that in so many of our*
> *tropical dependencies no attempt has been made*
> *to preserve for posterity any* adequate *portions of*
> *the native vegetation, especially*
> *of the virgin forests.*
> —ALFRED RUSSEL WALLACE
> The World of Life (*1911*)

In February of 1541, after serving with Pizarro in the conquest of
the Inca empire, a group of Spaniards led by Francisco de Orellana
left the city of Quito and went east, looking for new kingdoms to
conquer. They crossed the Paso de Guamani, a bleak Andean moor
distinguished chiefly by its constant cloud cover and cold, driving
rains, and from there they plunged down rugged slopes draped
with the mossy tangle of cloud forest vegetation. After ten months
of wandering in this dripping wilderness, Orellana and his men
had descended over 13,000 feet in elevation, but they were a
scant 100 miles east of Quito. When they emerged from the mist-
shrouded foothills of the Andes, they became the first Europeans
to enter the vast lowland rain forest of the Amazon basin. From
the junction of the Rios Coca and Napo near the base of the

Andes, the forest stretched unbroken save for scattered patches of natural savannah for over 2,000 miles to the Atlantic Ocean.

There are places in the American tropics where you can still imagine yourself in the shoes of the conquistadors, seeing places untouched by Western civilization. When I stood in the swirling mists of waterfalls deep in the cloud forest along Orellana's route, watching brilliant orange Andean Cocks-of-the-Rock cavorting in the dense canopy, or when I walked these same forests at night, plucking new species of frogs and lizards from the moss-cloaked vegetation that lines the streams, I found it easy to imagine that I was in the middle of uncharted wilderness. Such illusions were quickly shattered when I realized that the deep throb reverberating through the night was not the rumbling of the volcano Reventador, but the whine of pumps that push Amazonian oil up the trans-Andean pipeline. Civilization has come to these wild slopes, and even the great forests of the Amazon basin are no longer immune from the pulse of modern life.

People have lived in the lowland rain forests of the New World tropics for a long time, well over 10,000 years by even the most conservative estimates; but the destruction of rain forest habitats has accelerated tremendously in the past two decades. The tropical rain forests of Central and South America were the home of numbers of people prior to European colonization. Many parts of the Amazon basin were heavily settled when Orellana first traversed the region, and the three great civilizations of the New World tropics were dependent on the products of tropical forests. Although civilizations on a par with the Aztec, Mayan, or Incan never developed in the Amazon forest, the forest people had thriving cultures in parts of the Amazon basin, building their homes and villages on high banks and cultivating the rich bottomlands. For some reason, the Ecuadorian stretch of the Rio Napo was uninhabited when Orellana saw it, although its tributary, the Rio Aguarico, and the lower reaches of the Rio Napo in Peru, were inhabited. At some point, Quechua-speaking Indians settled along the banks of the Napo, carrying on subsistence agriculture, while more nomadic tribes hunted the deep forest.

Western culture eventually found its way into this remote section of the upper Amazon. The rubber boom touched the region; the Ecuadorian armed forces patrolled the Rio Napo; and a variety of naturalists, explorers, and missionaries paid visits of varying length. The region remained largely free of traditional colonization because of the prodigious difficulties of getting supplies and products in and out. The Andes effectively isolated it from the mainstream of Ecuadorian life (it was no simple matter to lead a mule train up Orellana's old route) and the long-standing enmity between Ecuadorians and Peruvians reduced the flow of traffic along the great rivers.

The pattern of life in this part of the world changed quickly with the opening of the oil fields at Lago Agrio in the 1960s. A pipeline was built to carry the oil from the wells over the Andes to the Pacific coast, and an all-weather road was built to service this pipeline. Large numbers of workers were recruited to build the road, the pipeline, and the wells, and with these workers came their families and people to service their needs. Although the oil development itself did not lead to extensive alteration of the rain forest habitat, the people who followed the newly opened roads caused drastic changes in the landscape. The forest was cut and cleared, farms and pastures sprouting up almost overnight. The road provided ready access to markets, and land that was once too difficult to settle became suddenly desirable.

The symbol of modern deforestation is the road. The roads that penetrate the lowland rain forests of tropical America don't resemble North American highways, despite their often grandiose names. The difficulties of building and maintaining roads in regions that receive 100 inches or more of rain each year are prodigious, and even the most well-traveled routes may be little more than a broad, muddy swath through the trees.

The paved highways that you can find in some rain forest regions are hardly any better. While waiting for buses on a paved stretch of the Panamerican Highway in western Ecuador, we used to watch with amusement the meanderings and weavings of vehicles as they dodged the potholes and cracks that littered the asphalt. From a distance it looked as though all the drivers were drunk as the vehicles crisscrossed the roadway from one shoulder to the other. The roads that lead in and through the tropical forests are far more than a way of getting from one place to another. They offer avenues of access, ways of getting goods to market and people to production, that in turn provide a new frontier for human populations growing at an exceedingly rapid rate. Sometimes roads are built specifically to encourage colonization, as in the ill-fated Trans-Amazon Highway, and sometimes they are built to serve other needs, as in the Quito–Lago Agrio Road; but people inevitably follow soon behind and begin the task of clearing the forest.

About half of the world's lowland tropical forests are in Latin America, the overwhelming majority in South America. The Amazon forest is the largest rain forest in the world. Although this forest does not cover as much area as the boreal forest of the Soviet Union, it is still an awesome expanse of greenery; if its boundaries coincided with a political border, it would be the ninth largest country in the world. These extraordinarily rich rain forests have come under increasing pressure from man in the twentieth century, and the savage, dangerous jungle of legend is falling easy prey to human development and exploitation.

The rate at which tropical rain forest is disappearing is hard to comprehend—if it continues at its present intensity, there will be little left of this facinating habitat by the end of the century. It is extremely difficult to obtain accurate figures on the rate of tropical deforestation because virtually all of this activity goes on without any monitoring by the nations involved. Norman Myers, an authority on tropical conservation, has estimated that about 95,000 square miles of tropical forest are lost each year, and similar estimates have been made independently by a number of tropical foresters. Although this figure is admittedly speculative, it is probably conservative, and it only hints at the true magnitude of the problem because not all tropical forest is being lost at the same rate. The situation in some Asian rain forests may have already passed the critical stage—they may disappear before the end of the decade.

The overall picture is not quite so bleak in tropical America. The rain forests in parts of the upper Amazon basin are still largely untouched, as are parts of the forest on the Guiana shield in northeastern South America. But there are some exceptionally endangered rain forests in tropical America, most notably the fascinating Atlantic coastal forests in southeastern Brazil and the unique rich forests of northwestern Ecuador.

The loss of tropical rain forest seems a subject far removed from everyday life here in North America, and it has not received the attention its significance warrants. Despite the rise of the environmentalist movement in the late 1960s, economic growth and exploitation still take precedence over environmental concerns. Serious concerns that touch close to home, like acid precipitation, seem to invoke only yawns and bad jokes among large segments of our population, and the people and institutions responsible often refuse even to admit that there are problems. It's not surprising that the rapid destruction of tropical rain forest has failed to capture the concern of the general public here in North America, even though it is a vital question that will eventually touch the lives of people who may never want to see the spreading buttresses of a giant kapok tree deep in the Amazon forest.

If the tropical rain forests are all cut down, we will never know what we have lost. The wealth of new species waiting to be discovered and described in the tropics has a tragic corollary—many species will go extinct before they are ever discovered. There is no way of knowing which species of rain forest plants or animals could make valuable contributions to human welfare. We have only begun to become aware of the biochemical diversity of tropical rain forest plants, but already they have made important contributions to modern health care by providing novel secondary compounds that can be utilized as drugs. More than 70 percent of the plants known to produce compounds with anticancerous properties are tropical, and the National Cancer Institute of the United States has recently admitted that the loss of tropical rain forest would have serious negative ramifications in its research.

Other rain forest plants may carry important genetic information that sophisticated plant breeders can use to modify and improve important crops. Since only the tiniest fraction of the rain forest flora has been studied, and many species have still to be discovered and described, it seems reasonable to assume that there is a potentially large store of organic compounds that would prove useful to humans. Conserving these potentially valuable natural resources should carry a powerful economic incentive for nations with extensive tropical rain forests.

Preservation of large tracts of rain forest may also be necessary for the continued utilization of important local resources. There have been proposals to develop some of the floodplain reaches of the Amazon basin for rice production. This scheme appears admirable on the surface: it would take advantage of places that flood regularly to grow a crop that is a staple of the local diet. The land is not currently being used to produce export goods, and the people who grow the crop would benefit themselves and their country by producing food where no other crop will grow. Yet even though the motives of people backing these schemes may be laudable (we'll give them the benefit of doubt), such schemes could prove disastrous. Michael Goulding of the Brazilian Institute of Fisheries has recently published data which suggest that flood-plain development would cause far more problems than it would solve for the people who live along the Amazon.

Although the flooded forests appear useless to man, lying under water half the year and growing few woods of commercial value, they are essential to the well-being of the Amazon's most important animal protein resource, its rich fisheries. Each year, fishes enter the bottomland forest with the rising waters of the rainy season, and eat the fruits and seeds that drop from the trees. During the rest of the year, when the rivers drop into their channels and the forest emerges from the water, many of these fishes go without food and take care of their reproductive duties. Without the forest, the fishes would have nothing to eat and the human residents would quickly lose their most important source of animal protein. Clearly, any intelligent development scheme in these forests must consider the life history patterns of the fishes; but without the basic biological data just beginning to be gathered, this is impossible. Had the forests been cleared before we learned about the fishes, this valuable resource would have been lost without a clue as to why.

Rain forests are not called rain forests without good reason. A dense mantle of tropical forest is one of the finest flood-control devices available. The forests suck up and hold the water, cycling it back into the atmosphere through the respiratory activities of the multitude of trees. When the forest is removed, heavy rains quickly run off the barren landscape, choking river channels with silt and causing frequent, unpredictable flooding. If the forest is removed from hilly country, the slopes are destabilized, and landslides and mudslides run rampant, destroying roads and losing valuable soil in the process.

The role of forest cover in maintaining tropical watersheds has received remarkably little attention, but this may prove to be one of the most significant tools that conservationists can use to argue for the protection of tropical rain forest. There is recent evidence which links deforestation in eastern Ecuador and Peru with a sharp increase in flooding elsewhere in the Amazon basin, yet loss of the rain forest that covers most of the basin may eventually result in the creation of desert conditions. This seeming paradox has a biological explanation. Much of the rain that falls in the Amazon—perhaps as much as half—is produced by the forest itself, through the transpiration of trees. The metabolism of the trees helps keep the air saturated with moisture; if the forest is cleared, this internal cycling of water is severed and increasing aridity may result. If enough forest is lost, average temperatures may rise because the intense tropical sun would fall on exposed land and global shifts in climate could occur. Computer simulations suggest that such climatic shifts would increase aridity even in the temperate latitudes, and thus have a severe agro-economic impact far beyond the tropics.

We feel that there are other arguments for preserving the tropical rain forest in addition to the pragmatic ones above. There is a value in pristine nature that cannot be assessed in terms of practicality, a numen that defies definition and makes it impossible to weigh values on an objective scale. Unfortunately, this is an argument that carries little weight when discussing the importance of preserving tropical rain forest because it almost always evokes images of benevolent but patronizing colonialism—the tropical rain forest as a zoo for the wealthy.

The responsibility for rain forest conservation does not fall solely on the shoulders of the tropical nations that hold the forests. Although it might appear that the inhabitants of these largely underdeveloped nations are the agents of destruction, the greed that fuels the destruction of these forests comes largely from developed temperate zone nations. North Americans use a disproportionate share of the planet's resources to fuel our life-styles. It has always struck us as amusing that many of the best-known environmentalists in the United States drive private cars instead of using public transportation. They have obviously made a decision to place speed and efficiency of private transportation ahead of their impact on limited resources. We are no less guilty of favoring convenience. Each time we eat an inexpensive fast-food hamburger, we contribute in a small way to the clearing of tropical forest, because much of the cheap beef imported for these burgers comes from Central and South America. The demand for export goods from developing nations is a major factor in the continuing decimation of the tropical rain forests. Your desire for an inexpensive banana to slice over your breakfast cereal produces economic pressures on tropical nations that are most easily relieved by clearing another patch of forest for a large banana plantation. But all is not hopeless. There are ways to slow and perhaps stop the flow of rain forest into cheap exports.

Given the economic state of most tropical nations, conservation of tropical forests must have an economic incentive. In North American conservation circles, there is continual conflict among those who believe that certain sorts of economic activities are compatible with the long-term health of the environment. If conservation efforts are to succeed in the rain forest, this conflict must be avoided.

We are not suggesting that nature reserves and national parks are frivolous in developing nations. They are an essential part of any conservation strategy and they have several economic incentives that tropical American nations might do well to heed. Properly placed, they can protect important watersheds as well as endemic flora and fauna; equally important, they can attract tourist dollars and raise national prestige. Indeed, long-term revenues from tourism greatly exceed the short-term gains resulting from rain forest clearing.

North Americans take great pride in their national parks. Both the United States and Canada have set aside large tracts of land to be maintained for the enjoyment of future generations, most of them created to preserve spectacular scenery or unique features of the landscape. Our desire to protect the unique and spectacular is understandable, but it is not a good idea to base a conservation strategy solely on protecting unique resources. It is just as important to protect the typical. The key to sound conservation lies in protecting habitats and ecosystems. Unfortunately, even people interested in nature find it difficult to get excited about habitats; their emotions, if not their concerns, center on specific plants or animals. This is why the United States has an Endangered Species Act rather than an Endangered Habitats Act, although the latter would be far more significant. The "cuter" an animal is, the more concerned people become with its survival. Most people sympathize with the plight of the Giant Panda, and there are even those who lament the decline of animals as unfuzzy as a crocodile or condor; but how many would care about a lichen or a beetle?

The best wildlife conservation groups are well aware of the primacy of habitat protection for effective wildlife conservation, yet it is no accident that the World Wildlife Fund uses a Giant Panda as its symbol. They know that it is easier to get their message across by focusing on animals with an intrinsic appeal to people, and they know that their efforts to protect these appealing species involve the entire habitat in which these animals live. There are many plants and animals besides pandas that live in the panda reserves of western China, and they all share the benefits of the panda's irresistible appeal. One of the great problems that conservationists face when they try to elicit concern about the disappearing tropical rain forest is the lack of a symbolic animal to focus upon. The tremendous diversity of life in these forests makes any individual species less conspicuous, and without an appealing animal to act as a symbol it is often difficult to rally public attention on the loss of an extraordinarily valuable habitat.

If establishment of national parks were enough to ensure habitat protection, the loss of rain forest in tropical America would not be the critical problem that it is. Unfortunately, park boundaries may be meaningful only on the maps of a bureaucrat in the capital city. There are many problems that face conservationists after parks and nature reserves have been established. The social and economic pressures responsible for deforestation in the first place do not change; rapidly growing human populations, combined with extreme imbalances in the distribution of wealth, place inexorable pressures on easily accessible parks. Developing nations don't have much to spend on nature protection, and the budgets available to protect the integrity of park boundaries are minuscule. National park services have little to spend on training wardens and guards, and in some countries park guards may be little more than poachers and woodcutters who receive a small government subsidy for destroying the very resources they should be protecting.

Even if a huge system of biological reserves could be established and maintained, the restricted distributions of many rain forest plant and animal species means that some species might go unprotected. There is a correlation between the area of a patch of habitat and the number of species it can support, and small reserves tend to lose species regardless of how well they are protected. Barro Colorado Island in Panama, the famous biological reserve maintained by the Smithsonian Tropical Research Institute, has lost 22 percent of its bird species since it was established in 1923. This species-area relationship has prompted some biologists to place great emphasis on determining the optimal sizes and shapes of nature reserves and national parks in tropical forests. Parks and reserves should be designed so as to protect the largest numbers of species, and if random extinctions could be lessened by taking into account sound biological principles, we would all be better off. No one can argue with this. But the conservation of tropical forests is as much a biological problem as it is a political and economic problem. Conservationists should not ignore biology; however, we believe that the most urgent priority lies in determining where parks and reserves should be established, and then trying to make them as large and numerous as is politically feasible.

Many conservationists may continue to despair of the future, and some already believe, deep in their hearts, that there is little hope of saving significant areas of pristine lowland rain forest in tropical America. We are not so pessimistic. There is still time to slow down, perhaps even to stop the present trend of tropical deforestation.

We find some comfort in history. The present cycle of deforestation in tropical America is not the first. Not only were there the cycles of natural deforestation and reforestation during the Pleistocene that led to much of the present diversity of tropical rain forest, but the impact of pre-Columbian civilizations was also considerable. The earliest Spanish visitors in Panama found vast plantations of corn and heavy human populations in regions that a century or so later were covered by an unbroken mantle of forest. Indian populations in regions of tropical rain forest were much higher before the conquest than many people assume; it was the diseases brought by Europeans that decimated the forest people and turned the rain forests back into wilderness. Although the return to primeval conditions may be slow—the distribution patterns of some rain forest plants evidently still show the effects of this pre-Columbian wave of deforestation—as long as the integrity of existing and planned reserves can be maintained, there is reason to hope that this cause is not a hopeless one.

There are positive steps the public can take to slow the trend of deforestation in the tropics. The easiest, of course, is to contribute money to conservation groups concerned with protecting rain forest habitats. The World Wildlife Fund, the Rare Animal Relief Effort of the National Audubon Society, the Nature Conservancy, and the New York Zoological Society all have active programs dealing with the Neotropical rain forests. If you contribute, make sure that you indicate clearly that the money is to go to their rain forest programs. These groups are making positive contributions on a variety of levels: they sponsor critical scientific research that has immediate implications for conservation, they deal with governments in trying to establish parks and reserves, they help establish private reserves in critical cases where governments might move too slowly, and they educate the citizens of rain forest countries in the value of the living forest.

Contributing money is an important gesture, but it is a passive one. We have tried to convey some of the essence of tropical nature in this book, but second-hand contact with the tropical rain forest is a far cry from actually being there. Perhaps the most significant thing you can do for the welfare of tropical rain forest is to visit one of the national parks in tropical America in order to see, smell, hear, and feel some of the things we have written about. Only then will your intellectual concern for the disappearance of tropical rain forest be translated into an emotional one that will spur you to help do something. Your simple presence will contribute in more ways than you might think. (The Appendix on pp. 219–33 gives some practical information about travel in tropical America.)

Some of the most outstanding successes along national park lines have been in Africa and Latin America. Without the protections afforded by these national parks, our planet's biological heritage would have suffered irreparable losses. Africa's large mammal fauna might already have been lost were it not for the game parks scattered across that continent. Similarly, Ecuador's Galapagos National Park has preserved one of the most fascinating wild places on our planet from destruction, and it has even begun to reverse some of the damage done to the islands before the park was established. One of the most innovative national park systems in the world is that of Costa Rica. Although North Americans are rightfully proud of their national park systems, the Costa Rican system puts them to shame in many respects. The land set aside for parks in Costa Rica was chosen to be representative of the diverse habitats in this tropical country. Costa Rica's national parks protect virtually every major habitat in tropical Central America, including lowland rain forest and deciduous forest, cloud forest, coral reefs, volcanos, and páramo. Other tropical American countries seem to be following Costa Rica's example, and virtually every tropical American habitat now has nominal protection as a park somewhere in Central and South America.

Successful national parks and reserves in tropical nations share one important characteristic, and this is something that we can't stress too strongly. They have succeeded because international attention has been focused on them. Tourism can be big business, and the lure of millions of dollars of foreign currency pumped into the economy by these parks has provided a strong economic incentive for conservation efforts in developing countries. Your visit will do more than simply bolster the local economy. It can lead to national pride in a natural heritage. Costa Ricans are very proud of their national park system, and this pride can only be strengthened as more and more people visit the parks. The long-term effects of these feelings are likely to be critical to the success of protecting tropical rain forests.

The best that we can hope for is what we ourselves have settled for, a strong system of national parks and reserves and perhaps a modicum of care and concern for those areas where development must proceed. In the process of developing North America, huge expanses of natural habitats were reduced to tiny enclaves. The tall grass prairie that supported what may have been the planet's most spectacular wildlife display, the great herds of bison, was all but eliminated as the land was tilled. Along the route from the lowland rain forests that once cloaked tropical America to the mix of ranches, farms, cities, and preserved areas that lies in the future, much that is irreplaceable will be lost. Species will disappear as we chew away at the forest.

Such extinctions are terrible, irretrievable losses. We must resist the coming of the dark age of biological simplicity that rain forest destruction will bring. Tinkering with the world is unavoidable. However, as Aldo Leopold once said, "The first rule of intelligent tinkering is to save all the parts."

TROPICAL TRAVEL—
A BEGINNER'S GUIDE

A visit to the rain forests of the New World tropics can be either a sublime experience or a hellish ordeal, just like a vacation anywhere else. A little preparation goes a long way toward ensuring that you enjoy yourself. Since you will find that practical information on seeing tropical nature is hard to come by, we offer some general advice here based on our own experience.

TOURS

An organized tour is the easiest way to see tropical rain forest, and it can be an excellent way to get a first-hand taste if you find a good package. An escorted tour has several advantages. Many of you will have a limited amount of time for a rain forest excursion, and a good tour can make efficient use of that time. You won't have to hassle with transportation, food, and accommodations, so you'll retain more time and energy to appreciate the forest. A good tour leader can tell you a lot about the natural history of the forest. He or she can let you know what to expect and what to look for, and perhaps identify some of the plants and animals that may pique your curiosity. Finally, some of the best places to stay deep in tropical rain forest are the "jungle lodges" operated by tour companies, and your only access to these places may be through taking a tour.

Nature touring in tropical America is becoming popular and a variety of tours are offered by an increasing number of operators. One thing to keep in mind is that most tour operators use the same facilities once you leave North America. A typical "jungle" tour to Peru or Ecuador will use the same lodge and local transportation regardless of who is selling it. However, as you will soon discover, the prices of these basically identical trips can vary considerably, some costing twice as much as others. There are a number of factors that affect the cost of a trip. We will discuss some of the more significant ones here.

Leaders

Most trips are accompanied by a naturalist or scientist who is supposed to guide you through the wonders of tropical nature. This person can be the most important part of a trip, because if he/she is knowledgeable and enthusiastic, you are sure to see and learn a lot. Some nature tours offer well-known scientists as naturalist leaders, and these tours are generally the more expensive ones because you are paying the scientist's expenses as well as your own. In certain cases, these scientists may never have been to the places you will be staying; although they may be able to tell you a lot about tropical natural history, they may not be able to show you as much as a local naturalist. Some of the less expensive nature tours use guides provided by the lodge, who may be familiar with local conditions but who are rarely able to provide you with much perspective on tropical ecology. The best tours—which are generally also the most expensive—offer both well-known scientists and local guides.

Schedules

If you want to see tropical rain forest rather than just say you've been there, you should look for tours that don't move around much. A tour that promises to take you to many different places in a short period will never give you time to become attuned to the tropical rain forest. Since transportation costs are often high, the more a tour moves around, the more expensive it will be. In this case you will benefit by looking for a relatively sedentary trip.

Options

Most tours to tropical rain forest offer you the opportunity to see Indian villages and missionary settlements. Some offer these as options while others include them in the cost of the package. Again, if you're interested in tropical nature, your best bet is the cheapest. Look for tours that offer these excursions as options. If you want to see the natural history of tropical rain forests, there will be little to hold your interest in the missionary camps or westernized Indian villages you will be taken to. The idea is to spend as much time as possible in the forest, drinking in as many sights, sounds, and smells as you can.

Accommodations

Although most tours use the same accommodations once you enter the forest (there are only a limited number of well-organized lodges deep in the rain forest), they vary widely in their choice of hotels in cities. If you are used to creature comforts, by all means go for packages that will stay in luxury hotels before and after your forest excursion. If this isn't important, look for the less expensive tours that simply say you will have comfortable lodging in the cities.

Group Size

In general, tours with small groups are more expensive than tours with large groups. Although most people seem to find small groups more desirable, we think there are some sound arguments for the larger groups aside from economy. While it is true that you will see almost nothing if you walk through the forest with forty other people, you will see little more if you are walking with ten. Ideally, you want to see the forest on your own terms, or perhaps with one or two others. As long as your tour offers you the opportunity to set off by yourself, it should make no difference whether you share your meals with six or sixty others. Small groups can sometimes be dreadful experiences if you don't get along with the others—your chances of finding sympathetic companions may be better if you have more people to choose from.

As you can see, the best tour for you may not necessarily be the fanciest and most expensive. Another thing to keep in mind is that tour operators don't necessarily run the best nature tours. Universities and museums often sponsor excellent extension courses and trips that allow you to write off part of your expenses as a donation. There are some alternatives in nature tourism that offer many of the benefits of group travel without the hassles of traveling alone in a strange culture. Earthwatch, for example, allows you to accompany scientists on field trips, many of which take you into prime Neotropical rain forest. You volunteer your services as a field assistant, and you receive in return knowledge about the general natural history of the area and insight into the process of field research and its implications.

However you choose to go, if you travel in a group there are certain things you must consider before you write a check and get a passport. If you aren't careful about choosing your trip, a tour to tropical rain forest can be a monumental waste of time and money.

Make sure that daily schedules accommodate the activity patterns of rain forest life. Beware of trips with rigid schedules and itineraries, particularly if you are locked into normal breakfast hours—if you want to see wildlife, you have to be in the forest before the sun comes up. A cup of coffee and some toast at 5:00 A.M. should be enough to keep you going until the midday meal, when you can gorge yourself and sleep through the heat of the afternoon. Make sure that your trip will offer at least one opportunity to take a long hike through the forest at night. Since most tour operators are reluctant to let you wander off alone at night, your tour leader will have to be willing to escort you.

There is one class of nature tour to tropical America that we feel we must warn you about. Unless you're a hard-core birder, you should probably avoid birding trips to the tropics. These trips are often too narrowly focused to provide you with much insight into the rain forest; their goal is to see as many different species of birds as possible in a limited amount of time. Some of the leaders of these birding trips may be unconcerned with anything without feathers, and even though such tours take you to some of the most interesting places in tropical America, they are not a good bet unless your overriding passion is for birds. If you're more interested in natural history than in life lists, you may be disappointed. There are other special-interest tours to the tropics that may share some of the same drawbacks, so you should consider your own interests carefully before signing up on such a tour. Some of the operators who offer birding tours may also offer more general natural history tours, and these are the ones to choose if your interests reach much beyond things avian.

GOING IT ALONE

The ideal way to savor tropical rain forest is to do it on your own. This is not as easy as an organized nature tour and in involves more preparation on your part; but if you have time and an adventurous spirit, you will see far more far better than you could hope to on any organized trip.

Tropical American countries have a different cultural background from most places in the United States or Canada. Consequently, most of you will be the victims of some degree of culture shock when you visit tropical rain forest. It is beyond the scope of this brief guide to delve into the details of Latin American culture so that you will be prepared to deal with its often perplexing ways. We highly recommend that you purchase the current edition of the *South American Handbook*, which is published annually by Trade and Travel Publications in Bath, England, and distributed in North America by Rand McNally. This book not only provides you with a wealth of tips on dealing with Latin American culture but also has the best practical information on local transportation, lodging, and dining in Latin America. It covers all tastes and budgets, from the spartan to the sybaritic, and it will pay for itself many times over. It is the only travel guide to South and Central America we have ever needed.

If you travel alone, you will have to learn the rudiments of the local language, which in most of Latin America is Spanish. The little phrase books should help, but keep in mind that vocabulary and pronunciation can vary widely, often within the same country. The same words can have startlingly different meanings in different countries, but as long as you struggle through with a smile you can probably get by. One thing to avoid, however, is thinking that if you speak English slowly enough, they will eventually understand you. The only English word that seems to be uniformly understood is obscene. There are a few places in tropical America where English is the dominant language, and if you're reluctant to struggle in Spanish or Portuguese you might venture there. In addition to former British colonies like Belize and Guyana, you can get by with English along the Caribbean coast of Costa Rica and in parts of Panama and Surinam.

Your biggest problem if you travel without a group will be getting to good lowland tropical rain forest. There is little good mature rain forest that is easily accessible. You may also find it difficult to arrange for accommodation in these forests, because primary rain forest and Western culture seem largely incompatible. Some of the best places to stay are the biological field stations scattered around in Central and South America; as a traveler, however, you are low on the list of priorities when it comes to reserving space. If you contact the people in charge well in advance, you may be able to schedule your trip so that you can stay there. This can be a tremendous advantage because field stations are often situated in the middle of good forest and there are scientists around from whom you might be able to learn quite a lot.

PAINFUL ENCOUNTERS

Virgin visitors to the tropics are inevitably concerned about being bitten, stung, or poisoned by a plethora of malevolent creatures. We won't deny that there are a host of nasty little creatures living in tropical rain forest, but with a modicum of common sense the forest is far less hazardous than any urban area in North America.

Poisonous snakes receive the most attention, yet we have seldom encountered them in Neotropical rain forests. You are far more likely to see a sidewinder in a California desert than you are to see a fer-de-lance in a Costa Rican forest, and your chances of finding a bushmaster in Ecuador are about the same as finding a rattlesnake in a Boston suburb—they're there, but you probably won't find one, even if you go looking for them. Despite their general scarcity, if you spend enough time in tropical rain forest you will eventually run across a venomous snake from time to time. Looking over my field notes, I seem to see an average of about one snake a day in tropical rain forest, with perhaps one individual in a hundred being a venomous species. Your chances of coming across one are probably slim (I am, after all, a herpetologist and I'm often looking for the things), but that is no reason to be imprudent.

There are two basic types of venomous snakes in tropical America, coral snakes and pit vipers. Coral snakes are usually banded with some combination of red, black, and yellow, as are many species of non-venomous snakes. Some people have learned to distinguish the harmless from the deadly by looking at the order of the color bands. In North America, the venomous coral snakes have red bands touching yellow bands while the nonvenomous species have red bands touching black bands. This does NOT work in tropical America! We have only two species of venomous coral snakes in the United States, while there are well over fifty in the American tropics. Some tropical coral snakes have no red banding, some have white instead of yellow bands, many have red bands touching black bands, and a few may lack bands completely.

There are only two reliable ways of distinguishing the venomous true coral snakes from their nonvenomous mimics. True coral snakes lack a loreal—a small scale between their nose and eye—and they have small fangs at the front of their jaw; needless to say, you have to be on intimate terms with the snake to detect either of these differences. The other venomous tropical American snakes are pit vipers, all of which have relatively broad, more or less triangular heads, with a large nostril-like opening between the eye and nose.

There is no need to peer carefully at the head of any snake you see to determine whether there is cause for alarm. Many of these snakes will attempt to flee as soon as they know you're there, and the rest will sit still, hoping you won't see them. None of these snakes is aggressive, and just as in North America, your only real risk is stepping on one. Your best protection against snakebite, therefore, is to keep your eyes open and be careful where you put your hands and feet. Birders are particularly prone to ignore this precaution because they often wander through the forest with their eyes aimed upward, so if you plan to concentrate on birds, you might want to walk in the company of people who will devote some attention to the ground.

You should also be aware that most tropical American forests have at least one species of venomous arboreal pit viper, so be cautious when you come across low-lying branches. For those of you who are amateur herpetologists and feel an urge to look at snakes in the hand, we strongly recommend that you avoid grabbing any snake with a banded dorsal pattern. Unless you're absolutely certain of a snake's identity, don't grab it.

Of far more serious concern are stinging insects. Colonies of wasps, ants, and bees abound in fallen logs, hollow trees, and tangled vegetation. You face a good chance of getting stung if you insist on climbing trees or sitting on dead logs on the forest floor. With a few exceptions, the stings of these creatures are no more serious than the stings of their temperate zone relatives. If you get stung by a wasp, scrape the detached stinger out gently with your fingernail—if you attempt to squeeze or pull it out, all you will do is pump more venom into the wound. If you're allergic to these stings, you should definitely carry your injection kit when you step out into the forest, and you might want to supplement this with one of the epinephrine inhalers used by asthmatics.

You should be particularly wary of fuzzy and spiny caterpillars. Attractive and cute though they may be, many can cause a caustic rash of almost supernatural pain. The little hairs and spines penetrate your skin and inject a powerful poison, so don't touch any caterpillar that looks the slightest bit hairy. Other insects to avoid include some brightly colored stinkbugs, which spray hot cyanide compounds when they are molested, and large kissing bugs that pack a walloping bite. Unless you're entomologically inclined, you would do best to avoid touching any large insect you see.

Scorpions, centipedes, and spiders can be locally common in lowland tropical rain forest but rarely constitute a serious threat. If you leave your shoes outside, you might want to shake them before you put them on; and if you're the extremely cautious type, you might want to shake your bedding before you retire.

As long as you show reasonable sense, none of the above nasties is likely to spoil your visit to tropical rain forest. One of us, whose major interest in insects lies in their food value for vertebrates, has never suffered from a nasty insect sting, while the other, who is continually poking around wasp and ant nests, has suffered from remarkably few painful encounters. However, even though stinging arthropods are not a major problem as long as you're reasonably cautious, almost every tropical naturalist will suffer the itchy attentions of a host of small arthropods.

Chiggers are perhaps the most common cause of tropical itches. Chiggers are tiny mites, barely visible to the unaided eye, who shout their presence with insidious itches. These are not the simple itches that attend mosquito bites (minor swellings that require scratching for a few hours at most), but raging, complex itches that come and go for days on end. Chiggers sit patiently on vegetation, waiting for a juicy mammal to pass their way. They jump aboard when you brush against the grass, and crawl over your clothing looking for a way to your succulent flesh. Once they find your skin, they crawl around until they find a nice tight place, usually where your clothing constricts against your skin, and there they burrow in.

Nothing happens for a day or two, and you might never suspect that you're feeding an army of mites. The chiggers release saliva containing digestive enzymes that dissolve your flesh into a palatable soup. If we could accept this insignificant loss, all would be well; but our bodies fight back, and this is what causes the itch. The itching lasts for about a week. During this period there is nothing you can do to make it stop. The itching isn't constant. It waxes and wanes on its own schedule— one moment your legs may be afire, then after a brief respite your waist flares up. You can scratch yourself raw in a futile attempt for relief, but there are two alternatives that provide similar gratification without risking infection. One technique, which came to Bill Haber after a heavy infestation of seed ticks, involves gently massaging the itch with a soft hairbrush rather than ragged fingernails. The other involves running water as hot as you can stand over the affected area. This method kills the chiggers, but hot running water may not be available, and you run some risk of putting water just a bit too hot on some particularly sensitive part of your body.

The best way to deal with chiggers is to avoid them, which is no more possible than exterminating cockroaches in a large urban apartment building. The most you can hope for is control, and the best method is to dust your clothing with powdered sulfur. Insect repellent also works, but most of these tend to vaporize quickly in tropical climates. Grassy areas where domestic animals live are particularly prone to chigger infestations, so avoid such areas whenever possible, even if it means walking a bit out of your way.

Mosquitoes and other biting flies are no more bothersome in tropical rain forests than they are in many temperate zone habitats. However, tropical flies can carry a variety of diseases, so you should take some care to reduce the number of bites you get. Mosquitoes are generally thickest near human habitation and small biting flies are particularly numerous on the exposed sandbanks of rivers during the dry season. Different species have different activity periods; some mosquitoes are most active during the day, while others are most active at night, and many of the small no-see-um flies are most bothersome in late afternoon. Insect repellents work fairly well, but they must be replenished often as they are quickly perspired away. They last a bit longer if they are applied to your clothing. A mosquito net is often necessary for sleeping, both at night and during afternoon siestas, and you may want to burn some of the pyrethrum coils (*espirales*) available in most tropical markets.

RAIN AND HEAT

Keep in mind that it isn't called rain forest out of whim. In most rain forests you should expect rain at any given time, even during the midst of the dry season. There is nothing you can do to prevent this that we are aware of, so you will have to learn to deal with it.

Every type of raingear we have tried has had drawbacks in lowland tropical rain forest. Standard parkas and raincoats are unbearable because of the perspiration that builds up inside. An unlined Gore-tex parka is a marked improvement, but you may find it uncomfortably warm inside and you will still get damp from perspiration. They can't keep you any drier than the air, and if the humidity is pushing a hundred percent, there is no way you can stay dry inside. Ponchos allow air to circulate a little better, but they tend to get in your way if you try doing anything other than walking or sitting. Although it may seem ludicrous, umbrellas are a reasonably good way of keeping dry, and they allow you to take photographs when it is raining.

We have found that the best way to deal with rain in tropical lowland rain forest is simply to ignore it. Since the rain is nearly always warm, even at night, getting drenched is no serious problem as long as your water-sensitive equipment is protected and you have dry clothes to change into back at camp or lodge. Wear a waterproof hat to keep your hair dry and just let the rest of yourself get wet. If you're wearing light clothing, it will dry out quickly once the rain stops.

Warmth and humidity offer ideal growing conditions for fungi, and if you're not careful, you may find these sprouting all over your body and through your gear. Feet are especially prone to fungal infections, so it is extremely important to keep them as dry as possible. Whenever we're in camp, we eschew shoes and socks, wearing sandals or thongs. Don't go barefoot outside, however, because parasitic worms and sharp palm spines have a way of finding exposed soles. Fungal rot can also sprout up elsewhere, especially in the crotch and armpits. Loose-fitting underwear (or none at all) lessens this risk, as do loose-fitting, light clothes. Daily washing is highly recommended, and you might want to dust yourself with baby powder from time to time. If you're especially prone to fungal infections, a talcum powder laced with a fungicide like tinactin can be helpful.

It may take a week or two for your temperate body to acclimate to the heat and humidity of the tropical climate. You will probably experience a degree of lassitude and a general loss of enthusiasm unless you make some adjustments, especially in diet. You should drink large quantities of fluid whenever possible (beer is particularly good) and salt your food more heavily than normal. This allows you to perspire more freely and thus keep cooler. It also helps reduce the chances of constipation, which is every bit as hazardous as diarrhea in tropical countries. A diet rich in grease will do much to pep you up, and its effects will be longer lasting than the quick sugar fix you can get from chocolate.

Those of you who wear glasses will find that the high humidity causes them to fog at inopportune times. Contact lenses are the best solution to this problem, but if you are unable or unwilling to wear them, you can try using skin diver's anti-fog solution on your lenses. This can be purchased at any good diving shop.

CLOTHING

We strongly recommend that you avoid blue jeans in the tropical rain forest. They may be comfortable and stylish when they're dry, but when wet they're a burden, and they take forever to dry in a rain forest climate. Light, loose-fitting cotton clothes are the most practical in this warm, wet region. Lightweight army fatigues are excellent, but they can lead to some problems if you are wandering in areas off the beaten path. You might be mistaken for a guerilla, which could be either good or bad, depending on who comes across you. We generally avoid the military look by wearing tan pants and light blue work shirts.

Long-sleeve shirts are more practical than T-shirts—you can roll the sleeves down if the mosquitoes become tiresome. Insect repellent lasts longer on clothing than it does on skin, and a good dousing in the morning might last all day.

One strategy we have found practical is to wear the same set of clothes in the field for a week or two at a time. As they get dirtier, you feel less reluctant to plunge into muddy, difficult places and are more at ease squatting and kneeling. When you get back to camp, you can quickly change into clean, dry clothes and get a whole new lease on life. We often take old shirts with us specifically for this heavy field use. At the end of the trip we can discard them and have less to carry.

At all costs avoid standard hiking boots. They are unbearably hot and their heavy lug soles pick up pounds of mud. Perhaps the most practical shoes are the army surplus jungle boots, with light canvas uppers and a sturdy sole. Their high tops allow you to tuck your pants inside, which will prevent unwanted nasties from sneaking in where the sun don't shine. Some friends prefer high-top sneakers, but the soles are a bit thin for our tastes. The nasty spines of palm trees can penetrate soft rubber like a hot knife through butter; we prefer the added security of the jungle boot's sole.

CAMPING AND BACKPACKING

The ideal forest shelter is a hammock with a rain fly, light blanket, and mosquito net, although it may require a bit of practice to sleep comfortably in a hammock. When you string your hammock, look for trees with little ant traffic. Generally you will be best off with a smaller tree. You might want to soak the ropes that support the hammock and fly with insect repellent just to make sure that nothing nasty gets curious. Tents, even the best ventilated, leave something to be desired because they must be pitched on the ground. If the ground is muddy, which is by no means unusual, you will have problems. If you must have a tent, the most practical are probably those with open no-see-um screening, which allow even the slightest breeze to waft through. Needless to say, these tents require a separate waterproof fly. Look for a high piece of ground, and be sure to trench the tent before the rain starts.

A backpacking stove is your best bet for cooking. You will have trouble locating the well-aged, dry wood that makes for roaring campfires in tropical rain forest. Keep in mind that white gas may not be available in most tropical countries. You can burn automobile gasoline in most backpacking stoves, but they will clog with appalling frequency and will require constant care. Look for stoves like the MSR, which will burn anything you can get into the fuel tank, or for stoves that feed on readily available kerosene. Remember that it is illegal to transport loaded fuel canisters on airplanes, so your fancy butane backpacking stoves should be left at home.

Inexpensive, lightweight cooking pots can be purchased at any general store in the tropics, but you may prefer to bring a compact, nesting cookset. Another item you will find essential for tropical camping is a cigarette lighter. Ordinary matches quickly become soggy in the super-humid environment, so you should carry either special waterproof matches or a lighter.

You should be wary about drinking water, even in the most pristine uninhabited rain forests. Tapirs have the odd habit of defecating in streams, and you can contract some remarkable cases of dysentery by drinking untreated water. Water can be treated by boiling, filtering, or adding chemicals.

Backpackers should be aware that Customs officials and police in some countries may discriminate against you. Internal-frame packs are less inflammatory than conventional open-frame packs, but they ride closer to your back and may be less comfortable to wear. Your best bet is to break your pack down and carry it in a large bag when you pass through Customs.

CAMERAS AND FILM

Most modern travelers keep a camera close at hand. Photography is an excellent way of capturing sights; however, there are certain problems you will consistently run across when you take your camera into tropical rain forest. We can't discuss the points of field nature photography here, but Alfred Blaker's *Field Photography: Beginning and Advanced Techniques* (Freeman) is an excellent guide that we recommend highly. What we will discuss briefly here are some of the special problems that plague rain forest photographers and how to get around them.

If you plan to take pictures in tropical rain forest, you can count on one thing: it will be dark. The forest floor, even on the sunniest tropical afternoons, is a deeply shaded world with distressingly little light for photography. There are several strategies you can use to deal with the dimness, each of which has its advantages and disadvantages.

There are a number of excellent fast color films available today, both for negatives and transparencies. They can often be rated at even higher speeds than indicated, as long as you tell your processor to make compensations. These high-speed films allow you to take photographs under low light conditions with little modification of normal techniques, but we rarely use them. Their major drawback lies in image quality. Although they give acceptable results, it is impossible to achieve the razor sharpness that we prefer. We generally use these films only when we need to photograph animals in motion.

The film we opt for is a fine-grain, high-resolution, relatively slow color transparency. This gives us the sharpness we prefer, but has significant drawbacks. In order to get good results in the dim light of the rain forest, you will need a tripod. Tripods are wonderful photographic tools, but they are bulky, heavy, and inconvenient. Although lightweight models are available, a tripod is not worth bothering with unless it is bulky, heavy, and inconvenient. The superlight models can't hold your camera steady enough for good results.

One way of getting high resolution while using slow films is to use artificial lighting. Electronic flash is the most practical system, but portable amateur units don't have enough power to be effective over long ranges. We generally use electronic flash only for close-up and night work, lugging along the tripod for general daytime use. Electronic flash is indispensable for close-up work in tropical rain forest.

Inexperienced photographers often hope for a nice sunny day so that they can have enough light to take pictures in the forest interior. In fact, if you take pictures in the interior of tropical rain forest on a sunny day hoping to capture the ethereal greenness that so delights your eyes, you will be sorely disappointed. The extreme contrasts between highlights and shadow are far beyond the range of any film; there is nothing you can do to ensure proper exposure of highlights and shadows with this lighting. In order to capture the forest interior, you need an overcast sky. Although there is not much light, the contrast between highlights and shadows is drastically reduced, and your film will be able to capture the richness of detail you see. If you don't have a tripod, you will need to set your camera on a rock or tree stump in order to use the four- to ten-second exposures that may be necessary. Be sure to check your film package for information on reciprocity failure (most color films require exposure adjustments and filtration for very slow shutter speeds).

You will need a rainproof container for your camera equipment. Make sure that you keep the film inside the airtight plastic containers in which it is packaged. To be doubly safe, you might want to keep these containers inside a plastic bag with a supply of desiccant, but we have never found this necessary on brief trips. When you go through airport security, keep all your film in a plastic bag that you can pull out and ask to have hand-checked. Ask politely and you should not be refused.

Equipment can make a difference if you spend much time in tropical rain forest. We shy away from automatic cameras because batteries drain more quickly in warm climates and electrical contacts get gummed up more quickly in humid climates. Most automatic cameras become non-functional if the electronics fail, while good mechanical cameras continue to function even if their batteries and meters fail. We rely on automatic cameras for much of our rain forest photography, but we always have a mechanical camera body for backup if the need arises (and it often has, especially when we spend more than a month or two in lowland rain forest). Good lenses are an important consideration, not so much for their optical superiority over bargain brands (which may be slim or nonexistent) but for their mechanical superiority. We have had several inexpensive lenses develop mold between lens elements in the warmth and humidity of tropical rain forest. This has never happened to our better lenses.

Finally, but most importantly, never take a new piece of camera equipment on an important trip without having tested it in advance. If you aren't familiar with your equipment and the basic techniques of nature photography, you are almost sure to be disappointed in the results. The flashiest new cameras are no guarantee of effortless success.

OTHER EQUIPMENT

Binoculars

You will want to have a pair of binoculars when you visit tropical rain forest, even if you're not a birder. Binoculars allow you a close-up look at epiphytes in the trees high above, and many other insights into the world of the forest. Even the least expensive binoculars are better than none at all, but if you plan to spend much time in the rain forest the best are a wise investment. The best binoculars are waterproof, internal-focus roof prism designs; they are generally expensive. Binoculars for rain forest use should have high light transmission because of the dim light that so often prevails, and they should have reasonably high magnification because of the height of the canopy. Our favorite binoculars are 10×40 Zeiss Dialyts.

Batteries

You will need batteries for many things, ranging from flashlights to electronic flash. Standard alkaline batteries are excellent if you are making a short trip, but for extended stays you will have to carry too many extra sets. We like the rechargeable nickel-cadmium batteries, but in order to use these you will need access to real electricity. If power is supplied by a generator, it may not run long enough to charge a battery fully in a single day. Most batteries require twelve to sixteen hours for a full charge. For electronic flash you might want to consider using a 510-volt photo battery. Although they are bulky, a single battery can charge several thousand flashes and will do so with almost instant cycling, a tremendous advantage for field photography.

Keep in mind that good batteries can be hard to find in most tropical American countries. The standard flashlight and penlight batteries they sell are cheap but almost worthless. You'll have to bring down all you will need.

Flashlights

The best light is a battery-powered headlamp. This will leave both hands free when you go for a walk through the forest at night. For camp use, a small penlight will come in handy.

WHAT TO BRING

Common pharmaceuticals can be bought over the counter in most Latin American countries, so you needn't worry about bringing along a huge medicine kit. Locally recommended treatments for gastro-intestinal distress often work better than anything you can drag along, anyhow. However, you should be aware that contraceptives are not easily obtained in most countries and that some common household drugs, such as aspirin, can be relatively expensive.

Always travel with a roll of toilet paper. There seems to be an endemic shortage of the stuff south of the United States.

Suitcases are impractical for most travel in tropical America. Soft bags hold more, are more durable and easier to carry. However, soft bags are generally not watertight, so you might want to carry a few heavy-duty trashbags for protection when the rain falls.

The following list is similar to ones we have provided field assistants in the past. Most people bring far too much clothing. If you follow our strategy of keeping one set of field clothes, you can get by with remarkably little. Should disaster strike, field clothes can be replaced easily and inexpensively. Note that the list mentions only field clothing—you can leave your traveling clothes in storage before you go to the forest if you bring along a small extra bag.

Field Clothing

2 pairs long pants: loose, fast-drying, cotton is ideal
4 light, long-sleeve cotton shirts
1 pair walking shorts
1 pair swimming trunks
4 sets of underwear (cotton is best; avoid heavy synthetics)
4 pairs socks (wool is best; avoid synthetics)
1 pair hiking shoes (jungle boots, high-top sneakers, or lightweight calf-high boots)
1 pair sneakers or thongs for camp use
1 folding sun hat (very important if you will be traveling by river)
1 poncho or unlined Gore-tex parka

Equipment

1 penlight
1 headlamp (plus several sets of batteries—a set of alkaline batteries is generally good for four to six hours of continuous use)
1 notebook (pencils are best for writing)
1 pocket knife (Swiss Army knives are perfect)
1 cigarette lighter (even if you don't smoke, they come in handy)
1 pair binoculars

FURTHER READING

We have compiled this partially annotated list of references for those of you who wish to delve more deeply into tropical nature. Our intent is to provide an introduction to the scientific literature and to acknowledge some of the biologists upon whose original research we have drawn. The listings are by no means exhaustive; we have tried to list here works that are synthetic in nature or that effectively review a large body of active scientific research. The bibliographies of these scientific reviews will open up a vast world of technical literature for those of you whose interests are especially piqued. Most of the books we have mentioned are in print, and should be available in large public or university libraries. Some of the scientific papers may be more difficult to locate but can probably be obtained on interlibrary loans.

GENERAL

Ayensu, E. S., ed. *Jungles*. New York: Crown, 1980.
  A well-illustrated general book on the biology of tropical forests.
Golley, F. B., and E. Medina, eds. *Tropical Ecological Systems: Trends in Terrestrial and Aquatic Research*. New York: Springer-Verlag, 1975.
MacArthur, R. H. *Geographical Ecology. Patterns in the Distribution of Species*. New York: Harper & Row, 1972.
  An excellent and succinct introduction to ecology that makes specific comparisons between tropical and temperate zone habitats.
Richards, P. W. *The Tropical Rain Forest: An Ecological Study*. Cambridge, Engl.: The University Press, 1952.

The classic work. Some of the information is dated, but this remains the most informative general text on the vegetation of lowland tropical rain forests.

FIELD GUIDES

The only field guides available for any group of New World tropical organisms deal with birds. We have also included references to some well-illustrated scientific works that can be used for field identification of other organisms. Although these references refer to specific areas, they can be useful elsewhere.

Plants

Allen, P. H. *The Rain Forests of Golfo Dulce*. Gainesville: University of Florida Press, 1956.

> Useful keys, with some illustrations, for rain forest trees on the southernmost tip of Costa Rica. Corcovado National Park is well covered by this book.

Croat, T. B. *Flora of Barro Colorado Island*. Stanford: Stanford University Press, 1978.

> An illustrated flora of the tropical moist forests of the famous biological preserve in Panama.

Dodson, C. H., and A. H. Gentry. "Flora of the Rio Palenque Science Center, Los Rios, Ecuador," *Selbyana*, 4 (1978), 1–628.

> Profusely illustrated with line drawings, this monograph treats the vascular plants of a western Ecuadorian lowland rain forest.

Amphibians and Reptiles

Duellman, W. E. "The Biology of an Equatorial Herpetofauna in Amazonian Ecuador," *Miscellaneous Publications, University of Kansas Museum of Natural History*, 65 (1978), 1–352.

> Black-and-white photos and selected colorplates of the amphibians and reptiles of a rich locality in the Amazon forest.

Birds

Davis, L. I. *A Field Guide to the Birds of Mexico and Central America*. Austin: University of Texas Press, 1972.

> Illustrates many of the birds to be found in Central American rain forests but suffers from poor written descriptions and peculiar nomenclature.

Meyer de Schauensee, R., and W. H. Phelps, Jr. *A Guide to the Birds of Venezuela*. Princeton: Princeton University Press, 1978.

The annotated illustrations by Guy Tudor are superbly done; if space is a problem, the plates can be removed and the text left at home. Particularly useful for Amazonian birds.

Ridgely, R. S. *A Guide to the Birds of Panama.* Princeton: Princeton University Press, 1976.

An exceptional field guide, useful in Costa Rica, western Colombia, and western Ecuador as well as Panama. In contrast to most field guides, the text is as fine as the illustrations.

Introduction: A TEMPERATE VIEW OF TROPICAL LIFE
Chapter 1. IN THE REALM OF THE TROPICS

The books listed below are accounts of travel and nature in the tropics written by naturalists trained in the temperate zones. The older ones give insight into a world that really no longer exists, while the more recent ones hint of some of the pleasures still to be had.

Bates, H. W. *The Naturalist on the River Amazons.* London: John Murray, 1864. Reprinted by the University of California Press, Berkeley.

Belt, T. *The Naturalist in Nicaragua.* London, 1874.

Carr, A. F. *High Jungles and Low.* Gainesville: University of Florida Press, 1953.

Skutch, A. F. *A Naturalist in Costa Rica.* Gainesville: University of Florida Press, 1971.

――――. *A Bird Watcher's Adventures in Tropical America.* Austin: University of Texas Press, 1977.

――――. *A Naturalist on a Tropical Farm.* Berkeley: University of California Press, 1980.

Spruce, R. *Notes of a Botanist on the Amazon and Andes,* 2 vols., edited by A. R. Wallace. London. 1908. Reprinted by Johnson Reprints, New York.

Wallace, A. R. *A Narrative of Travels on the Amazon and Rio Negro.* London: Ward, Lock & Co., 1889. Reprinted by Dover Books, New York, 1972.

Chapter 2. FERTILITY

Montgomery, G. G., and M. E. Sunquist. "Impact of Sloths on Neotropical Forest Energy Flow and Nutrient Cycling," in Golley and Medina, eds., *Tropical Ecological Systems: Trends in Terrestrial and Aquatic Research, op. cit.,* pp. 69–98.

Chapter 3. CANYONS OF LIGHT

Denslow, S. "Gap Partitioning among Tropical Rainforest Trees," *Biotropica*, 12 (1980), 47–55.

Halle, F., R. A. A. Ordeman, and P. B. Tomlinson. *Tropical Trees and Forests: An Architectural Analysis.* Berlin: Springer-Verlag, 1978.

Hartschorn, G. S. "Neotropical Forest Dynamics," *Biotropica*, 12 (1980), 23–30.

Horn, H. S. "Markovian Processes of Forest Succession," in M. Cody and J. M. Diamond, eds., *Ecology and Evolution of Communities.* Cambridge, Mass.: Harvard University Press, 1975, pp. 196–211.

Strong, D. R., Jr. "Epiphyte Loads, Treefalls and Perennial Forest Disruption: A Mechanism for Maintaining Higher Tree Species Richness in the Tropics without Animals," *Journal of Biogeography*, 4 (1977), 215–218.

Tomlinson, P. B., and M. H. Zimmermann, eds. *Tropical Trees as Living Systems.* Cambridge, Engl.: The University Press, 1978.

Chapter 4. HANGERS-ON

Darwin, C. R. *The Movements and Habits of Climbing Plants.* London: John Murray, 1876.

Dressler, R. L. *The Orchids.* Cambridge, Mass.: Harvard University Press, 1981.

Putz, F. E. "Lianas vs. Trees," *Biotropica*, 12 (1980), 224–225.

Ray, T. S., Jr. "Slow-motion World of Plant 'Behavior' Visible in Rain Forest," *Smithsonian* (March 1979), 121–130.

Chapter 5. MATAPALO

Janzen, D. H. "How to Be a Fig," *Annual Review of Ecology and Systematics*, 10 (1979), 13–51.

Ramirez-B., W. "Evolution of the Strangling Habit in *Ficus* L., Subgenus *Urostigma* (Moraceae)," *Brenesia*, 12–13 (1977), 11–19.

Chapter 6. LISTEN TO THE FLOWERS

Dodson, C. H. "Coevolution of Orchids and Bees," in L. H. Gilbert and P. H. Raven, eds., *Coevolution of Plants and Animals.* Austin: University of Texas Press, 1975, pp. 91–99.

Faegri, K., and L. van der Pijl. *The Principles of Pollination Ecology.* Oxford: Pergamon Press, 1966.

Janzen, D. H. "Euglossine Bees as Long-distance Pollinators of Tropical Plants," *Science*, 171 (1971), 203–205.

Van der Pijl, L., and C. H. Dodson. *Orchid Flowers: Their Pollination and Evolution.* Coral Gables, Fla.: University of Miami Press, 1966.

Chapter 7. "EAT ME"

Howe, H. F. "Bird Activity and Seed Dispersal of a Tropical Wet Forest Tree," *Ecology,* 58 (1977), 539–550.

————. "Monkey Dispersal and Waste of a Neotropical Fruit," *Ecology,* 61 (1980), 944–959.

Janzen, D. H. *Ecology of Plants in the Tropics.* London: Edward Arnold, 1975.

McKey, D. "The Ecology of Coevolved Seed Dispersal Systems," in Gilbert and Raven, eds., *Coevolution of Plants and Animals, op. cit.,* pp. 159–191.

Opler, P. A., H. G. Baker, and G. W. Frankie. "Plant Reproductive Characteristics During Secondary Succession in Neotropical Lowland Forest Ecosystems," *Biotropica,* 12 (1980), 40–46.

Chapter 8. BUGS AND DRUGS

Bucherl, W., and E. E. Buckley. *Venomous Animals and Their Venoms.* Vol. 2: *Venomous Vertebrates.* New York: Academic Press, 1971.
    See papers by Deulofeu and Ruveda and by Meyer and Linde for discussion of toad venoms.

Janzen, D. H. "Tropical Blackwater Rivers, Animals, and Mast Fruiting by the Dipterocarpaceae," *Biotropica,* 6 (1974), 69–103.

Lamb, F. B. *Wizard of the Upper Amazon: The Story of Manuel Córdova-Rios.* Boston: Houghton Mifflin, 1974.
    A fascinating account of the role of hallucinogenic drugs in Amazonian Indian culture.

Schultes, R. E., and A. Hofmann. *Plants of the Gods: Origins of Hallucinogenic Use.* New York: McGraw-Hill, 1979.

Smith, N. G. *Smithsonian Institution Research Reports* [Report on *Urania* Research], 34 (1981), 4–7.

Chapter 9. CREEPING SOCIALISTS

Chapter 10. ARMY ANTS

Bentley, B. L. "Extrafloral Nectaries and Protection by Pugnacious Bodyguards," *Annual Review of Ecology and Systematics,* 8 (1977), 407–427.

Janzen, D. H. "Coevolution of Mutualism Between Ants and Acacias in Central America," *Evolution,* 20 (1966), 249–275.

————. "Allelopathy by Myrmecophytes: The Ant *Azteca* and an Allelo-
pathic Agent of *Cecropia*," *Ecology*, 50 (1969), 147–153.

Jeanne, R. L. "A Latitudinal Gradient in Rates of Ant Predation,"
Ecology, 60 (1979), 1211–1224.

Ray, T. S., and C. C. Andrews. "Ant Butterflies: Butterflies that Follow
Army Ants to Feed on Antbird Droppings," *Science*, 210 (1980),
1147–1148.

Schneirla, T. C. *Army Ants: A Study in Social Organization*, edited by
H. R. Topoff. San Francisco: W. H. Freeman, 1971.

Wilson, E. O. *The Insect Societies*. Cambridge, Mass.: Harvard University Press, 1971.

Chapter 11. ARTFUL GUISES

Cott, H. B. *Adaptive Coloration in Animals*. London: Methuen, 1940.

Greene, H. W., and R. W. McDiarmid. "Coral Snake Mimicry: Does It
Occur?" *Science*, 213 (1981), 1207–1212.

Myers, C. W., J. W. Daly, and B. Malkin. "A Dangerously Toxic New
Frog (*Phyllobates*) Used by Emberá Indians of Western Colombia,
with Discussion of Blowgun Fabrication and Dart Poisoning," *Bulletin
of the American Museum of Natural History*, 161 (1978), 307–366.

Smith, S. M. "Coral Snake Pattern Recognition and Stimulus Generalization by Naive Great Kiskadees (Aves: Tyrannidae)," *Nature*, 265
(1977), 535–536.

Wickler, W. *Mimicry in Plants and Animals*. New York: World University Library, McGraw-Hill, 1968.

Chapter 12. SOUTHBOUND

Fitzpatrick, J. W. "Northern Birds at Home in the Tropics," *Natural
History*, 91 (1982), 40–47.

Keast, A., and E. S. Morton, eds. *Migrant Birds in the Neotropics:
Ecology, Behavior, Distribution, and Conservation*. Washington, D.C.:
Smithsonian Institution Press, 1980.

Lack, D. *Ecological Adaptations for Breeding in Birds*. London: Chap-
man & Hall, 1968.

Skutch, A. F. *A Naturalist on a Tropical Farm, op. cit.*, pp. 280–295.

Chapter 13. JERRY'S MAGGOT

Smith, N. G. "On the Advantages of Being Parasitized," *Nature*, 219
(1968), 690–694.

Chapter 14. SINGING IN THE RAIN

Crump, M. L. "Reproductive Strategies in a Tropical Anuran Community," *Miscellaneous Publications, University of Kansas Museum of Natural History*, 61 (1974), 1–68.

Heyer, W. R. "The Adaptive Ecology of the Species Groups of the Genus *Leptodactylus* (Amphibia: Leptodactylidae)," *Evolution*, 23 (1969), 421–428.

Lamotte, M., and J. Lescure. "Tendances adaptives a l'affranchissement du milieu aquatique chez les amphibiens anoures," *Terre et la Vie*, 2 (1977), 225–312.

McDiarmid, R. W. "Evolution of Parental Care in Frogs," in G. M. Burghardt and M. Bekoff, eds., *The Development of Behavior: Comparative and Evolutionary Aspects*. New York: Garland, 1978, pp. 127–147.

Weygoldt, P. "Complex Brood Care and Reproductive Behavior in Captive Poison-arrow Frogs, *Dendrobates pumilio* O. Schmidt," *Behavioral Ecology and Sociobiology*, 7 (1980), 329–332.

Chapter 15. NIGHT WALKS

Ryan, M. J., M. D. Tuttle, and A. S. Rand. "Bat Predation and Sexual Advertisement in a Neotropical Anuran," *American Naturalist*, 119 (1982), 136–139.

Tuttle, M. D., and M. J. Ryan. "Bat Predation and the Evolution of Frog Vocalizations in the Neotropics," *Science*, 214 (1981), 677–678.

Chapter 16. THE ETERNAL TROPICS

Endler, J. A. "Problems in Distinguishing Historical from Ecological Factors in Biogeography," *American Zoologist*, 22 (1982), 441–452.

Flenley, J. *The Equatorial Rain Forest: A Geological History*. London: Butterworth, 1979.

Haffer, J. "Avian Speciation in Tropical South America, with a Systematic Survey of the Toucans (Ramphastidae) and Jacamars (Galbulidae)," *Publications of the Nuttal Ornithological Club*, 14 (1974), 1–390.

Mayr, E. *Animal Species and Evolution*. Cambridge, Mass.: The Belknap Press of Harvard University Press, 1963.

Prance, Ghillean T., *The Biological Model of Diversification in the Tropics*, Columbia University Press, 1981.

Vanzolini, P. E., and E. E. Williams. "South American Anoles: The Geographic Differentiation and Evolution of the *Anolis chrysolepis*

Species Group (Sauria: Iguanidae)," *Arquivos de Zoologia* (São Paulo), 19 (1970), 1–298.

Chapter 17.   PARADISE LOST?

Mergen, F. ed. *Tropical Forests: Utilization and Conservation.* New Haven: Yale School of Forestry and Environmental Studies, 1981.

Myers, N. *The Sinking Ark.* Oxford: Pergamon Press, 1979.

————. *Conversion of Tropical Moist Forests.* Washington, D.C.: National Academy of Sciences, 1980.

Prance, G. T., and T. S. Elias, eds. *Extinction Is Forever: Threatened and Endangered Species of Plants in the Americas and Their Significance in Ecosystems Today and in the Future.* New York: New York Botanical Gardens, 1977.

Terborgh, J. W. "Preservation of Natural Diversity: The Problem of Extinction-Prone Species," *BioScience*, 24 (1974), 715–722.

Willis, E. O. "Populations and Local Extinctions of Birds on Barro Colorado Island, Panama," *Ecological Monographs*, 44 (1974), 153–169.

INDEX

ADRIAN FORSYTH
holds a Ph.D. in biology from Harvard University.
He won the Canadian National Magazine Award
for Science Writing in 1982 and 1983,
the first author to win the award twice.

KEN MIYATA
also held a Ph.D. in biology from Harvard University,
and worked for the Nature Conservancy in Washington, D.C.
He died in an accident late in 1983.